Advance Praise for *Downstream from Here*

"When Charles Eisendrath extolls fly fishing, or extracting maple syrup from his farm's trees, or the wonders and perils of his past life as a foreign correspondent, he coaxes readers to his campfire and mesmerizes us with glorious stories. The stories, as with Thomas Jefferson's from Monticello, are really love poems—to Eisendrath's Michigan Overlook Farm, to its shimmering and stormy lakes, to its varied trees and wildlife and fish, to his devotion to family, and to a love for journalism exceeded only by his love for the wondrous outdoors."

— **KEN AULETTA, author, media columnist,** *The New Yorker*

"Written with the eye of a journalist, the prose of a novelist and the wit of a humorist, *Downstream from Here* takes you on a long walk down the path that leads to a life truly lived. Prepare to be inspired."

— **JEFF DANIELS**

"*Downstream from Here* is neither a pilgrim's nor a rogue's progress, but a sybarite's unabashed plea for sufferance. Eisendrath is a likeably voluble, well-informed Virgil through the rounds of his own life's considerable exploits. And it all works here. His memoir seeks not so much regulation redemption and transcendence as corroboration that human life is, in fact, worth living— especially, it must be admitted, *his*."

— **RICHARD FORD**

"Too often we are told we have to choose between living wide or living deep, between traveling across the surface of the earth, or coming to truly know and love one place. But Charles Eisendrath has done both in his rich life. This is the memoir of a foreign correspondent and a journalism mentor and yet a man who is spiritually rooted at his beloved Overlook Farm. The essays that he has written about this life are a joy!"

— **ELLEN GOODMAN**

"Charles Eisendrath could be fearing for his life while interviewing a Chilean dictator after a bloody coup. Or he may be chatting with a Michigan fisherman at sunrise. He comes to both conversations with the same humility and infectious curiosity. And that's the beauty of this book. As he reflects on his journey, he tells us it's okay to crave both adventure and quiet moments with people we love. In the end, what really is fulfillment? You'll leave this book in a better place to find it."

— DAVID GREENE, author, co-host "Morning Edition," NPR

"Whether he's covering a coup, surviving a plane crash, learning how to tap a Michigan maple or pitching his patented wood-burning barbecue cooker, former *Time* correspondent Charles Eisendrath's *Downstream from Here* offers a great read. From his rural Michigan "spirit home," as he calls it, Eisendrath offers us an eclectic collection of essays that highlight the value of place in our emotional lives. With wit and wisdom, he revisits the past and helps us to feel better about the future."

— CLARENCE PAGE, author, columnist, *The Chicago Tribune*

"*Downstream from Here* is a trip home, to the home you dream of and which may not exist for you but—lucky for us—it does for Charles Eisendrath, a reporter, orchardist, teacher, inventor, a father and son and husband whose love of the outdoors is matched by his astonishing attention to its joys and depths. This book comes along with you long after a passage is finished. It speaks to you in a voice beautiful and poignant, a poem about longing, achievements, disappointments and, ultimately, joy."

— DOUG STANTON, author, co-founder,
The National Writers Series

"Charles Eisendrath writes that "Journalists spend their lives looking out the window." In this marvelous memoir, he lets us look back in that same window to a family farm in northern Michigan, and how it relates to a fascinating international life. *Downstream from Here* is a paean to place and to family, with a cover by one son, drawings by the other, and a counter-intuitive explanation for why one of the country's most engaging reporters invented a disruptive cooking device called Grillworks."

— ARI WEINZWEIG, author, co-founding partner,
Zingerman's community of businesses

DOWNSTREAM FROM HERE

MISSION POINT PRESS

Published by Mission Point Press
2554 Chandler Rd.
Traverse City, MI 49696
(231) 421-9513
www.MissionPointPress.com

Readers are encouraged to go to www.MissionPointPress.com
to contact the author or to find information on how
to buy this book in bulk at a discounted rate.

ISBN: 978-1-943995-99-8
Library of Congress Control Number: 2019934405

Printed in the United States of America

DOWNSTREAM FROM HERE

A BIG LIFE IN A SMALL PLACE

CHARLES R. EISENDRATH

MISSION POINT PRESS

TO JULIA, WHO TAUGHT ME HOW TO HAVE A CLOSE FAMILY

No. 2061

Abstract of Title

TO

THE FOLLOWING DESCRIBED REAL ESTATE

SITUATED IN

Number 1.

"The East Half (E½) of the Southwest Fractional Quarter (SW fr'l ¼) and Government Lot One (1) of Section Twenty-two (22) Township Thirty-three (33) North of Range Seven (7) West."

Number 2.

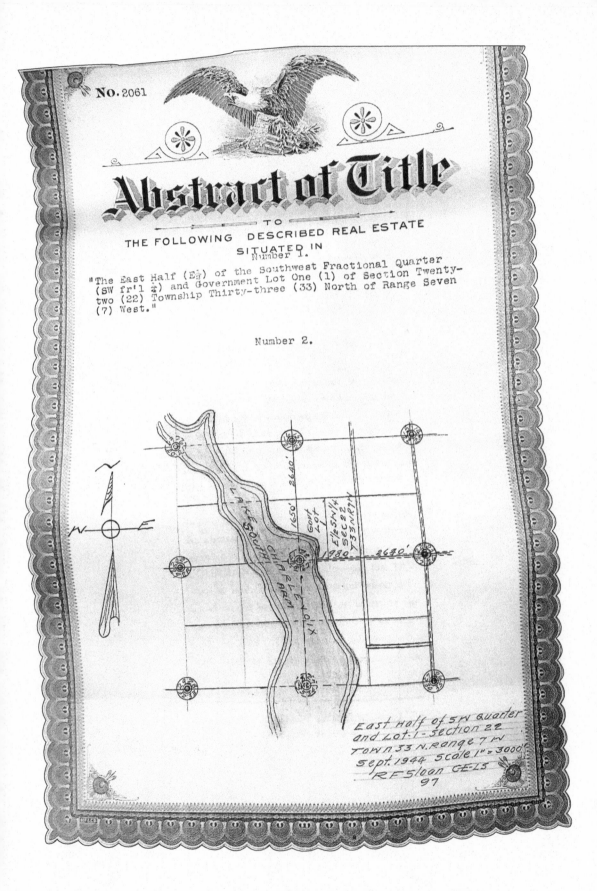

East Half of SW quarter
and Lot-1-Section 22
Town 33 N. Range 7 W
Sept. 1944   Scale 1" = 3000'
R. F. Sloan GE-15
97

CONTENTS

WHERE THE FRONTIER WENT

Mapling seemed a part-time no-brainer for my new retirement from the University of Michigan. The comforting thought that trees aren't tapped until they're at least my age suggested peak production years ahead. Also, the product is the color implied by the term "golden" years. The technique is suitably old as well. The vastly overpriced sliver of land I'd bought to restore the farm's original outline included a venerable sugar shack. We would refurbish it, and mapling would pour over a post-academic life like syrup over pancakes.

You have to begin with a huge reservoir of such reassurance because there's so much to drain hope. Let's start with weather. With cherries, we sweat early warmth, late frost and, of course, not too little moisture, not too much wind. Maples? The sap begins rising in the few weeks when late winter melts fitfully into early spring—you can put your ear to a tree and hear it roar. But for usably-high sugar content, sap must rise and then fall back again to the roots, means days above freezing, nights well below. This requires meteorological precision that often derails. Not to mention the exhausting effort of moving around in two to three feet of snow.

Then there's the actual making of the stuff. We need forty gallons of sap to boil a single gallon of syrup over a wood fire. That means collecting, seasoning, splitting and feeding the evaporator five pieces of cordwood every seven minutes, or about sixty an hour, all by hand. It was going very well, actually. In the first three days of the season we had made

THE LOST SON'S SNOWSHOE HARE

forty-nine gallons, more than the entire trial run last year. I was away at a meeting in the city when Joshua, our maplemeister, called at about 11 AM. A flue pipe had gotten too hot, igniting a nearby beam. "It's burning," he said. "All of it."

In twenty minutes it was gone—the charming old, rough cedar shack; the gleaming new stainless tanks and processing equipment; a dozen face cords of hardwood; the generator; and a hefty log splitter. The fire left everything white ash or twisted metal. It even knocked out the well we'd re-dug the year before. I felt as devastated as the pocked cement floor that had supported it all, including my retirement reveries.

I should have known that the sense of loss wouldn't last—not *that* kind of devastation in *this* particular place. Thirty years earlier, at about the same time of year, I had idiotically let my eleven-year-old disappear with his Christmas shotgun late one afternoon with heavy snow coming in on a southwest wind. He was after snowshoe hare among thick cedars. One muffled shot, then another—and then nothing for too long, with too much snow and too much darkness. Panicked, I made a call to a neighbor. Fifteen minutes later *five* trucks with as many snowmobiles arrived. As they deployed and revved up for the search, in trudged son Benjamin, proudly holding his prized hare high in the headlights.

There was no call for help after the sugar shack fire, but something similar happened anyway. People hereabouts monitor police radio scanners. The first clue to community response arrived with a cord of split hardwood dumped where we needed it. No notice or explanation—everyone knew the snow lay too deep for wood-gathering. Another cord followed, and an offer of much, much more. Derek Ross, the maple equipment dealer located across the Mackinac Bridge in the Upper Peninsula, couldn't find a truck or a driver on Sunday, so he overloaded a trailer with a complete set of replacement gear and delivered it himself. A neighbor appeared on a John Deere with wheels huge enough to haul it the half-mile through the drifts.

Over the next two days a northern Michigan polymath named Rob Vincent gathered an impromptu rescue team. Up went canvas/wood/tin/whatever structures as mysterious in combination as the names of its crew: Darwin Sherlock, the rangy lead carpenter. Maplemeister Joshua, as in he who accomplished much with little. Uncle Swain, the object of whose affection reciprocated in a tight sweater even on the snowmobile commute, but was in fact a dachshund named Clyde. Everyone, it seemed, had some connection with mapling. This included the insurance adjuster, who knew it was now or not at all for our season and supported an advance payment from the company. We were collecting sap again in new tanks four days after the fire, boiling it in six.

Our firestorm took place at the same time that the country was struggling with a firestorm of political dissension and a blizzard of tweets out of Washington. I've taken to reciting our sugar shack story during sessions of dispiriting national angst, often to people far away who have never experienced life at a place like Overlook Farm. The response is a kind of shock and awe about things going *right* against the odds.

THESE ESSAYS EXPLORE a variety of human love that doesn't ask anything in return, but sometimes receives it anyway, although in ways you need to learn how to feel. It's about love of where you live, but only sometimes, while telling yourself and others how you want to live there more. Love for this kind of place isn't like love for other things. Yes, you can wear things you love, eat or drink them, do them, appreciate them, care for them as you would for people, gardens, pets or collections. But these are all ephemeral *in-love-with* kinds of loves. These essays are about the loves of a place you inhabit only temporarily, but which inhabit you permanently. And here again, loves, plural, is no typo.

Without any attempt at continuity, I have returned to Charlevoix County, at least briefly, every one of my seventy-eight years. During the

MARK HAMPTON, OUR BEST MAN AND DECORATOR TO
A SUCCESSION OF FIRST LADIES AND SOCIETY ULTRAS,
DASHED OFF THIS WATERCOLOR IN 1963 WITH "THE FARM
IS HOPELESS, DON'T CHANGE A THING." WE DIDN'T.

last thirty of them, intermittent summing up of what a place can mean
in a single human life — mine — love, singular, has increasingly felt like
a linguistic tic. Our greatest artists and social scientists have expended
entire careers extolling / explaining / weeping about the infinite varieties
of love, and I've come around to agreeing that there are as many kinds of
love as there are objects deserving of it. Put differently, the optic of this
book examines one place from the perspective of many loves — each with
its own history, characters and characteristics. You may see it as some version of your life, too, if you take the time to examine the things that grow
lives of their own while staying where you left them between visits. It's all
there, waiting for you, just downstream from where you are right now.

Yes, this demands huge amounts of time, that most precious and only
completely never-expandable quantity, but it's worth it because, as the
comic strip "Steve Roper" wisely said, "Your life is what happens while

you're making other plans." Place, home, that most essential compendium of spirit and experience, gets short shrift in *curricula vitae*, rating only the name of a town, as if a neighborhood, a backyard, a winding path, a favorite tree didn't matter. With a few exceptions for the house-involved like Thomas Jefferson, even full-scale biographies focus on the doing, and how the doing was done rather than the where and how. Or, *how* the *where* influenced all else. For me, it was when I began calling Overlook Farm my spirit home that I became increasingly interested in the *where* of my unexamined time and why it was that the *where* was becoming the single root for doings otherwise as hard to trace back to the individual points of origin as leaves blown from a single tree in a forest.

Much in these essays concerns loss. Much that is happening to America these days smacks of losing touch with our essential greatness, part of which is the frontier appreciation of collaboration. It is knitted into our national fabric and worn on battlefields around the world. I would bet a new set of mapling equipment that experiences like mine seem normal not only in little places like East Jordan, Michigan, but also in small parts of big cities where people build things together. Instances of the frontier spirit at work are scattered across America like rescue lights in the gloom of a blizzard after dark.

December 20, "Crash Day,[1]" 2018
Overlook Farm

---

1   An annual family anniversary, see page 227.

PART 1

WRITTEN IN TREES

Finding Where Home Really Is

August, 1984

When you come home, your feet travel faster than your head. In 1973, shaken up by harrowing images from Pinochet's new Chile, there was a lot to get used to. Along with quotidian politics—after years abroad during which nothing seemed quotidian—the other attitude-changing encounter was with the social/personal theories of someone who lived 2200 years ago, someone whose writing I'd under-appreciated as a teenager.

I learned about Aristotle in 1958 at Yale, where, with seventeen years of life experience, I had come to New Haven from St. Louis to study philosophy. It wasn't at all clear to me what philosophy was, exactly. What mattered was how deep it sounded. Anything that sounded deep attracted me because it seemed, well, adult. Philosophy! What could be more exciting? Adults were the ones who understood things, right? For reasons known only to Yale, I was given advance placement to skip summary courses and was placed in a department sub-field of a subject I'd never heard of in and of itself: Ethics. And Ethics required me to write a paper on "Aristotle's Notion of Wisdom."

I read and read. I made lists. I made two columns of words and drew lines between them, trying to figure out whether enjoyment really meant fun or whether Mr. Aristotle had in mind something more like "sacrifice." Suddenly, my seventeen years' worth of knowledge seemed painfully—shriekingly—inadequate to transport me across an intellectual inky black sea. While my philosophy major ended before I could actually elect it, or finish freshman year, or pass my first philosophy course, or even complete the first assignment, this void loomed like the combination of a dream you can't exit and a night that won't end. I sensed something essential there, as a steering wheel to a properly driven car. But for about twenty years I decided to forget it.

According to the ambulatory university named Aristotle, Wisdom equals Excellence in the Art of Living. In many ways—though not all—that little equation and its permanent psychic encystment was what my parents bought with four years of full tuition payments to the Yale Corporation. It was a bargain. When the shooting in Santiago stopped and I made my way out on a UN rescue plane, Aristotle's equation, dormant since Ethics I, suddenly began kicking like whatever agitates Mexican jumping beans against the walls of the mental cyst. Wisdom surely did not mean getting killed in somebody else's war by accident or design.

What happened during the week of September 11, 1973, was the biggest story of my career, the most dangerous period of my life and it occurred a decade before Gail Sheehy published *Passages*. Twenty years later I began the essays that have become this book, realizing that I had been just shy of twenty when Mr. Aristotle equipped me with a personal philosophy and the hapless instructor made sure I would take no more philosophy courses.

Aristotle thought that happiness was the goal in life; and wisdom, the means of getting it. Or even better, embodying it. It took beginning a new life in a country that seemed decidedly home and not-home for me to see the wisdom in that two-thousand-year-old text, and it was at Overlook Farm where I would begin to practice "excellence in the art of living."

IF "THE LAND REMEMBERS" is the stuff of legend, the houses on it tend to get edited out as just one more needless thing in our frequent remodeling, rebuilding, redevelopment or moving. But if you refuse the sensible abridgment of unused items and discarded dreams, if you let a place stand still, no matter how far away you go or how different you become, a home naturally accretes reminders of progenitors, their friends, treasures, mistakes, trophies. For example, when we (infrequently) "reorganize" the attic, I must deal yet again with the meticulous scrapbooks my father kept of French cathedrals toured while he, like the twentieth century, was in his twenties. There is the photo of him with Jerome Hill, a railroad scion and future art dealer; and Robert Osborne, the Pulitzer-winning political cartoonist of World War II—all of them impossibly young and picnicking with the Fitzgeralds, Scott and Zelda. As with the cathedrals, there was no explanation. My father, devoted to art all his life, believed in the power of the image to explain itself unaided.

Elsewhere, everywhere, anywhere, there are relics of old passions. Kitchen stools covered with indigo tie-dyes from coverage of the Biafran War, my first. A shelf of Russian novels, others about collecting mushrooms. Some books are bubbles that pop into the memory stew, like

THE GREAT INDOORSMAN WHO BOUGHT A FARM TO STAY AWAY FROM HIS MOTHER-IN-LAW

my pride in a 1969 scoop (insufficiently celebrated, I thought) about the joys of single-malt whisky, then unknown in the U.S. There are the bespoke English kites and their enormous wooden reels that we slung under our first-born's blue English perambulator. The thing was the size of a rowboat, and rocked like one on Sunday walks to the Kensington Palace Garden pitch. When the Queen Mum's red helicopter flew over us to take her to lunch with her granddaughter, Princess Meg, a bobby would bark "Strike kites!" and we scrambled like boys playing soldiers. It all reverberates.

Our children, and now grandchildren, ignore the clutter on their playroom wall, but adult visitors don't. Neither do we. To us it's "the ancestor room," hung haphazardly during a three-day drizzle with butterfly nets, canoe paddles, boat steering wheels, grill crank wheels, baby shoes, mounted fish, pince-nez and childhood Leonardos. And, of course, photos. My grandchildren call me "Pops." Well, there's my own Pops in

5

the three-piece tweed suit he wore while catching large tuna caught off Catalina in the 1920s. All around the player piano—from his place in Charlevoix—the photos go back beyond grandparents on both sides. The first Charlevoix vacationers in the 1880s, from my side; on Julia's, Supreme Court Justice Benjamin Cardozo and Emma Lazarus, who gave the Statue of Liberty the poem, "Give me your poor, your hungry...."

Scrapbook living comes quite naturally if you let it. The American Housing Survey estimates there are around six million "second homes," although it notes the difficulty in defining that status. Many of them stay in the family far longer than principal residences. Why? Taxes on appreciated value, for sure. But I think it's more because, if you let them, they can make a more complete you of you: a history of what became your future.

True scrapbooks have a chronological order. Memoirs have a narrative arc. Here, the only logical progression can be read in the inescapable march of technology. In these essays written between 1983 and 2018, typefaces grew smoother as many of the human faces described crinkled. The originals of both are preserved—viewpoints from the moment of writing and publishing and also from succeeding generations of machines. These begin with a beloved portable Olivetti, Model 32, with a Time Inc. plaque on its blue case; and an antique Underwood Model 5, its architecture open to view like the Eiffel Tower's; and on to various computers (I skipped the electric typewriter phase). Each recalls a time, a mood. Like the various kinds of loves for a place, affection for the different expressions of these faces that gaze back at me is definitely plural, and no typographical error there, either.

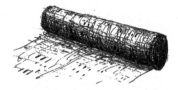

July, 1997

It is April, 1974. Ben is 5 years old and in love with his Juan Peron generalissimo's hat. Mark, 2 ½, sucks his beloved plastic nipple pacifier that Irene, our muchacha, has informed us is called a chupete, or 'pe,' for short. He does this nonstop. They are both wearing blood-red ponchos with black stripes from the Salta region of northwestern Argentina. But this is northwestern Michigan, and Julia is helping me load a music roll on the player piano.

The song is "Waiting for the Robert E. Lee." At my boys' ages, I would play it the way Mark sucks his 'pe.' Nonstop. All over the world, sealed off in a memory cell lined with mental lead to prevent degradation or dilution, is a memory secret even from me: of all things, the image of an oblong, rectangular box made of cheap paper board with a frayed orange label on top. "Checked out," it says, "from the St. Louis Public Library, date Mar. 19, 1913." As a child dreaming away rainy afternoons in a living room corner of my grandparents' cottage in Charlevoix, I loved thinking that someone in my family had been alive and doing something I could visualize in those ancient days. Even better, here was indisputable proof that grownups could do something as dumb as leave a library fine running at two cents a day…forever.

In the classic pattern of American memory shredding, my mother presided over the sale of the house we all called "415 Michigan Avenue." Never just "415" or "the cottage." Whole lifetimes of memories and associations fade into walls at the moment of title change, and can't be evoked because the new occupants of the house hold only the keys to the door. For me, the real keys to that house were its views through the lopsided branches of a lone, signal white pine toward an open ocean called Lake Michigan, and an upright player piano made by the Franklin company of Philadelphia that joined my family a half-century before I was born. While digging the song out of the roll cabinet, I have explained the magic of this old instrument to the boys, whose eyes have grown wide enough to receive all the miracles of the world. They push closer against Julia, silent. The music starts, the rhythm slows, mimicking the rotation of a riverboat paddle wheel:

Way down on the levee,

In old Alabamee,

There's Daddy and Mammy,

There's Ephram and Sammy....

Something is happening in my chest. I can't breathe. Something's going on in my head, too. Consciousness goes blank. The boys and Julia blur into moving colors. I hear myself make a loud, unfamiliar sound and feel my head jerk up and down. "Dad's CRYING!" Benjamin reports. I have never done that in front of them, or Julia, for that matter. She is smiling at me in a new way. "I think we're home," I say as she takes me in her arms and I sense why she's a wonderful mother.

The Way Home

July, 1987

Going back where you belong, or once belonged, or could belong, is dependent on age, health, finances, computer baseball software, travel, cooking—you get the idea—and can mean everything and not much. Returning to a place my parents owned longer than any other white people in the area—but never lived in—and which became the first home I ever owned—also *in absentia*—was as much spiritual and political as geographical. Going home meant America and America meant the farm.

The road back to America and Overlook Farm began in Anatolia with a yellow message under my hotel room door. It was August 1972, two months after the Watergate "plumbers" arrests and late in the endgame called Vietnam. I had covered neither, but the rogue war and outlaw presidency reached me anyway. Like my country's spirit, my own was about to darken.

The telex under my hotel door in Turkey announced that *Time* Managing Editor Henry Grunwald had decreed—for unexplained and, to me, inexplicable reasons—that the magazine would do a crash cover story on the international drug trade. At that point I was an acting bureau chief. I would have seven days to put it together. Reporting, that is, the short book that would be condensed to about the 40:1 ratio of maple sap to syrup—as I later learned in northern Michigan—before being poured out to readers.

Little ironies did not escape me. For months, my bureau got yawns from New York about a proposed major investigative update on the

PARIS, 1972

still-unsolved "French Connection" in the drug trade, the same drug trade that had raised such a stir as a 1971 Gene Hackman movie. And this moment, when I was being summarily ordered back to base, I was engaged in one of the little stratagems that so frequently backfire—trying to increase my editors' appreciation for the big story by getting a little quickie of more immediate concern, i.e. domestic politics, into the magazine.

Poppies had been cultivated in Turkey longer than Kansas has grown corn, producing no more local addiction problems than corn flakes. But the Nixon administration hoped to wipe out the U.S. heroin problem by destroying the Turkish poppies. My story, I hoped, would show the pathetic hopelessness of combating the American drug problem anywhere but at home.[2]

That story went on hold. I raced back to Paris, and from the airport straight to the bureau which I put on "war footing," meaning as close to an around-the-clock operation as we could manage to report, write and then have the telex room retype for transmission to New York. The enormous mound of copy for such enterprises amounted to a kind of journalistic *gourmandise*, invented for the pleasure of Henry Luce. Luce wanted to make sure that he and his editors had all the information possible on a topic selected for *The Weekly Newsmagazine*, even if they decided not to use it. Since he always paid better than any competition in the print media, much of the chaff was of considerable literary merit; in fact, it was distributed for a period as a separate syndication service. But in a "crash" story situation like this one, there was no time for much digging on our

---

2   Hindsight proved me wrong and also right. The policy I thought was hopeless succeeded in Turkey, but merely shifted the drug trade, first to "the Golden Triangle" in Southeast Asia and then to South America where we continue the same policies, curing others in order to avoid taking the medicine we prescribe.

own. Our investigations, as someone put it, would have to be investigating what other people had already investigated. To this end, I knew of a *le Monde* staffer who'd spent months fathoming the mysterious inability of French police to find the "*labos*" around Marseilles where opium gum became heroin. I hired him. He turned in six pages; I edited them to three.

The telex room of the Paris bureau was a sizable operation, employing three people full time. In those pre-fax days, it processed copy from *Time, Life, Fortune, Sports Illustrated* and Time-Life Books. And the stories weren't just from Paris, but from much of Western Europe as well as colonial holdovers like North Africa and Vietnam. It was a situation made for a "little light intelligence work." As such, the telex room refused to transmit the three pages on The French Connection. All of *les typistes* were French nationals, none of them journalists. It was "a police problem," I was told, not part of journalism. Some tense sparring indicated that this was not a debatable point. So without saying anything more, I left the room and dictated the pages by phone to the London bureau for transmission. The telex room in London—which probably served the same ancillary function for British intelligence as ours did for the French—absolutely loved my situation. New York used two paragraphs:

> *Typically, the big-time operators deal in more than just drugs…*
> *…By some accounts, French smugglers are into something far more complex. It is said that the SDECE, France's CIA, has quietly engaged Paris- and Marseille-based smugglers to move arms to a number of Middle East countries. These secret arms shipments are said to enable France to bolster its export arms industry and its influence in the Middle East, while it continues to adhere publicly to its 1968 total embargo on weapons sales to the belligerent nations of the region.*
>
> *The theory goes that arms and ammunition are turned over to established smugglers and shipped in compartments concealed in specially fitted vehicles. The underworld then takes advantage of the arrangement: on the return trip, the same compartments are filled with drugs. (Time, European edition 9.4.72, "Search and Destroy—The War on Drugs," p.13)*

ANATOLIAN GROWERS SAID ASKING THEM TO STOP
PLANTING OPIUM POPPIES WAS LIKE TELLING KANSAS
FARMERS TO STOP GROWING CORN

Those brief passages changed my life. Until then, my main fear as a journalist was failing to get something, or getting it wrong. Now I learned that getting something right could be worse, or at least it got me thinking about the possibility.

Insubordination in the telex room had merely confirmed conventional wisdom. Every correspondent learned within weeks of arrival that big foreign news operations in Paris always included someone who worked with French security. It was also a given that your telephones were bugged and that you would know it because the system — installed by the Gestapo during the Nazi occupation and not updated in France's long neglect of its infrastructure — was pretty crude. Sometimes you could listen to *them* while they listened to *you*. But until the "Search and Destroy" cover story, all this was hearsay. Surprises now popped up in unsettling sequence. At the office, and then at home, we began hearing someone we weren't talking to take a deep breath now and then and, occasionally, what sounded like the clink of a coffee cup. After a few weeks, anger defeated apprehension. I launched a loud, rude and lengthy soliloquy at the agent I imagined having just listened to my conversation with my mother in St. Louis. The tap couldn't have been of much value because the lines cleared the next day, sometime between dinner and midnight.

Thuggery I took more seriously. It had never occurred to me that my own government might actually behave as governments do in the John le Carré novels I devoured. Unprepared, I was shaken on several levels by a call from "the political reporting section" of the U.S. embassy, an American voice warning me to clear the bureau immediately of all personnel because of a letter bomb threat. True, the Israeli embassy was next door. On the other hand, American embassies had no "political reporting" sections. Nor was there anything unusual going on in the Middle East.

My standard practice in sensitive stories was to talk to my sources immediately after publication. As part of this cover story package, I had reported in an accompanying "sidebar" on a Paris-based U.S. drug agent, describing his courage in a dangerous job. Given the flattery, I wasn't ready for his fury. He further surprised me with an invitation to lunch to discuss the story, designating a restaurant near the *Assemblée Nationale*. That was my first experience with La Bourgogne where, I learned, much of the dirty work of French politics had been transacted for decades. The gold lettering on its crimson awning shimmered in the sunshine of an immaculate spring day. As I approached, the agent and a colleague got up from their table and escorted me—one on each side, lightly, but gripping my elbows—to another table where four men sat, eyeing us in silence.

"You wanted to know what Monsieur Eisendrath looks like," my source told them in place of introductions. "Take a good look." Until then, I hadn't processed what being held by the elbows meant. Now it was obvious. The escort continued on to yet another nearby table where I was invited to sit down. I assumed the explanation to be intentionally ominous: "About those four over there," said the agent. "Two are *ours*, two are *theirs*."

NEW FRIGHTS BLOT OUT remote implications, so I didn't understand until much later that a drug story that began in central Anatolia and closed at a Paris café was what launched us out of foreign correspondence and toward northern Michigan. Our next vocational transit

13

lounge? Another unlikely place—Punta del Este, Uruguay, the Riviera of southern South America.

Tourists avoid the place in September for the same reasons that Jones Beach holds few attractions for New Yorkers in January. When Julia and I arrived with the boys, the only swimmers were penguins. On the other hand, we weren't tourists. We were short-term refugees. Another call from the American embassy had suggested that I take my family on an impromptu vacation.

"When might it be suggested that I do that?"

"According to our information," said the friend on the ambassador's staff in Buenos Aires, "leaving any time between now [11 AM] and about five this afternoon should be okay."

The problem was that Juan Peron had recently returned to Argentina and my coverage had documented the inability of this octogenarian dictator to tolerate democracy, as he had promised to one group of followers from an eighteen-year exile, or to dictate efficiently, which he had promised to another. Rival *Peronista* factions representing ideologies ranging from Marxism to fascism regularly shot it out, knifed it out and caused one another to "be disappeared"—*desaparecidos*—a chilling term of phrase. Terrorism was rampant, and victims included journalists. Louis Uchitelle of the AP had taken a bomb in the kitchen of his apartment, where his wife and young daughters spent a great deal of time (but were elsewhere, fortunately). Several Argentine reporters had been found in the city garbage dump, murdered. Guerrilla armies like ERP (People's Revolutionary Army) had made a business of kidnapping executives, whereby capitalist ransom funded Marxism.

My sources estimated guerrilla strength to be several times what the embassy was reporting to the community of American businessmen in Buenos Aires, but the more these guerrilla exploits confirmed my figures, the less friendly would be the reception from my countrymen in the business community. While police stations were being dynamited, while colleagues were being kidnapped and sometimes killed, while the executives themselves regularly decamped for the safety of Uruguay following specific threats, they also managed to sink ever deeper into denial. Their worst fear wasn't loss of life, it was loss of *career*. Crazy, I thought. Only when I revisited this in the peace of a northern Michigan summer did it dawn on me that my own priorities were just as warped. Yes, the search for truth aims higher than mere business, but still — there I was with a wife and two young children, decamping for Uruguay like the executives I'd thought seriously misguided.

Time's cover story on Juan Peron arrived on newsstands complete with an inflammatory corner slash. Peron's acolytes were particularly infuriated by my reporting the simple fact that the fascist and Marxist elements of *Peronismo* were at war with each other and that *el Caudillo* — The Strongman, as they called him — no longer had the strength for strongman rule. Even more powerful was an image by Horacio Villalobos, a young Argentine freelancer I'd sent to Ezeiza Airport. Instead of photographing Peron deplaning, he got an image of a Peronista from one faction dangling by his fingers from a nearby pedestrian overpass while a man from a rival faction was cutting off those fingers with a large knife.

Once in the safety of Uruguay's Punta de Este, the Eisendraths found themselves to be just another group of refugees in a resort famous for accommodating those on the run. One night our waiter pointed out that the aging figure seated with a gorgeous young thing at the next table was the overthrown president of Brazil. After more than ten days exile I received a summons (as always, a telex under the door), and at first the message boded well. *Time's* Santiago stringer had lined up an interview with Chile's besieged socialist president, Salvador Allende. My embassy contact confirmed that it was safe for the family to return to Buenos Aires, albeit on a state of alert. It seemed that with the arrival of a new edition of *Time*, the Argentine threats had calmed down, or at least other targets had been selected. I would escort Julia, Ben and Mark to our apartment, then continue on to Santiago, where my interview was scheduled for 8 AM, Monday, September 11 at the Moneda Palace. What I soon learned was that a coup was also scheduled for that time and day.

FROM NOTES DATED SEPTEMBER 10, 1973

In Santiago, I take a taxi to dinner with classmate Peter Bell, whose thinking I've admired since discussions shared at Book and Snake, one of Yale's secret societies. Now running the Ford Foundation office, he's a perfect source. Peter's other guest is Enrique Santos, a Uruguayan who heads a United Nations Relief Agency. They confirm what my taxi driver had announced with great solemnity—that there will be a coup the next morning. Yet that's nothing new, including the confidence. The city has been paved with rumors for weeks. Early the next morning, however, it's for real.

It's 7:30 am and I've downed my much-loved early breakfast at Santiago's spectacular wrought-iron fish market: black coffee with ceviche so fresh the Humboldt Current salts your nostrils. Begun as attempts for impromptu access to Allende, known for such meetings there, these visits had become an indulgence. Journalism might fail but not the adoption of a lifelong proclivity for fish market breakfasts. Walking back to the Hotel Carrera, troops at double-time march blocked the way, materializing from shadows at every approach to Constitution Square. Oddly, but somehow endearingly, they wear the same slightly outdated uniforms that the Pentagon had sent to my non-essential unit of the Maryland National Guard while new issue went off to Vietnam. A recoilless rifle opened up without warning a few feet from my left ear. Like an unforgettable refrain, the metallic ringing becomes a permanent reminder of the early morning of September 11, 1973.

At first, it isn't clear whether this is a coup or an elaborate intimidation of President Allende, whose office in the Moneda Palace faces the Square. Troops begin the same "search-and-clear" urban combat maneuvers I learned in my own training: You get control of the stairways all the way to the top of a building and then herd the prisoners down to the street, hands clasped atop heads. But it quickly becomes clear that this is no drill. Also, that something is very, very wrong. Judging from the firing inside the buildings, the Chilean Army is taking control of the stairs, all right. But their prisoners are being forced out of upstairs windows at gunpoint. One man who survives his fall to the pavement tries to wriggle behind a park bench. He is shot dead. Clearly my 8:30 interview with Salvador Allende is going to be—rescheduled—maybe into eternity.

This would be my third war, following Northern Ireland and Biafra, and correspondents have set routines in situations like the one unfolding in Santiago. You get a hotel room on a high floor so that any "incoming" from the street will angle harmlessly up into the ceiling. You fill wastebaskets and anything else that will hold water, because water will probably get scarce. You plan to sleep rolled up in a mattress near what you hope is a bearing wall or, if things really get heavy, inside the mattress inside the bathtub. I went about this small business with the television on and also the portable radio I always carried with me.

Whatever the communication techniques of the age may be, sudden inaccessibility to them is like entering a tunnel with no light at the other end. You can feel the forces carrying you deeper, without any hint of where, or if, you'll come out. There's a feeling of weightlessness and that neither right and left nor up and down matter. I had long known that ignoring a telephone is as difficult as not answering your mother's voice[3], the Chilean coup taught me that the light of a monitor screen holds similar power.[4] Its sudden dark brought terror from some corner of the psyche I hadn't known existed. The ability to perceive and be perceived by the rest of contemporary mankind had vanished.

There had been televised indications of the problems to come that day. "A Midsummer Night's Dream" appeared where national news had been. Then, reflecting what was happening in the Chileans' world, it was broadcast again—upside down. Maybe it was a warning from desperate technicians that the long-awaited *golpe* was underway, but it wasn't long before someone in authority took note of the message and the screen's life narrowed to a single bright dot, shrinking the pool of normalcy to a circle as small as the drain at the bottom of a sink. All communications whirlpooled down that drain. The phone died. The radio played Bee-

---

3   The cell phone changed that dramatically.
4   In 1973, this meant television only.

YOU DON'T GET TO CHOOSE
WHO LAUNCHES YOUR CAREER,
AS AGNEW INADVERTENTLY DID
FOR ME. AN INTERVIEW ON THE
CAMPAIGN PLANE, 1968

thoven, interrupted by static that sounded like gunfire, or *vice versa*—either equally likely. A voice announced *"Bando Número Uno"* to a city that knew what was going on, but not what it meant. It was "Order Number One" from the country's new *Número Uno*, General Augusto Pinochet Ugarte, and the order meant that all activity outside the home would shut down at sundown. Or else, what? Or else anyone defying a dusk-to-dawn curfew would be shot dead. Then another drain moment, a hiss signifying the death of radio. The hotel switchboard announced no further calls into Chile, or out of it (although that part turned out to have intermittent sputters of life). From my window, the peaks of the Andes suddenly looked like jail bars.

Salvador Allende's brain was blown out of his skull[5] not long after I was to have seen him, and with his life also ended the world's only Marxist national regime brought to power in free elections. Was there American involvement in the take-down? Denied at official levels, this was a matter of faith by all factions in Chile and assumed by those of us who covered it, although we lacked any confirmation we could use. Not being able to report what the feeling in your reportorial bones tells you is a particularly painful journalistic paralysis. Five years before I had had a bad case of it when I knew from any number of circumstantial inputs that Vice President Spiro Agnew was a crook. But all I could do, lacking hard evidence, was report the foibles I encountered during his campaign for office. Confirmation in Chile wouldn't happen until well after the first phase of the coup, when the long-distance truckers whose strike had crippled the economy admitted taking bribes from the CIA. But nothing prevented me reporting what I could see and hear—the carnage being wrought by those the U.S. was helping to power, some of it visible from my hotel window. As in France, and then Argentina, straight reporting

---

5   Some later reported that he had shot himself.

18

would run me afoul of my own country's policies, with the Chileans acting in concert.

After putting my room in order for a siege, I spent a few hours gathering what information I could by eyeball. This meant watching Hawker Siddeley fighter-bombers come in at the level of the hotel's rooftop restaurant vantage point. To call it "a deafening roar" is like describing lightening as "very bright." Jet afterburners at close range and without ear protection can cause a kind of synesthesia, like when you're not sure, for an instant, whether you've heard a light or seen the noise because the sound's in your eyes, too. The rockets shattered Allende's office across the Square—exactly where my interview was to have been, at precisely that time. The view from the hotel window would have included my fragmentation along with his.

Meanwhile, the Hotel Carrera's frantic manager was pounding on doors, trying to herd us into a designated shelter in the basement—a routine familiar to many war correspondents. At first, the business executives were proudly protective of the lovely young girls who had been with them in their rooms. After a few hours, when conversation became the only amusement in our quasi-prison, they invited the rest of us poor celibates to join their tables for verbal relief. I ended up alone and facing a wall, writing up an eyewitness scene-setter for the coup story.

For weeks, the canny Nina Lindley, *Time's* longtime office manager in Buenos Aires, had packed me off on each trip to Chile with a suitcase stuffed with cosmetics, stockings and female underthings. I was to present them to "The Telex Ladies" at the Hotel Carrera, who punched copy into telex tape which was then bounced off a satellite for transmission to the Time-Life Building in New York. I had the silent telex room punch the tape for me, then I put it in my shirt pocket for some modicum of safekeeping until I was able to send it from somewhere, somehow, to someone. But I never used it because one of the recipients of my little bribes buzzed my room. "We've got a line out, but only to Mendoza [Argentina], and we don't know for how long," said the operator, thereby seriously endangering herself. "Do you want it?"

I wasn't ready for a *telephone* line, and certainly not to Mendoza, where I knew nobody. But panic adrenalin reminded me that I was *supposed* to know somebody in Mendoza, a man I'd intended to meet as a source for a planned wine story during a vacation weekend with Julia. The source ran an American library and his number remained in my book of contacts. Miraculously, he was a former UPI reporter and in short order he'd taken the dictation and signed off to relay my story to New York.

Although privately gloating about what I knew would be a world scoop, I decided that prudence demanded keeping my giddy little success strictly to myself. Luck is a lot like Tolstoy's comment about happiness in the opening line of *Anna Karenina*: "All happy families are the same; each unhappy family is unhappy in its own way." In the chaos that follows fresh killing, all is rumor, facts are for later. While a hundred or so of us misinformed each other in the basement of the Carrera, thousands of others were imprisoned in the national soccer stadium where many were raped, tortured and murdered. Among them was Charles Horman, an idealistic young American with socialist leanings who liked to hang out with us in the hotel bar. Horman became the posthumous subject of the best-seller, *Missing*, and the attending Costa-Gavras film starring Jack Lemmon. Like happiness, luck often doesn't last very long. I might as well have shouted my scoop with a megaphone. The Junta, of course, had been listening.

At the Junta's first press conference, hosted by spokesman Federico Willoughby, the tiny band of foreign reporters in Santiago learned that the ground rules would be different in this particular "salvation of the country." For example, there would be no censorship nor expulsion from the country, standard practice in such situations. By then, however, we had heard the bursts of dawn and dusk curfew gunfire. We'd also heard rumors about a colleague from Brazilian radio being taken to the soccer stadium-slash-impromptu prison.

If we erred by Junta standards without being silenced or thrown out, someone asked, then what could we expect? "The opposite," said Willoughby, which we assumed meant being thrown into the stadium. The briefing was brevity itself, called only to announce Allende's death (suicide, officially), claim victory, deny defections within the military and debunk the presumed "outside influence" from the CIA. Picking up his assault rifle, which he had pointedly rested between his microphone and his audience, Willoughby asked "the man from *Time*" to identify himself. I was escorted to a back room for some special instruction. A Junta telephone intercept had picked up my dictation session and hadn't liked the sound of it.

Willoughby locked the door behind us, muffling the hubbub my colleagues made as I was escorted away. It wasn't lost on me that whatever went on in this room would be lost to them as well. I was informed that *Time's* stringer was a member of Allende's Socialist party—true—and that "We [the Junta] want him"—which I could not let happen. Mario Planet had worked for *Time* for many years. Any harm to him, I warned them, would be in the issue of the magazine immediately following the resumption of Chilean communication with the rest of the world. Now that the threat had been made, even an "accident" would be attributed to the Junta, and the Junta staked its success on recognition by the U.S. and foreign investment—investment by precisely the kind of multinational company executives who read *Time* and *Fortune*. My pitch to save Planet was that the Junta's own self-interest required that corporate America hear nothing negative about the treatment of Time Inc.'s personnel while reporting the first weeks of its "New Chile."

It wasn't just my stringer's fate that I worried about. I had a distinct feeling of uncertainty about my own. This was the era of Watergate; the Nixon Presidency was consumed by anger and increasingly paranoid. In the U.S., a plane carrying the wife of a Watergate operative and a large amount of alleged hush money mysteriously crashed in a Chicago suburb. Field agents trained in the arts of the black side of intelligence were given a degree of operational latitude that Senator Frank Church's later investigation exposed as harmful to U.S. foreign policy. The agency was consequently downsized and brought under tighter surveillance. But that was then and this was now, and lacking conformation of U.S. involvement, I could only report speculation. Personally, however, I lived by the assumption of serious personal risk. To what length would renegade spooks go in a cover-up? The thought of my own government out of control at such a moment left me with a far greater unease than I had felt in Paris, where threats came from "their guys," not ours. In Santiago there was no *Time* bureau, a much smaller group of friends and a far larger feeling of being vulnerable to violence that could easily be made to appear random.

Fortunately, there was a counter-balance to full-blown paranoia. True, my personal situation was discomfiting. Professionally, however, things were decidedly brighter: While I was locked in, my competition was locked out of Chile and the big story.

Awaiting a response for the first interview with Pinochet, I reported as much as possible on foot between curfews. I checked in at the AP office, which occupied a low floor in a building directly opposite the Defense Ministry, from which the coup had been directed. Its staffers had hidden under their desks as the place was raked with small arms fire. There was plenty of material for a piece on the AP situation, but the first thing I learned was that the police had been there, looking for *me*.

It was time to get out of Santiago. I called Ambassador Nathanial Davis at all hours at his office and at home for a seat on the first plane. If the idea of being terrified by bloodiness and, at the same time, demanding an interview with the man who might be directing it seems surreal, well, welcome to foreign correspondence.

By the time I was summoned to the Defense Ministry, I had been in semi-hiding for almost a week, keeping up the harassing calls to Ambassador Davis, which no doubt doubled as a kind of threat. To the embassy I insisted that I was still functioning as a journalist reporting the coup, something I hoped they might communicate to the Junta: harm to me would add weight to reports of U.S. complicity.[6]

These were strange days. Chile's excellent wine was free in many bars because the supply of foreign bottles quickly ran out—one could appear with any sort of container and it was cheerfully filled. Everything was suddenly for sale, but only in dollars. At dusk, with the onset of the Junta's curfew and the regulatory procedure of gunfire, convoys of army trucks drove slowly through the streets. In one I noted bloody arms and legs protruding from the cargo bin; Chile's new leadership was not wed to the subtler forms of intimidation. The Hotel Carrera's elevator operators, who normally transformed the rickety cages into foreign exchange booths on unscheduled stops between floors, ceased their bulge-pocket moonlight banking after the first police sweep.

When I got the interview, I wasn't at all sure what awaited me at the

---

6   I ultimately concluded that U.S. efforts to destabilize Allende came through the Nixon/Kissinger White House, leaving the embassy free to truthfully report non-involvement.

WORLD SCOOP—FIRST INTERVIEW WITH
AUGUSTO PINOCHET, FOUR DAYS AFTER HIS COUP

headquarters of an army that only a few days earlier had sent out MPs to arrest me. Somehow, I thought, looking formal, even diplomatic, might be good protection. I still owned one London suit, a blue chalk-stripe, and I wore it like armor. Pinochet didn't have to take special care with his clothes to send me a message; he received me in the Wehrmacht-style uniform of the Chilean army, which meant something special to me as a Jew whose first conscious memories were of World War II. I shivered a little. The interview itself had an aura of lethal comedy. The Chilean Junta, and maybe even U.S. intelligence services, were going to try to convince the world that Allende had to go because of personal profligacy! Aides produced the sort of photo albums that preserve U.S. high school graduations and wedding parties within bogus-leather covers. The albums were filled with color photos showing spent bottles of Chivas Regal and young girls in suggestive poses—evidence, explained briefing officers in tones of civics teachers, of general disarray instead of the dignified business of governing in the Moneda Palace. The last photos were supposed to verify the Junta's account of Allende's suicide by showing something identified as human brain splattered on a sofa.

We had all heard reports that a new, strictly capitalist "Chicago Economy," designed by Prof. Milton Friedman, would be introduced to replace Allende's socialist administration. I hadn't thought about how literally or how quickly that might be done until Pinochet introduced his economics aides to me: in their minds I represented *Fortune*—"Our Bible," as Pinochet's "Chicago boys" called Time, Inc.'s prestigious monthly. As a Chicago native, I easily picked out the broad Chicago "A's" in their accented English. *Time* ran a Villa-Lobos photo of the scowling general in full uniform with crossed arms, documenting his intention to do whatever was necessary to rid the country of Marxism. In Santiago, it was made clear that as many people as necessary would die in the radical transformation of Chile.

WITH ITS LONG, NARROW TOPOGRAPHY bordered entirely by mountains, sea and desert, Chile is not an easy country to flee—and I was far from the only person with a need to get out. When the United Nations finally succeeded in securing a plane to carry passengers over the still-sealed borders, a strange group assembled. Most of us were shaken because we understood what was happening and found it sickening. There were exceptions, however. One of the activities interrupted by the coup that week was a tour by University of Michigan's water polo team: Blond giants had been seen tossing Frisbees in streets otherwise emptied by curfew and gunfire. This sent Chileans into awe and their handlers into conniptions, but the team was among the first chosen to be escorted out of the country unharmed. So was a woman in a crimson dress and copper hair that might have been natural forty years ago. It was this eye-catcher, I was told in whispers, who owned an International Telephone & Telegraph-controlled company that supplied a "hard-wire" communications link to CIA headquarters. In fact, I had spotted her before in the port city of Viña del Mar, where I'd raced to-and-from during open curfew, both to remove myself from Santiago and to look for evidence of a reported U.S. naval presence. (I saw none.) She, or rather someone playing her, turned up as a bit actor in "Missing"—Costa-Gravas' attention to detail was impressive. The depiction, even though unexplained in the film, hinted at the possibility of very private communications between those in the know within the most public of media.

One of the few others who *absolutely* understood what was going on became an important source for everything I used in later reports, with the exception of his own identity. The tall, distinguished-looking American might well have been who he said he was — a retired colonel in the U.S. Army. He certainly knew who I was before I introduced myself, and he wanted to tell a tale, but only if our plane — a propeller craft that flew through passes in the Andes rather than over them — managed to land us safely in Argentina. He was too shaken to talk right then, he said. Suddenly, I felt better about my own collywobbles.

IMAGE CREDIT: FROM THE PAGES OF TIME. TIME AND THE TIME LOGO ARE REGISTERED TRADEMARKS OF TIME USA, LLC, USED UNDER LICENSE.

We — all of us except the water polo players and the "lady in red" — boarded the plane in the kind of trauma that expressed itself best in horror stories medicated with the bottles of Chilean red Cabernet that Hugh O'Shaunessey of the *Financial Times* and I carried aboard and guzzled together. What greeted us at the military airport outside Buenos Aires was a wall of shouting humanity, or rather that sub-breed of yelling, sleeve-yanking humanity that is journalists firing questions and clawing at anybody in an airline uniform for a ride into a place that departing passengers, like us, had so ardently wanted to leave. While I enjoyed being lionized for the eyewitness scoop and the first interview of Pinochet, this taste of the other side of my profession — the pursued source — got me thinking in broader terms. Before the rough stuff in Europe, and now again in South America, I'd never focused on the magnitude of what the trade-offs of journalism could entail. On the plane out of Chile, I'd begun wondering about the life I was leading and how it stacked up to possible alternatives. Why, exactly, had I gotten myself into something that required practicing the art of survival while describing other peoples' wars? Like the race back to Paris from Turkey to report the drug story, the flight to Buenos

Aires was taking me toward a different kind of life. I could *feel* it coming, but it still wasn't something I could yet think about clearly.

In the splendor of the Plaza Hotel, built to showcase long-ago opulent stability, the mysterious "colonel" shook things up further. After showing me an ordinary, civilian U.S. passport and making elaborate denials about representing the CIA or any U.S. government entity, he told a tale I considered so sensitive that I arranged to have it hand-delivered to my editors. As far as I know, it is still the only hard proof from inside Junta headquarters of the executions immediately following Allende's death. It was certainly the only first-hand account from the only American purportedly actually there during the coup. I never learned why my editors chose to do nothing with it.

> *To: Murray J. Gart*
> *Chief of Correspondents*
> *Time-Life News Service*
> *New York*
>
> *From: Eisendrath, Baires (Buenos Aires)*
>
> *STRICTLY CONFIDENTIAL*
>
> *On my way out of Chile Sept. 19, I encountered the bizarre fellow herein described, and shortly thereafter his equally bizarre story. The casualties involved confirm my suspicions and those of most other journalists who were in Santiago during the fighting. The rest (possible U.S. involvement) runs directly counter to information from sources on both the right and left in Chile.*
>
> *A man who now heads a highly-reputable U.S. outfit in Chile, and whom I knew ten years ago at Yale, told me as I was about to board a plane Santiago–B.A. Wednesday that there would be "a high CIA official" on the special, UN flight. The "official," my former schoolmate said, was scared almost out of his wits because of recent dealings with the Chilean military during the coup, during which time many Chilean leftists had seen him. The "official," whom my schoolmate knew, had seen incredible things which I*

should know about, I was briefly introduced at the airport, and a meeting was set up for B.A.

At 11 AM, Thursday morning I met the "high official" in the Plaza Hotel. We spoke for about two hours in the cafeteria, bar, and then during a short walk outside. He denied being with the CIA, identifying himself as an independent investment banker named Robert Kimbrough, with telephone contacts Stateside ▬▬▬ *or* ▬▬▬▬▬. *By the end of my talk, the picture was anything but clear. I had a distinct impression that I was being used for something (which always makes me balk); that I didn't have the whole story (which usually makes me hesitate); and that the information should be checked thoroughly before use.*

Here is the outline: Kimbrough denied being with the CIA, but said instead he had arrived a few days before the coup "completely independently" on behalf of some former friends in Gen. Chennault's World War II China air operation. These pals apparently now hold high positions with Hughes Aircraft. His mission: to investigate the alleged presence of three Chinese and three Japanese communist agents mysteriously arrived in Santiago.

This mission, however, became less important after the coup began than the establishment of a secure line of communication out of Santiago to North America. This, he said, had been accomplished through the Hughes Aircraft Corp. The need for such might be necessary in case Americans had to be evacuated quickly form Santiago, since the U.S. Embassy was in no position to call in an airlift in a country the U.S. does not recognize.

Kimbrough identified himself as acting "completely independently" on behalf of his old pals who direct Hughes Aircraft, which he inferred retains interests in Chile. He said that in his opinion there was a great likelihood of a leftist counterattack within the next two weeks, and an even greater likelihood that it would not be directed against the military, since this would be suicidal. Instead, the left would begin a massive assassination and kidnapping campaign against foreigners from nations friendly to the Junta. Americans would be target No. 1, and would be caught in a murderous cross-fire.

He estimated that 9,000 people had been killed so far in Chile, most of them in summary executions or in the process of being rounded up. He said he had been in the Junta headquarters during the coup, and had personally seen 200 shot after interrogations not even sufficient to provide positive identifications. A former U.S. airforce interrogator himself in the Far East, Kimbrough said the Junta's procedures made him "sick."

What was a U.S. citizen doing in Junta headquarters during the revolution? His story was complicated. Stripped of details, however, here it is: He was following the three Chinese Communists when the fighting broke out, catching him unaware because it came "five days early." After a series of adventures, a Chilean Air Force general drove by. Kimbrough explained his predicament and that he was a retired military officer. He ended up in headquarters because that was where the Chilean general was urgently headed, and stayed there for the rest of the curfew days because once the officers learned of his experience and former professional calling, they let him stay. In fact, he stayed without sleep for three days.

As we parted in B.A., he gave me the number of the man in Santiago whose telex is supposedly coup-proof. "Deliver the merchandise," he said, would be the code message for the arrival of some sort of airlift (The Hughes Company plane? A B-52?) Kimbrough was full of military and right-wing jargon, and urged me to use the number, but only for myself or for other "good Americans."

Perhaps some of this fits in with jigsaws in Washington or elsewhere. At any rate, it must not go out without extensive checking, and certainly none of it should be routed into Chile in query form either by telephone or telex. To protect our people in Chile, this information must be very carefully handled. A message from me, "Nice job," will mean to get out of Chile immediately.

Time, Inc. called its in-house newsletter *FYI*, which in important ways reflected a now-vanished culture that thrived when the adventuresome, sometimes wacky spirit of journalists was supported by salaries and expense accounts that encouraged both. Relentlessly upbeat, the issue quoted below also included classified offerings of Hasselblad camera accessories, special left-handed golf clubs with a custom leather bag and a Riverside Drive penthouse with a "capable Jamaican housekeeper." Its coverage of my drama in Santiago:

September 24, 1973
Scooping the Coup *by Daphne Hurford*

Buenos Aires Bureau Chief Charles Eisendrath was one of the few foreign journalists in Santiago during Chile's recent bloody revolution. Hours after his arrival, on Monday, Sept. 10, he found himself cloistered in the Hotel Carrera, across the street from La Moneda, the presidential palace where Salvador Allende Gossens — and his Marxist democracy — lay dead. All communication was canceled, and a 24-hour curfew imposed by the military government. Says Charlie: "When the shooting got ridiculous Tuesday morning and I learned from the radio that fighter planes would soon be attacking a building located just a slight margin of error from my hotel room, I moved my office, where I was typing those forever unsent advisories to TIME's World editor, from the bedroom to the bathroom. Bathrooms are good bunkers because they have an extra wall and because you don't have to risk going anywhere else to do anything that you really must *do when people are shooting at each other and maybe you."*

Journalists in the Carrera gratefully accepted the hotel's gift of candles in case lights went out (they did) but avoided elevators, preferring to scale 16 flights of stairs rather than risk getting trapped between floors in a power failure. They also became expert at adjusting curtains and venetian blinds to make them look closed, as requested by the hotel and demanded by the army, while still providing a view of the square.

"Slats were painstakingly angled up and down for vision," Charlie remembers, "curtains oh-so-slowly pulled. But by Wednesday all that delicatesse had become unnecessary. Many of the artfully arranged windows and sashes had been cleanly shot out by then."

After having his window shot out, Eisendrath "slept on a mattress pulled off the bed with another mattress propped up as a shield against flying glass and shrapnel."

Although Eisendrath was safe, he was enduring the journalist's ultimate frustration: he couldn't get his story out. Eisendrath, thumbing desperately through a notebook full of names of possible news sources in Argentina, decided to try calling a contact in Mendoza, the biggest Argentine city near the Chilean border, whom he had never met but had intended to interview some day. The call went through and for an hour Charlie dictated his story to a surprised but helpful Argentine.

An hour later, the Chilean regime clamped down nationwide censorship.

By Friday the fighting was over, the curfew partially lifted, and life started again in Santiago.

Early Sunday morning Eisendrath got a call through to New York and instead of reaching the Time Inc. operator found himself talking to somebody in the computer room:

Eisendrath: This is Charles Eisendrath calling from Santiago de Chile.

Computer Room Man (with marvelous New York accent): So?

E: Is anybody in the Cable Room?

CRM: How should I know?

E: Could you take a look? You're on the same floor.

CRM: Look, mister, I'm trying to close TIME magazine and you're asking me to go clear to the other end of the hall.

E: That's nothing. I'm trying to close TIME magazine from the other end of the world.

CRM: Well, if you feel that way about it, buddy...

Adds Charlie: "Fortunately for both of us, the mag had already closed tight. But when I asked his name, the line went dead."

Later that day Charlie interviewed Gen. Augusto Pinochet Ugarte, President of the junta. Speaking of censorship, Charlie told Pinochet "that their system could not have been better calculated to get the junta bad press, and that while it could not really hurt its media enemies, it would alienate anybody with an open mind, since it is difficult to write objectively with a gun at one's head." A few hours later a junta decree lifted both censorship and restrictions on the movements of foreign reporters. A junta spokesman said that TIME's campaign had been responsible. On Tuesday, Sept. 18, Charlie cabled New York: "The weekly newsmagazine can and should rightly take pride in the lifting yesterday of censorship on outgoing Chilean news. We brought it about. For my part, I take as much pride in that as anything in my reportorial career."

Turbulence is nothing new to Eisendrath, who came to Time Inc. in 1968 and has covered the vice-presidential campaign of Spiro Agnew, fighting in Northern Ireland, opium production in Turkey and the recent return to Argentina of Juan Peron. He is now back in Argentina with his family.

"It's like living with an echo," says Julia Eisendrath, describing the life of a foreign correspondent's wife. "You know he's out there writing the original. But by the time he comes back we have read the headlines. So he fills in what it was like to produce them. As for worry, this time was typical. I only really felt down the day he got back, totally unannounced, as always. I guess I should know by now that when I get scared for him he is about to walk in the door. But somehow, I don't."

While it was fine and somehow life-affirming to fit the coup into *Time's* overall optimism, what I learned from "Colonel Robert Kimbrough" confirmed what I had suspected but couldn't bring myself to accept as a patriot; that the routine course of following my trade—which was finding truth and reporting it to the largest print audience in America—could land me in situations where I didn't think I could rely on my own government. I had covered civil wars in Northern Ireland and Nigeria (Biafra) with no more than the usual concerns. What I now felt was different. I found that I couldn't trust my reflexes, even in Buenos Aires. The city was calmer than Santiago, for sure, but still dangerous for young American families like mine. I wrapped up the week's coverage, arranged for a replacement to come from the Rio de Janeiro bureau and asked for R&R leave. Ben Cate, *Time's* new chief of correspondents, refused the request. Cate loved playing the tough guy and affected odd bits of military terminology. Never, however, had he covered a war. I felt there was no reason to honor his judgment—let alone abide it—and decided to depart anyway, leaving word that I could be reached at a farm in northern Michigan. Three days later Julia, the boys and I were on a plane headed home, bound for Traverse City and then East Jordan.

The morning after our arrival at the farm produced a bizarre confirmation of basic survival reflexes: I woke up *under* our bed, looking up at a box spring and wondering how and why I got there. Down on Lake Charlevoix, a shot still echoed in motionless air. Then two more. It was duck season—as good a time as any, I thought, sandwiched between floorboards and bed slats, to get myself out of war footing and calmed down.

There would be battles of a different sort to fight at the Time-Life Building in Rockefeller Center. If certainly not mild—with charges of "insubordination" and "immediate transfer from Buenos Aires"—they seemed winnable. After two weeks at the farm I felt ready for a few days of *mano-a-mano* office politics, winning leave to finish the assignment in Buenos Aires. There, my last act was a return to Chile. Our stringer Mario Planet reported that the *tanques* (armored personnel carriers) that had put him under de facto house arrest during the coup had returned. He expected to soon be headed to the stadium unless *Time* intervened. I picked him up in person, handed him a ticket and escorted him into exile—on a commercial flight, this time. He was lucky to still be alive. Several thousand Allende supporters detained during my visit had died in the intervening weeks. To me, the deadly silence of the place was symbolized by the immaculately whitewashed walls of the city. The exuberant, scarlet political slogans of socialism were gone. Santiago had been calmed down too, by force.

HOW MUCH OF TRAUMA or triumph do you report? If you're a journalist, all of it. But at the moment, I'm a mere memorialist. Reporting the news can be like my childhood passion of collecting butterflies at Overlook Farm. The bright wing powder—millions of individual grains—affects you and defines the subject like facts in a new story. Then other "facts" present themselves, to be collected in another box, much like the news cycle. The whole collection doesn't come into focus until academics open it years later as "primary source material" to be examined and disputed like any other bunch of dead insects on pins.

I think it's the effect of personal drama that matters. In the eight days beginning early Monday, September 11, 1973, I had my share of both journalistic triumph and personal trauma. What should the balance be? I would begin looking for it in the October hills of northern Michigan, where the blood red around me was leaves turning color against the calm blue of sky and lake, and the shooting was aimed at ducks.

A SENSE OF PLACE

August, 1987

If you expected a piece about a cherry orchard in northern Michigan to start with cherries, orchards or Michigan, I have already disappointed you. This one begins at la Chapelle de Bragny, a small, as these things go, Burgundian chateau owned, as it has been for centuries, by the de Carmoy family. The count's name is Hervé, and he has many commendable qualities—earned as well as inherited. Hervé and his effervescent wife, Roseline de Rohan (part of the Chandon family, as in Moet & Chandon), were relatively new at the *grand seigneur* role, having taken over the place only a few years previously from *Papa*. The little theatrics played by these aristocrats in their thirties were for the benefit of the town. In de Carmoy eyes, their every move was watched. This couple, who literally owned the town, felt themselves checked for shortcomings daily. Were they elegant enough, kind enough, generous enough to be permitted to lord it over the rest? Hervé and Roseline spent their vacations making sure they looked and comported themselves accordingly, *de rigueur*. Their house-guests, ditto.

I asked Hervé why he went to the trouble of maintaining a chateau. Beside the enormous expense, it was clear that even a decision about what the children should wear on a tennis court required deliberation. "With us, this has been going on for 500 years and it will keep going on for another 500," he said. "The town expects certain things from us. A certain standard. We play our roles. We do our best. But it does seem that every 200 years or so, they cut off our heads."

BOUGHT "AS-IS" IN 1944—NO HEAT, NO ELECTRICITY,
NO PLUMBING, BUT LESS MOTHER-IN-LAW, TOO

Leave la Chapelle for, say, Provence? Might as well ask the steeple to separate itself from the chapel of Bragny. To the likes of us, who owned no home base in our own country and, during six years of married life, had moved five times, this dedication to place was a new way of going at the business of life. Or, to be exact, an extremely old one new to us. Nevermind religion—even in terms of geography, we had neither church nor steeple to mark home from a distance.

I found this baselessness deeply unsatisfactory. I did not want to tour around the rest of my life as an observer, the way I was cruising the Vietnamese peace talks, European politics and the drug trade as a professional outsider. Against the model of the de Carmoys and la Chapelle, with its commitments and its finality, the butterfly nature of what we were doing struck me as flighty to the point of embarrassment.

At thirty-two, I had witnessed, analyzed and communicated U.S. presidential elections, the Prince of Wales' investiture, de Gaulle's funeral and the Biafran War for a magazine with the biggest audience in the world. But where was *my* story? La Chapelle got me thinking in a new way. I had no la Chapelle. My little family was a tree without roots. I would grow some.

LIKE MANY A COUNTRY HOUSE, Overlook Farm began as a marital evasion. My mother adored spending summers where she had as a girl, in a white-frame "cottage" with paint always so new you could see your reflection in the green shutters as well as the windows. Four-fifteen Michigan Avenue had cedar strip sleeping porches with nothing but a few yards of darkness separating you from the sounds Lake Michigan made at night. My father thought Charlevoix was beautiful—how could he not? Facing the big lake from high sand bluffs, a gem called Lake Charlevoix to the east and the perfect natural harbor of Round Lake between, the place dazzles. In truth, he appreciated how it looked, but hated what it was. An esthete, he found resorts intellectually sterile and liked their socializing even less. He grew to positively loathe his in-laws, May and Charlie Rice, people given to closing off the street when even the nine-bedroom "cottage" could not accommodate the mob of 200 invited guests. But he conceded defeat, admitting that he must buy something in or near my mother's family and the site of her childhood nostalgia. His instructions to the realtor became a legend[7]: "Find me something with a body of water between me and May Rice, and I'll take it." His two-week vacation ended, he departed for Chicago.

The plan of exclusion worked. Somehow, the one-toot ferry ride across the South Arm of Lake Charlevoix (the world's shortest, according to an old *Ripley's Believe It or Not* column mounted on board under glass) cut the number of in-law visits satisfyingly. Or maybe, it just seemed that way to my father. To the amazement of everyone, he pronounced the dilapidated place "perfect" and committed to buying it sight unseen.

It is not at all clear that my mother knew it was a done deal before the dutiful young wife wrote this letter about things (acreage, soil and well water quality, price, taxes) that to her husband were not nearly as important as seeing less of her mother:

Sept 7, 1944 Thursday night
415 Michigan Avenue
Charlevoix, Michigan

Bill Darling. This has been a day! Starting at 6:30 this morning when

---

7   As did the realtor himself, Earl Young, originator of Charlevoix's "mushroom houses."

Charles awakened me, until this moment at 8:45 pm, when I have tucked in the last young 'un, and can finally tell all that has occurred. Everything reached a climax today, and all that I shall report is the result of many conversations in the course of several days, so I can't give you a play-by-play account. When the deed was finally consummated this afternoon I tried to send you a 'My God, I am shot' telegram, but (Western Union) wouldn't take it.[8]

The name of the place is Overlook Farm; the address is Route 2, East Jordan, Mich. The tax bill is assessed $2600, approximately half the value—but what the hell! It's a divine place, and I'm thrilled.

THE OUTDOORS GIRL WHO
MARRIED AN ESTHETE, BECAME
A BOTANY PROFESSOR AND
STEERED THE FARM TO ME

FREUD WAS RIGHT ABOUT OEDIPUS. I read those letters in 1985, a few days after my mother's death. As she had revealed herself at thirty-five, I fell in love with her on the spot. At forty-four, I was experiencing her youth while being about as much senior to her as my father had been when they met at a picnic on the point of an island visible from the farm they bought a decade later. Time added yet another coincidence: In her letter, my mother was doing all her bubbling at precisely the same age I would be when I came to know Overlook Farm for the first time as the owner. That was, of course, long before the farm showed me what la Chapelle taught Hervé de Carmoy—that attachment to land goes beyond family history and remains unexplained. Can't be explained. That's probably the most important thing the place taught me. Without using an analogy, can anyone describe the color blue? Or middle "C?" Or love?

---

8   Because of the word "shot." It was wartime, after all.

Within a very few minutes of meeting Julia on a blind date, I'd said to myself, "Wrap it up, I'll take it." As the song goes, "Fools give you reasons, wise men never try."

The year after buying Overlook, on the day World War II ended, my mother wrote again, this time to express the joy and relief of a young Jewish mother who had bought a Smith & Wesson .38 caliber revolver to deal with the marauding Nazis she envisaged storming the beaches of Lake Michigan. I still have it, along with a photo of her at the wheel of a Red Cross army truck, both of them tucked away on a bookshelf at the farm.

THE RECORD OF THAT FIRST TRIP to Overlook was written in trees. Experience imprints most indelibly because, like an image, there is no first screening by reason, logic or even intuition. That is why political cartoons are the first target of censorship. It also explains why I learned so much in the decade between inheriting the farm and reading my mother's letter. The education began in 1972, after a flight from Paris to Traverse City, the nearest airport. Our eldest was the age I had been when my screaming awakened my mother rudely enough for her to put it in a letter. Ben's younger brother was an infant, and their mother had seen the place only once before.

I had never before planted a tree and knew nothing about them. If you had asked me about the root structures of various species, I would have resented it. Like all confirmed urbanites, I knew that roots went down, and *that* was all anyone needed to know. Complementing this total lack of competence was the utter lack of need for more trees. Trees were mostly what the place was. One hundred of 146 acres was woods. In the five acres around the house, you couldn't walk more than fifty feet without encountering a birch, beech, white pine, honey locust, cedar, ash or one of the thirty ancient apple trees from its days as a commercial orchard. And the huge, lyre-branch willow with its big toe tap-root in the septic line? It swayed at the slightest provocation, with the smug good fortune of those with inherited nourishment.

My new compulsion for Landscaping 101 had nothing to do with Overlook Farm or its management requirements. The size of the place—rather the size of the care-taking—overwhelmed any sense of

scale I had managed to develop as a perennial apartment renter in Baltimore,
Washington, London and Paris. The trees
I planted—or I should say transplanted,
because they were all seedlings sprouted
here and there around the place—served
more as markers of my local known world.
The tiny bit of terrain I thought I might
be able to deal with. They are still there.
I look at each of them every morning.
They remind me that roots determine
range, that innovation starts with what's
available, that the gap between us and our
parents recedes and that recycling includes
the thought process. Not bad for two little
cedars and three white pines.

```
Living Abroad          1970

What should be easy is impossible.
What should be impossible is amusing.
What should be amusing is exasperating.
What should be exasperating is boring.
What should be boring is impossible.
What should be impossible is easy.
```

IN PARIS, I WROTE MYSELF A MEMO
ABOUT LIVING ABROAD THAT
ENDED UP AT THE FARM

Our 1972 inspection trip lasted ten days. By the end, I had acquired enough sense to buy a 1965 International Harvest-er Scout, red and white, complete with the snowplow that said "this-is-home." It cost $1,200. We then returned to "the big world" of inter-national journalism, where there were premiers to be interviewed and power dinner parties to attend and an elegant apartment in the 16th ar-rondissement. In our absence—and several dimensions removed—the tiny cedars disappeared in the seven-foot luxuriance of big bluestem grass.

And so things remained until the economics of northern Michigan transformed life and property. In 1975 I took a two-thirds pay cut, leav-ing *Time* to start over as an assistant professor at University of Michigan. Up until then, lake frontage hadn't been particularly valuable. Suddenly, it was everything, lifting property values along with ruinous taxes. Time for a new strategy: from now on, luxuries needed to support themselves.

I consulted the Sherman brothers. Their home farm, a cherry orchard, was just down the road, and I had known them since their father bought the property and a small cannery in East Jordan. It was a good relation-ship, strong enough for me to march into their offices, kick filthy garden-ing boots up on a desk and say how much I had come to dislike the local sociology. *I* was supposed to be the rich outsider with the hobby farm, I told them. *They* were the hardscrabble locals. Things had gone wrong because while I'd been running around the world, they'd built lakefront homes — homes I could not come close to affording. "Fix the sociology, please," I said. They laughed and opened their ledgers to where it showed the rent on our fields: They were paying $400 to us and $10,000 to Mrs. McDonald up the road for similar acreage.

"Two generations of you have asked the wrong question," announced Bill Sherman, who had forsaken a career in diplomacy to run the family business. "Ask us about cherries."

The next morning, I walked off an orchard with Bob Sherman, and the following April, Ted Sherman planted 1,100 trees. An additional 800 were added the next year. Three springs later they turned the hillside light pink. Another three, and the fruit came in — and with it, money to support the place.

OURS WAS A SAVIOR ORCHARD and my favored path to salvation led straight east from the kitchen door, between a pair of lilacs and another of crabapples, out between the cedars I had once carried on the blade of a shovel, sometimes wearing a son in a backpack. Twenty years later the cedars were fifty feet high, with lower branches that made a wall. I cut an arch through the wall and a swath through a transept of grass.

Yes, sometimes it did seem like walking into a country church, but a change in the weather, mood, or both could make it more like a sea that parts on cue. The path leads east towards sunrise and is only half as wide as the grass is tall. In a good wind from the north or south, with the bluestem whiskers sweeping your face like spray, you are Moses delivering the Israelites. Follow on and there seems a promised land beyond a River Jordan called Mountain Road.

In the right conditions, young white pines grow eighteen inches a year, a pace that slows as they reach maximum height. Last year, I noticed that the three I had planted to define the known world were slowing down. The spaces between groups of branches, which indicate how much a conifer has grown in a year, had decreased to five or six inches at the top. My little trees were catching up to a pine my parents had planted not long after my mother wrote her letters. Time to write some of this down.

TO BE A MICRO-JEFFERSON

July, 1992

Even on jets, you don't get from Buenos Aires to East Jordan unexhausted, particularly if the travel includes two small children. They sleep for now. So does Julia. The plane swims along above a monotony of squares. Slowly, so slowly, the way dreams can glide above consciousness before picking out anything to land on, I begin to realize that the graph paper landscape of the northern Midwest satisfies me in a way far different from mountain ranges, the quirky cultivation patterns of Europe, or even the charming, stone-fence outlines of the eastern United States. Aesthetics have nothing to do with it. The grid makes me feel full in the way of a lunch counter pork chop on a long road trip.

The platting of the upper middle-western U.S. equals squares of exactly 160 acres. Nearly every road and field runs due east-west or north-south with utter and sometimes comical disregard of natural features. Small lakes take bites out of squares, large ones leave them looking like the scrap heap in a jigsaw factory. I learned about the platting from an inspired, high school history teacher and used it against snobby Easterners in college: Of course Midwesterners *are* squares; Jefferson, himself, made us so. In France I ingratiated myself to the cultural hegemonists with reports that it had been their (Enlightenment) thoughts in Jefferson's brain that determined the political geography of the American heartland—England merely supplied the language for signposts. What I hadn't realized was that, for me, the patchwork spread out on the soft landscape was the quilt of home.

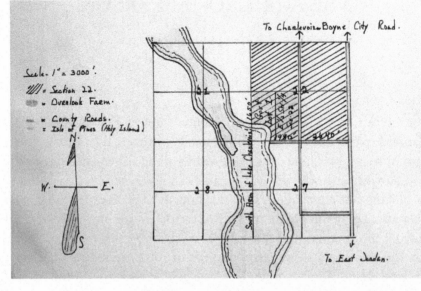

Overlook Farm was purchased in September, 1944, from Mrs. Marie Howe. The farm lies in Eveline Township, Charlevoix County, Michigan, and consists of the East ½ of the Southwest quarter of Section 22, plus Government Lot No. 1.

MY MOTHER CHECKED OUT EVERYTHING FROM
THE OFFICIAL RECORDS—EXCEPT WHETHER HER HUSBAND
HAD ALREADY BOUGHT THE PROPERTY

In 1787, at age forty-four, Jefferson radicalized himself on a trip to Nîmes where the Maison Carrée (Square House)—a miraculously-preserved Greco-Roman temple—brought on an epiphany that became the vision of public architecture for the United States. Greek purity of form dictated rectangles and circles and dimensions that could be left to aesthetic golden harmonies. His buildings at the University of Virginia have been copied in glory and banality in every state ever since.

Jefferson never visited the Northwest Territories (later Michigan, Minnesota, Wisconsin, Illinois, Indiana and Ohio), nor had he anything beyond the sketchiest description of its soil types. He nonetheless confidently concluded that the ancient world gave him everything he needed to impose political form on an area somewhat larger than the thirteen colonies. As a large landowner himself, he calculated that it would require precisely 160 acres to provide the food, the fuel and the wealth to create the class of yeoman farmers he saw as the most suitable inheritors of the new world.

Overlook Farm was 146 acres—a quarter section less a five-acre bite taken out of the southwest corner by Lake Charlevoix, plus another strip lost in an easement my father sold to a neighbor. In our newly inherited home, the first Julia and I had ever owned, we would be the heirs of Thomas Jefferson. But to us, as urban sophisticates, the countryside and the yeomanship required to manage it remained to be learned. We'd come back to America after seven years abroad to take a fellowship I'd won at the University of Michigan. But when the leave of absence from *Time* ended, Overlook Farm had begun to feel like the beginning of something. To friends, we explained that we wanted to settle down, that I liked the idea of teaching. The real attraction—not letting a career get in the way of the serious work of building a life—sounded too grandiose. Like my hero's, my life would be anchored in a farm and a university. Also like him, most of my learning would come from the farm.

The chance to become a micro-Jefferson carried certain obligations it seemed to me, the highest and hardest being keeping the focus on the development of the (my) big picture. In our century, individual life components tend to take over—they demand that, in fact. *Time* magazine had done so utterly and the bargain was pure Faust. In accepting the position with *Time*, I sacrificed a regular newspaper byline for first-rate personal instruction in foreign languages, world politics and a great salary at the public's expense. Grandly, I thought of myself as a sort of emergency room clinician, helping the world understand itself while also providing essential information for leaders to use when making life or death decisions. What I hadn't factored was strain; administering journalistic first aid when a must-do story concerning a pop election, or even a pop musician, could rush me elsewhere when I should have been, for example, focusing on the birth of our first child—or just being home. Control? I had considerable over the version of some events read by four million people. Over what I did with my time on earth, however, I had none.

The dinner party Julia spent days preparing at our house—at which I was absent, having just left for Orly Airport—became a marital emblem.

Journalists spend their lives looking out the window. There's always plenty going on, to be sure. Without drawing the shades in any way, the appeal of Jefferson's model of a life was that it promised far more than introspection. To the bedevilment of those around him—and the delight of his biographers—Jefferson let the building blocks of his identity spill out of his imagination and into actual walls, structures, an entire city. Architecture was merely one set of whims. Beyond politics and diplomacy spread mechanical engineering, agriculture, high-end gourmandizing, oenology, forestry and, of course, writing, which he mastered, and economics, which, endearingly, he did not.

We are all the sum of those who have gone before. Molecular biologists study the systems of a cell. Geneticists trace the families. Journalists compile the record and historians explain how it all extends itself, but since one group can't know all the facts, and the other generally writes long after the fact, the accounts of both are star-gazings of one sort or another. Why not learn how to learn by learning how to do? Why couldn't we go backwards and forwards at the same time, intro-prospecting what's gone into our gene pool by letting it come out as the future unfolded? Each of us is a family album that few of us take the time to reference. The trick is learning how to read the pages while making new ones at the same time. The page-turning trick happens by itself, you just need to pay attention.

For me, the first entries in a new album sprouted pale green from the white pines delineating "the known world," as I thought of it, around the house. I'd planted them during our first visit to Overlook from Paris, two years before. Since then, I'd moved around and the trees had grown. That growth was the new comparative dimension, the pages to be referenced, reflected and then extended. Why the developing passion for white pines? It wasn't just their height against the sky and the way their needles could tell you the speed of the wind; I loved them for their metaphor. Want to understand how inspiration works? Watch a white pine grow. Nobody in my world, with the blindness of sophistication, would have expected the complexity, violence and speed shown by a little conifer in April. Tiny brown clusters of buds shaded into yellowing brown, then yellowish green. What had looked like fish scales lying flat became needles overnight. The stubby little fingers took the form of, well, limbs. Within six weeks, the tree added eighteen inches in height, enough to notice the difference and to remind me that I wasn't the only impatient being on this farm. And the miracles went beyond size. For everything that grew straight up, there were several going sideways. Starved for sunlight, water or something else, some pine limbs sprouted only one or two buds. The bumptious had eight or nine. Pinch off any of them and the tree would not—I repeat—*would not ever* grow in that direction.

Within 146 acres of strict, rational, ninety-degree Jeffersonian rationality, I had just learned something from a tree. Clearly, my life was going to change — or at least it could change, if I didn't cut off the wrong bud. What I didn't realize until later was that the tree had something to say about Mr. Jefferson, too. By hiding part of his life to maintain the rest of it—the part lived with Sally Hemings and their children—he pruned his own existence as surely as the pine I shaped with the pinch of two fingers.

Meanwhile, in the woods far beyond the limits of the known world marked by my yard-side pines, I sensed not only Jeffersonian straight lines and right angles, but also the wandering lives of my parents, grandparents, neighbors and creatures—ghosts with power, cunning and laughter. I would not be exploring this property alone.

PART 2

TURTLE IN THE ROAD

TWO BULLDOZERS & SOME GHOSTS

July, 1993

Just because you decide to fancy yourself a micro-Jefferson — meaning that you adopt the style while knowing full well that you lack the talent — doesn't mean the woods won't surprise you. All the *savoir faire* in the world couldn't do that. It might also scare you. At age eight I was sure "wild dogs" lived out where the orchard rows surrendered to open fields and then the woods. Dad helped me build a two-board platform in the apple tree where I could wait for darkness. He explained that no dog could climb the ladder slats we'd nailed to the trunk. The idea was to have me prove to myself that these creatures did not exist, because I clearly didn't believe *him*. The proof? That I would not be eaten on that particular night.

It did make sense, but such technicalities didn't interest me. In the creeping lateness that grays the line between hayfield and trees, visions of wild dogs floated low in the night mist, slinking closer and darker as the lightning bugs came out. A psychiatrist once suggested that my horror of wild dogs probably represented fears of my father, who could be fierce, indeed — nostrils flared, eyes narrowed, wolf-like. But only maybe. In at least one way I suppose the shrink was right. If I hadn't been more afraid of my father than of the wild dogs, wouldn't I have broken the promise and gone inside before he came to lead me, a shivering boy, back toward the kitchen light? On the other hand, he alone tried to get me to overcome the terror.

CHARLES M. RICE, "POPS,"
PIED PIPER GRANDFATHER

PHOTO CREDIT: LAWRENCE ABT

Overlook Farm's woods seemed more ominous and scary than any others, even the ones nearby where real bears lived. But that connection between fear and family went unnoticed for years—until a series of drought summers dried up our swamp. Swamps are where deer hide when wounded. Nearly impassable underfoot, with hidden logs to trap your en-oozed boots and full of equally bedeviling entanglements above, they offer everything wildlife needs most and likes best. A swamp's thick cover hides recovery rooms with cafeterias. They provide water and greenness when all else is brown. There are berries and roots, frogs and beetles and secluded, easy meals for all kinds of creatures including, of course, each other.

As it turned out, after hours and hundreds of dollars of telling stories to a silent psychiatrist, my grandfather Pops lived in that swamp, as far as my psyche was concerned. He was a ghost. It also turned out that my fears, at least one of them, was that I would lose him. That's why the drying up was so devastating.

CHARLES RICE, MY POPS, was a bundle of contradictions wrapped up as an Edwardian lawyer who stood six-foot-one—a towering height among us—with a nose crumpled on the Washington University football team. He loved dancing, but wheezed asthmatically after only a few of the fast steps he favored. And he loved the solitude of day-long walks in the woods, using wildflowers as an excuse and a bucket of blaze paint to compensate for the complete lack of any sense of direction. Be that as it may, if you had asked him the way home after he had splattered yet another birch as signpost, he would have answered with great authority based on nothing whatsoever.

I don't know any more about my grandfather than you do about yours; a few scraps of memory and bright, little stones of fact. It had been his parents, Jonathan and Aurelia Rice, who "discovered" Charlevoix County, shortly before the turn of the Nineteenth Century, as a place to escape from the heat and yellow fever of St. Louis. That generation-before-highways would load their cars on barges bound up the Mississippi, Illinois and Chicago rivers for trans-shipment by either lake steamer or train to Petoskey, Michigan. There, the "Williams" of their world—always Black, always in black livery—who had traveled ahead of the families, would be ready at train-side for the short, rutted drive to the "cottage," in our case a large affair overlooking Lake Michigan.

Pops' father, an immigrant from Ba-

"GRANDPA," (ACTUALLY GREAT GRANDPA) GOLDMAN; CONFEDERATE DRUMMER BOY, COTTON BROKER, DEVELOPER, WITH MY UNUSABLE PEARL--AND-DIAMOND STICKPIN

varia, made his money in Rice-Stix Dry Goods. The logo, deeply chiseled into a massive brownstone cornerstone, survived the business, defunct by the time it was pointed out to me on a childhood mission in downtown St. Louis. That cornerstone was the first revelation that the name of somebody I actually knew—in this case me and my middle name—could become something so eternal-looking. Natural, I guess, being young. Nobody I knew had yet acquired a gravestone.

Pops married into the May department store family through the Goldmans. Grandpa Goldman (the name stuck well beyond generational accuracy) was not long off the boat when he joined the Confederate Army of Georgia as a fifteen-year-old drummer boy. In that era, drums and bugles were the main battlefield communication system. Soldiers probably had a hard time with a boy's English that sounded more like Bavarian German, but his drum had no accent when ordering retreat or, in this case, probably more advances. He was present at Chickamauga, a major Southern victory at a huge cost of spilled gore.

When the fighting stopped, Jacob Goldman migrated north toward opportunity in the booming city of St. Louis. With him came hundreds of pounds of Confederate currency stuffed into an oversize cedar trunk. The money was to be used in beginning a new life but, mysteriously, his adopted country had ruled the paper worthless. Nevertheless, he somehow found the resources to establish the Lesser Goldman Cotton Company on the cobblestone levee. He made a fortune on Mississippi steamboats, providing the means for desperate growers to ship their crops downriver to New Orleans and on to the mills of England. That cedar trunk now holds bulky featherbeds at Overlook Farm. When we decided to devote a downstairs room to family photos that had stayed too long in the dark, Grandpa Goldman's portrait went up, showing a pear-shaped man in a frock coat, diamond stickpin, smokestack cigar and an expression to be dreaded in, say, a used car salesman.

Pops married Jacob Goldman's daughter, May (Margaret) Nanette Goldman, after founding Lewis, Rice, Tucker Allen & Chubb. The composition of Jewish and Gentile partners was rare and is important to our story, because although they mixed freely in business, social life in Charlevoix country—where Pops and May chose to spend their summers—remained strictly segregated into the 1960s, and its clubs still are today. Pops also became the May Company's lawyer. Argumentative? He had no problem whatever arguing the opposite side of even his own example.

You could call him a passionate man, and he was passionate about swamps. Swamps let him combine nature and lawyerly explanation, given the right jury. Often that was me. Pops taught me how to fish—or rather to love fishing—and he was anything but a purist. Our sorties took time out to chase painted turtles when they came up for air near the boat. We marveled at the lethal—to insects—flick of a leopard frog's tongue or we paused to discuss the advantages of swimming backwards to a crayfish. In adult company, he would rumble on about things I don't remember very well, but probably included male roles, the law, responsibilities, that sort of thing. Everything he said about swamps, however, stuck:

There's a pink lady-slipper, no, don't touch; the yellow ones come before, see the dead stalk over there? See the bit of yellow? Those little things like clams with hairy lips? They're sun-dews, and they eat bugs. Yes, really. For something to eat, that's why. That flying thing? It's called a darning needle, because that long, green body looks like something to sew socks with. If you see one up close, there's a forked thing on the end; it's an 'ovipositor.' Comes from Latin, which if you like science as much as I do you'll have to learn [he hadn't and I didn't]; means 'egg-putter.' That's what she does with that—puts eggs where she wants them. Bet there's a snake under the rowboat, let's have a look?

As the drought set in, the routes I'd walked with Pops didn't change, but much else did. My mother was still alive when we stopped seeing the snapping turtle. The duck hawk abandoned its nest, and even the tree frog screeching went dead. Mythic figures leave behind trails of aphorisms, and one of Pops' was, *In times of drought, all signs fail.* Long after death, he still intones it to me with suitable gravity, always in a fedora that had been on life support for decades.

In 1981, in a panic, I called the School of Natural Resources at the University of Michigan. Yes, after much talk, a professor would trade a day of salmon fishing for an analysis of whether the clear-cut timbering nearby could have killed my grandfather—er, the swamp. After his tour, he left a sampling tool with which Ben and I cut soil cores in suffocating heat. But nope, no grounds for a lawsuit. The water visible in these "pothole marshes" varied naturally with the water table. Scrape away the brush and muck and it'll be there, lying on top of an impermeable layer of clay. Having never thought much about them before, I began thinking about bulldozers.

Ever wonder just how much tickle you can get mushing mud and pushing stuff around with a bulldozer? Well, it's just obscene, that's how much. And God, had Charlie Rice ever loved pushing stuff around. In the 1920s, he'd 'dozed away the gravel at his place in the Ozark Mountains so he could see the water running over the limestone creek beds, repurposed as roads. They were terrible roads, of course, but that wasn't the point. Poetry was the point. Specifically, delight in unexpected beauty. In the thick Missouri heat, your car splashing rainbows and diadems on the stream banks where he'd transplanted wildflowers, you could imagine a mahogany speedboat raising a rooster-tail in the cool water of Lake Charlevoix.

My turn came in northern Michigan. When the county road-crew season ended in late fall, the owner of the biggest bulldozer in East Jordan agreed to lesser work like "mucking out your swamp." Every year there was less water showing, each summer Pops' bog-loving flowers and creatures were disappearing under a mat of grass. Maybe, if we scraped that smothering layer away, they would come back—and at some unconscious level, maybe the past, too. I stood behind the seat as we smashed our way along a ravine toward the target, only to almost lose the machine after clearing a puddle-sized area of water. Turns out, it had once been a shallow lake and our weight was sending us toward the ancient bottom. The bulldozer man couldn't afford what it would cost to haul out a several-ton, stymied main source of income. Ghosts, however, aren't at all like bulldozers. If you submerge them, they reappear anywhere and without warning, just like your grandfather's blazes on a trail when you don't know you've been lost.

My eyes had been opened by a clanking machine that dismissed the barriers separating past from future, editing the swamp with an angled steel blade as if mounds of glop were so much excess verbiage. Some ghost or another had been on the lookout and, unsurprisingly, a second bulldozer project came to mind the next year. This time it called for a small machine to snake between trees. The steep, logging two-track on our south line—the one we used to get to the beach—had invited unwanted interest from the County Road Commission. I feared our isolation would disappear with a paved, all-access boat launch, so we stopped using it, hoping that a combination of erosion, sabotage and a legal challenge would make the problem go away. But we still needed a way to get to the lake. The new road was sited far from a property line with the advantage that, with its gentler grades, it wouldn't wash out when the snow went off. But that meant a mile-long loop starting due north in order to end up due west—it was four times the old, straight shot to the water.

A man considerably older than Pops was when he died was yelling at me from the controls of a Caterpillar D-4, the blade turning up the semen-like smells of stripped-back forest. Ahead, Ben, Pop's twelve-year-old great-grandson, raced from tree to tree, tying orange surveying tape to mark the trees to be spared on our march to the lake. Ben was the sort of child who took tiger swallowtail butterflies on "flies" with thread tied to one of their legs. On the walk to school he would lose himself following beetles. After the fourth call from his first grade teacher about tardy arrivals at Burns Park School—two blocks from home—and unable to shake his "I go straight there" explanation, I shadowed him. He didn't even make it down the front walk before a bug crossed his path. Ben was on the case. He followed it through the hedge. A cardinal flew by. He watched it alight here, then there. It sang, he listened. Pretty soon he saw a cat sitting in the sun. I gave up my campaign.

Ben opposed all tree-taking on principle, so our route fluttered with orange tape warnings. The Caterpillar man, of course, preferred leveling everything in front of his blade. My own plans had started with retaining privacy, but became bogged down in a swamp of another kind called Eveline Township politics. Suddenly, however, bureaucratic wrangling didn't matter. We had cleared, ditched and graveled the first sharp drop in the new road. We'd doubled back south, past the site of the homesteader's cabin, and had poked a hole in the forest wall at the edge of what had been his clearing. And there, dead ahead of the blade, was a silver birch sporting a bright blaze of Federal Blue—the same color as the shutters of our house, the same color worn by farm boys gone off to fight Grandpa Goldman's side in the Civil War. Ben was just a few years shy of the age when his great-great-grandpa drummed his messages at Chickamauga, and I really wasn't ready for that ghost to materialize. But the blaze of Federal Blue on the birch up ahead was Charlie Rice, bright as ink on paper. We had linked up with one of his trails.

"This way, Chips," I heard him say, his white undershirt splotched with sweat and paint. More birches and light gray beeches marked where we would make our roadbed. Four generations heading to the lake in a new way, our way.

TURTLE IN THE ROAD

July, 1993

In July of 1975—too late, really—I started a piece I'll finish even later. It's a muggy, southeast-windy morning and through the open window of my second-floor study comes the throbbing roar of two shaking teams rushing to get 180,000 pounds of cherries off the trees before the rain. My twenty-two-year-old lede had been inspired by a tourist—or "fudgie," as they're called hereabout—and this seems to need a digression before I even ingress into an essay. The term says a lot about our adoptive region.

In 1887, there wasn't much to see for the few visitors who came to Mackinac Island, other than the fort used successively by French, English and American forces to prevent the other from sailing through the Straits of Mackinac and into the booming trade in Great Lakes furs. Enter Henry and Jerome "Rome" Murdick, sailmakers in an oncoming age of steamships. More to the point, also enter Henry's wife, Sara, with her recipes, talent and a large, white marble counter on which her confectionary performances became an attraction in themselves while sail-making went on in the back. Success, of course, brought the compliment of copycats. Soon several competitors opened on the Island and later, even on Martha's Vineyard in faraway Massachusetts.

In short, fudge came to represent Mackinac, Mackinaw and eventually all of northern Michigan to the outsiders who come to visit. Lots of resorts have emblematic foods using emblematic ingredients, like Maryland crabs. Mackinac fudge, however, is indeed unique in that there is nothing native about it or its ingredients except its marketing, which has proven sufficient. It is delivered all over the country and attracts queues among the 15,000 "fudgies" who each day disembark on an island whose population freezes back in winter to 492, according to the most recent census.

But its real interest comes in translation. Being a fudgie means you don't understand and probably don't care. It means you come from somewhere beyond the undeclared geopolitical unit called "Up North." To those who live north of the diagonal southwest/northeast snow line that crosses the state at a town called Standish, everything else is "Down Below." This makes some sense when you're looking at a map of Michigan with nothing but a sliver of the northern peninsula between, say, East Jordan and Canada. All else lies south and, therefore, "below."

Canada itself is the single anomaly. Although ninety percent of the Canadian population lives south of northern Michigan, Canada is never, ever, Down Below. Nor is it Up North, a term up-northers reserve for themselves. Canada is just Canada, or "across the Straits" (of Mackinac). Geography doesn't matter. I've never heard the location of Boston debated here, but Boston would surely be Down Below. During the Cold War, people did talk about Moscow. Moscow, 500 miles farther north than northern Michigan, would also be Down Below. Nothing here is more Down Below, however, than Detroit. Down Below means "different" and, unlike vision, hearing or any other sensory perceptions, proximity magnifies emotions that lie inert in the viscera. Detroit is the most different place on earth. Industrial, unionized, Black, big.

Charlevoix's winter population is 2,500. Of the thousands more who crowd its city limits in July and August, most present no particular fudge-based taxonomy problems. Quite another matter, however, are the families of the Belvedere Club (founded in 1878) who have rented their large, charmingly trimmed wooden "cottages" for generations at a time. Or the Chicago Club people (established in 1881) who hide from view behind an island they own and keep unoccupied and fully wooded as a barrier against the boaters who might—gasp—glimpse them while passing through Round Lake harbor. Then, over on the "Big Lake," i.e. Lake Michigan, there's a street called Michigan Avenue. But a street name isn't what "Michigan Avenue" is to this subset of fudgies. To them, Michigan Avenue means their summer crowd, no matter what their actual Charlevoix address. In the old days, its four blocks, from the channel bridge to Mr. Hooker's "Paddock," were the social hub of a Jewish aristocracy drawn mostly from the Midwest and South, with an additional smattering from the East, but none, early on, from Detroit, the nearest big city. Three complete sets of mirror images in a very, very small town.

I grew up part of the "Michigan Avenue" group that actually lived on Michigan Avenue. The Chicago contingent included the Blocks of Inland Steel, the Loebs and Rosenwalds of Sears-Roebuck, the Guthmans in real estate, my father's family of Monarch Leather, the Silberman's and the Moseses. My mother's side included the Rices of Rice-Stix Dry Goods, the Goldmans and the Lessers of Lesser-Goldman Cotton Company. A smattering of Godchauxes and Lemanns represented New Orleans; the Oppenheimers, Memphis; and the Steinerts, Boston. Cincinattians were the biggest group: the Lazaruses of Federated Department stores, the Adlers of Adler Yarns, the Josephs, the Wylers, the Iglaurers, the Gluecks, the Westons, the Strauses. Later there were the Broders, Rothchilds, Kleins, Friedmans, Okrents and, notably, the Gilberts, Edith becoming the Doyenne of Michigan Avenue lore. None matched the truly baronial stature later made famous in Stephen Birmingham's *Our Crowd*— their wealth hadn't been amassed as early as the New York legacies he described, nor were their factories as big — but wealthy and snobbish they certainly were, on about the same level as the gentiles they emulated.

There was no intermarriage, and not even any summer socializing. My great grandfather Goldman bought property from the Teasdale family for Hortense Place, a grandiose development in St. Louis named for his daughter. The two families, however, did not cross paths in Charlevoix. Grandfather Rice did business all year with the May Company clients summering just across Round Lake; my grandmother headed the St. Louis Red Cross during World War II, the Conference of Christians and Jews somewhat later and served on the St. Louis Symphony Board much of her adult life. But they never crossed the seasonal and social Gaza Strip of Charlevoix's one-street, five-block downtown. The protestants felt superior to Catholics and the German Jews disdained the "Russians," by which they meant co-religionists from all over Eastern Europe. Except for Dr. Gib Saltonstall,

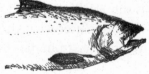

few of the year-rounders figured into the social consciousness of fudgies of whatever persuasion.

Segregation extended beyond socializing and into the resort sports of golf and tennis, with separate and unequal facilities for each. My invitation to play tennis at Belvedere as a high school senior came as something of a Michigan Avenue astonishment. My grandmother, for example, regarded fellow Jews as north—far north—of Blacks, but just as certainly south of Gentiles. This was 1958, four years after the U.S. Supreme Court decided Brown v Board of Education and when much in our hometown of St. Louis remained segregated. Still, she angrily accused me of "passing" at Belvedere where she thought I wasn't welcome.

Which brings us to an image in another distinct social mirror. While white fudgies on both sides of Round Lake held themselves apart by religion, the Blacks—whom both regarded as a servant class—mingled freely. Robert (never Bob) Jones, my grandparents' "man" in the 1950s, was the only member of the Rice household who had crossed the barriers—marked and otherwise—between the shaded lawns of the Belvedere Club and the rest of the town. Among these chauffeur/butler/toters, however, a boss's social standing mattered. One memorable 3 AM, Robert took me largemouth bass fishing with "the men." We of the Michigan Avenue group picked our way in the humid dark to the stash of rowboats, arriving before anyone else at the appointed spot on the shore of Lake 26. But no one launched until the Belvedere and Chicago Club men showed up, the soft conversation leaving a clear mark on my eleven-year-old and lone white self. Their subservience was nothing new—I had seen these men wait for my family and their friends—the surprise was that it extended beyond race into social standing.

There were other firsts that night. I had never fished with anyone except my grandfather, never fished largemouth, never fished at night. The boats maneuvered silently in weed beds so shallow that water hardly covered the oar blades. Fish feeding on the surface sounded like rock splashes: I had never *heard* fish before. My Heddon Crazy Crawler looked like a fat mouse with the gaudy paint job of the cars of the day and heavy, chrome side-flippers that made it sound like a kitchen faucet when I dragged it back after a cast. The 1950s bass loved it. Would fish take something like that now, when our cars have lost their tail fins?

The men's signal for going home was when the sun rose high enough to attract the mud turtles to their logs. It was Sunday, meaning church for Belvedere and Chicago Club families. The men of Michigan Avenue's non-temple-going Jews packed up, too. I didn't mind. By that time I had a fish nice enough for a Belvedere man to snap me with his Brownie Hawkeye, and I liked the idea of keeping a schedule according to what turtles did.

Turtles had been a kind of sacred icon since the first time—was I really only six?—my grandfather put me on his lap to steer the big, gray LaSalle sedan with electric windows and "free-wheeling." (I never did and still don't know what that was, exactly.) Up the hill from the Ironton Ferry, where my adventure began, a mud turtle appeared ahead on the macadam. I felt larger hands over mine on the wheel and the car came to a stop on the gravel shoulder, paused, and backed up. "We'll take him to where he won't get hurt," Pops explained. He might as well have told me the world would end if I ever passed a turtle where it might get squashed.

Turtles react to rain the way I do to a sunny morning with a breeze; they want to try something new. And this is how they end up, if they're lucky. You let little ones clunk their way around the floor of a car until you get to water safe for them. All you can do with a really big snapper is nudge it back into the grass. I have a whole memory file of turtle-in-the-road images. It's a quirk—I remember them the way I do people's eye color—I'm better at this than I am at names.

Anyone along with Pops that day would have had a stash of such memories by the time they turned thirty, my age in July of 1971, when a big Buick braked at a sight that the driver, a fudgie, wasn't ready for. Our red and white International Harvester Scout with a snowplow hoist up front, a spotlight on the roof, trailer hitch out back and scars of twelve seasons showing all over was pulled over on the shoulder of Ferry Road. A forty-pound snapping turtle—a good twenty-four inches across—alternately hissed and lunged at the window scraper I was using to prod it to safety. The man who got out of the sparkling Buick might as well have come from Mars, or really any planet with Kmarts. Although mercifully receding elsewhere, the seasonal tide of pastel, double-knit leisure suits had only recently engulfed northern Michigan. But the fudgie knew local color when he saw it, and pulled back so the women in his car (interestingly, feminism has brought no demand for, say, "fudgette") could see what he had found.

A local — me, as he perceived things — wearing a grease-brimmed baseball hat, T-shirt, filthy shorts and combat boots had jumped out of the battered old Scout in the full drench of an afternoon shower. Clearly, this fellow was about to do something quaint. The huge turtle with moss on its back was worth a picture all by itself.

"You eat those?" he asked me.

Journalists of my age don't think of themselves as members of society, whether this involves joining political parties or geographic groupings like "locals." We don't join organizations, we avoid causes and look with suspicion on women and ethnic colleagues who advocate and march. There is something inconsistent between the role of professional observer and participation. We tend to call the rest of the world "real people" because, instead of describing things, like us, they *do* things. In my mind's eye that afternoon, I was still a flashy foreign correspondent from *Time* who would be on a plane jetting somewhere else in a few minutes — at the very least a dinner party where I would amuse my companions with tales of turtles. Or, the tale of being taken for a local by a paunchy Middle-Westerner positively swathed in woven plastic and driving a car painted like a color chart.

Mr. Doubleknit was so vexed by what I told him I was doing that he climbed back inside his bloated vehicle-version of a Michelin Man. The idea of someone looking like me playing good Samaritan to a slimy, ugly creature just didn't fit the fudgie view of locals.

"Anyways," I heard him sermonize as he drove off, "like I say, they make 'em into soup."

The minor scrambling of his fudgie self-image was nothing compared to what he did to mine. Under the jumpsuit, was the man comfortable in his own skin? Probably. Could I say the same? Can you wear more than one skin? Can you be a part-time "real person?" This, I came to realize, was what was happening to me. Or maybe, what leaving the kaleidoscope life I had been living as a foreign correspondent to resume old psychic roots at a family farm was doing to me. What sort of hybrid was I becoming? What I loved about the identity crisis was that cosmic questions could be raised by a turtle that decided to take advantage of wet macadam to move his house to another locale.

THE NAME, SIZE & SHAPE OF BOATS

July, 2006

Size, not century, seems to have always determined the kind of name a vessel gets. The large usually bear serious names, whether of ownership association (the doomed lake freighter *Edmund Fitzgerald*), function (the ferry *Beaver Islander*), or image (our local icebreaker, the *Steelhead*). Naval lore from our shores and beyond resonates with vessels called *Constitution, Indefatigable, Victory, Invincible*. For the small, it's unclear why size inspires playfulness, particularly since large dreams often inspire the names: *Bank Account, At Last, Wet Dream* and dozens of others are afloat in Lake Charlevoix alone.

The vintage lake tug that tends the barges at Ironton is all business with its high, bandaged bow, low working afterdeck and a record of jobs and mishaps written all over its black hull and green wheelhouse. Her name, *American Girl*, didn't catch on until I realized what she means to me: She's a floating hat-check girl when I'm outbound on a fishing run to the Big Lake. Coming home, I tip my cap to my old *American Girl* at the mouth of the narrows. She's my favorite because she looks just right. What does that mean? Picture how your own favorite American girl makes you feel when you look at her. What should be up is up, what's down is fine that way. She's built to take you where you want to go.

My own boat history begins with the *Lazy Ike*, a name only indirectly linked to the late-1940s hero worship of the general who won World War II. Eisenhower was such a powerful icon that any boy with "Eisen" as the first two syllables of his last name was automatically called "Ike," which

BOBBY, BUZZY, ME AND JAY JUST BEFORE
THROWING UP IN THE SOUTH ARM

in my case, slopped over to the boat. The main inspiration, however, honored one of those improbably red, white and black wooden fishing lures that promises "Will Catch the Big Ones." That was enough for me.

I still hadn't caught anything with it when my father somehow produced a twelve-foot, green plywood rowboat with a five-horsepower outboard. Not that Dad was a boater. He neither knew nor cared to know anything about the outdoor life that so powerfully called me from every magazine and boy's adventure book. The *Lazy Ike's* first sortie met the standard I've used ever since for a successful adventure: Nevermind enjoyable; the story must be memorable.

The idea was for my father and me to set out alone from the shore in front of my grandparents' beach "cottage" and fish all the way to Overlook Farm, fifteen miles and two lakes away. Huge, albeit unconscious symbolism at work here: to be departing from in-laws my father detested, with a son to whom he had only recently taken interest and an activity the son knew more about than he did. Every time I think of that day—lunch packed by the cottage kitchen staff in a wicker basket that went soggy within the first three minutes—the memory comes paired with another from forty years later.

I am seated in my psychiatrist's office, muttering on and on as one does in one's forties about my father's tangle of emotional and intellectual legacies. The doctor, who almost never said anything beyond, "How did that make you feel?" actually interrupted the story of this trip to observe, "It sounds like your father did the best he could."

I have never wondered until right now why we set off when we did. It may have been that this particular day, bright and blustery, was the only time that fit in with my grandmother's elaborate social schedule. Or, possibly, my astonished enthusiasm to be actually setting out in a boat with my father overwhelmed whatever else was going on in his mind. Most probably for this most impractical of intellectuals, seafaring conditions weren't his concern. In his mind, boating meant getting in and going somewhere, like in a car. As we planned the day at breakfast, the Big Lake was calm. It almost always is at that hour, usually signifying nothing about what might follow. By the time we flipped the boat over on the sand, there was considerable surf. As Dad pushed off, each wave broke, first over me, then the stern, then heaving my father back on the stones. I flailed away at the oars. The propeller sounded like a hammer on steel as it bashed into rocks. Somehow, we got beyond the first line of breakers. Somehow, we got the engine started, with him holding the boat steady in chest-deep water. Problem: He was out of the boat, which did not have gears. He hung from the bow, one leg over a gunwale. My instructions were an unspecific, "Keep going." Gradually, more of him followed.

We made it to the Charlevoix channel light where waves from the rear pushed us any way they wanted, sometimes helplessly toward the cement breakwater. Then we were through Round Lake, the town's natural harbor, and out into the main body of Lake Charlevoix. My father, visibly relieved, said, "Aren't we supposed to be fishing?"

One of the many odd features of all of our sporting adventures together — there were two — was that we actually got what we — I — was after. I clipped on the *Lazy Ike* lure and paid out as much line as Pops seemed to have done in our trips together on the *William*. There was no need for the buckets Pops would sling alongside to slow his mahogany runabout to trolling speed; as my father remarked, our slow was slow enough to challenge the concept of forward motion. In place of the connection between the speed at which a lure travels through water and a fish on the line, there was ...

64

no connection, whatever. For Dad, lunch relieved the tedium of "nothing whatever happening." And the ruination of sandwiches by inundation actually helped by giving us something to do; locating the bits and crumbles we didn't need to wring out first.

When the steelhead hit—I still remember it—I thought at first that something terrible had happened to the rod, reel, boat, maybe the world. As steelhead do, this one jumped repeatedly, took line, dove. I don't remember anything about my father's reaction except that he seemed to have no concept that anything unusual was happening. To him, the consummate non-angler, when you went fishing, you caught a fish. When you'd caught it, you pulled up your line and did something else.

That's what we did. Me? Thrilled. Him? I don't know about him. That was the summer he'd come into the living room where I was dreaming over a copy of *The Fisherman's Encyclopedia*. I was nine. "Charles," he said, "let's become acquainted." He must have thought a boat might float a new relationship.

THE SECOND AND FINAL joint sporting adventure involved ducks. In St. Louis, everyone's father except mine hunted ducks. My dad didn't even seem to know any of those hunting dads, at least anyone he felt right about asking to take us. Nevertheless, we found ourselves one day in the *Lazy Ike*—which we'd transported south on top of a sedan—headed for Lake Alton, where a Mississippi dam had created an impoundment sprinkled with rental duck blinds. But which blind was ours? The rental man had described architectural features that may have distinguished it to real hunters; to us his directions meant something like "go find the fish" at an aquarium entrance. So ... how about the one over there, the one with a duck perched on it? I was in the stern, steering.

"Shoot!"

I had never heard Dad say anything in quite that tone.

"Shoot! SHOOT!"

The gun, of course, wasn't ready, but the duck, obligingly, stayed put. I raised the gun. Dad hunched down, hands over ears. I shot over his head. Amazingly, the bird and, it must be admitted, part of the blind, splashed into the water. Dinner that night included the first of many stories about "Charles and the psychopathic duck," which was probably a mud hen. Even I had to accept that it didn't taste quite right.

Lazy Ike II never carried the numeral. At thirteen, I considered myself to have graduated definitively from rowboats. There was no reason to cause anyone to wonder what sort of embarrassing little peanut the *Lazy Ike I* might have been. With the pride of an admiral, I stuck the black letters on both sides of the white, fiberglass bow. Fifteen feet long, with wooden decking forward and between the front benches, *Lazy Ike (II)* had a real steering wheel, not an outboard handle. From my seat in the stern I could not only navigate, but also keep track of the fuel; check the oily, ever-rising bilge; bail with a succession of cans, cups and scoops; and be deliciously deafened by the power of twenty-five horses somehow contained within a green Johnson Outboard Motor housing. Total cost: $250 with trailer.

It was fast, very fast. Faster than any of the larger, newer, less porous boats my Charlevoix crowd had. It was so improbably fast—with just the last foot or so in the water when it was up on plane—that friends from that era still ask about the *Lazy Ike*, even though some other part of their memory knows it long ago floated away from all of us with the rest of the 1950s. Maybe it's their way of remembering the days when, at the end of clear August afternoons, the horizon turned light green. And if you looked straight up at the enveloping blue, you seemed enclosed in a color-coded school folder containing your most important records.

BOATS WERE CARS before we could drive and thoroughly intoxicating. We could go anywhere reachable by water, which included the most worthwhile things—girls, movies, hamburgers, each other's houses. *Lazy Ike* put the farm within socializing distance. In twenty minutes, I could roar flat-out up the South Arm, through The Narrows—then without a "no wake" zone—and straight to "Uncle" Jimmy Ries's dock.

That's where the girls were, because that's where the water skiing was. Uncle Jimmy would arrive with several of them—girls too young to drive themselves, but not too young for me to ogle—in a white Cadillac convertible as long as his unimaginably wonderful Century speedboat, the one with white accents framing luminous mahogany planking like a sign that said "unattainable." Uncle Jimmy was probably in his late sixties, certainly too old for our parents to have *not* worried about his focus. Nobody said much, however, until he invited Suzy Grate to move to Cincinnati with him. At seventeen—an older woman to me—Suzy was the summer goddess I worshiped but never touched. Years later I saw her again as Suzy Ries, then a wealthy widow. There is some justice in the world: When she shook my hand it was as if the marble Venus has stepped from a pedestal and asked for a light.

Jimmy had "the boat," but the *Lazy Ike* had advantages. When the lake was too rough for skiing, we—I don't remember the girls ever following—could go where it was calm. We could night ski and, if we hit a sailboat regatta buoy in the dark, creating a huge welt across the chest, we could explain that it had been caused by something harmless-sounding, like falling over a bicycle. The boat's property of being a car before a car carried a broader message, too: Solve the transportation problem and anywhere was accessible from the farm. When the time came to decide whether I would make Overlook my principal inheritance—even though I was outbound to a life I saw as permanently based abroad as a foreign correspondent—I knew at some inchoate level that this seemingly isolated property could be made part of a broader life.

Yes, I went away. In the album my mother kept called "Overlook Farm," the last pictures of me with *Lazy Ike* are of water skiing with my father, him at the controls, wearing a baffled look. There's another of him, looking at the starter rope as if he were pulling at the head of a rattlesnake. Nothing further, not even a shard of memory about the fate of this talisman vessel of our relationship.

LIKE SO MANY THINGS that had become central, even emblematic, boats disappeared from my life along with fishing and hunting. Only vestiges lingered. Along with the white buck shoes and other stuff I considered important on the drive to freshman orientation was my .22 rifle:

Yale had no objection, but told me cars were not for first-year students. Occasionally I'd walk the New Haven Railroad tracks where they went through woods, more homesick for the farm than planning to actually hunt something. During reporting assignments much later, with the little Winchester following me around Europe and South America, I caught myself imagining it in my hands when evocative landscapes appeared.

Then, in Buenos Aires, I bought a sailboat from a Kodak executive who had been sent home after too many kidnapping threats. I didn't name our graceful wooden sloop, probably because it was linked too closely with the terrorism leading up to Argentina's Dirty War. We cruised the tan River Plate between Buenos Aires and Montevideo mostly for peace of mind. Offshore it was easier to ignore the very distinct possibilities of kidnapping, or worse, for us or the boys. Somehow, no name meant detachment, like, "We're really not here." If that sounds crazy, think of how much more insane it was for the thirty-two-year-old me to have had a family there at all. One rationalization: We wouldn't be there very long, due home within sixteen months.

Home, of course, turned out to be Overlook Farm. The boys were three and five, and I knew right away that the place would teach them what it taught me: that before the adult world allowed automotive liberation, boats gave you the freedom to fish, explore, join friends, find girls. And so came a series of them, towing in their wakes an extended second childhood I could share with my sons. In a way it was like growing up again by starting over when they started, and all of it stuck together by the most powerful interpersonal glue: being foolish together.

Our first boat was found in the attic of a Charlevoix marina. A wooden, lapstrake, sixteen-foot Thompson runabout that I hadn't seen since boyhood. Everything about it was as familiar as a high school girlfriend and, in fact, it had belonged to Hamilton Moses, father of Penny and Jill, two of the lithesomes always ahead of me in the water ski line. With its original '58 Evinrude 35-horsepower outboard and trailer, it cost $500 and was immediately, adoringly named *Happy Daze* by Ben, who even at ten knew his way around words. His captain's hat with that lettering still hangs in the farm mudroom.

Some years later, and after a new engine—distracted by adolescent annoyance from Ben, I neglected to mix oil with the gasoline—and

BEN AND A BLUE-WATER BOAT THAT COULD SLIDE
RIGHT UP ONTO A BEACH WITH HIS CATCH

several family refinishing efforts that left the woodwork still locked in steady decline, *Happy Daze* was replaced with a seventeen-foot Thompson inboard/outboard. I should have known it wasn't for me. In this sort of boat, the drive shaft sticks out improbably and inelegantly from the transom, right at the water line. It also had a "bow-rider" configuration up front. To me, both went against all instincts for keeping water on the other side of a hull. I find it significant that alone in the lineup of Overlook boats, it's the only name I can't bring to the surface. I do, however, remember spending dozens of hours, and when that failed, hundreds of dollars—both resented—removing all traces of its former name, *Sundance*.

We sold the inboard/outboard to our plumber for a song and bought a twenty-two-foot Catalina swing-keel sloop. Still in a hangover from Paris and the general aura of foreign correspondence, not to mention the amount of alcohol we all drank then—first round of Scotch when on deadline, 10 AM, without comment—I renamed it *Bateau Ivre*. Julia never liked the idea of naming a boat for a poem by Arthur Rimbaud called "Drunken Boat" and I should have listened. Especially, I soon learned, as the idea was neither original nor even unusual. Local waters bobbed with boats inspired by a French surrealist who stopped writing at twenty-one and died at thirty-seven. My choice seemed as worrisomely trite as *Sundance*.

Everything changed for the better the year Ben went off to the University of Vermont, beginning with a boat ruining our first "Parents Weekend," at least for Julia. The boat and I met on a blind date. Just after 7 AM on my morning walk, there she was. It was love at first sight. A Platonic form of jaunty, she dressed up an otherwise unremarkable marina near the Lake Champlain ferry docks. The place wasn't open, but that didn't matter; I had already as much as bought her and could think of nothing else. Even worse for Julia, Ben was quite happy with the course change of conversation from classes and professors to boats and future fishing.

It was the first boat I called "she," and her inspirational bow belonged to the raw hull of a Maine lobster boat, twenty-two feet long and awaiting customized outfitting. I opted for outboard power—for ease of storage and repair—and a canvas top instead of the traditional wood. Everything else was strictly Maine. Not only Maine, but Beal's Island, Maine, built to the specifications of Calvin Beal, whom I learned deserved his legend. A stubby skeg keel produced the steady handling of something much bigger, which Ben and I discovered on the way home, unable to pass open waters without "just a little splash." No nasty surprises, and we even caught a respectable salmon. Admiring, acquisitive glances followed us at launch sites. Even offers to buy "Right now. Cash." Something new and wonderful: We were traveling with a nautical starlet! I'd paid $26,000 and was offered twice that by a guy who witnessed our spin at the eastern end of Lake Ontario. Hell, I would have paid twice as much, too. You don't get to feel like that very often.

As always with true love, finding the right name for her scrambled the best of ingredients into a throw-away omelet. The right recipe came from our friend Bill Sherman, the eldest of the three brothers who ran the cannery where our cherries ended up. He had taken to teasing me about being a "cherry baron"—food-processor-talk for the growers who always (according to them) want more for their crop than merited. Of all people, my natively unboaty mate solved the bedeviling nautical problem. Julia still insists that the name she blurted was intended as sarcasm, but to me, its pure inspiration was palpable: *Cherry Baron* she would be.

Why are boats, particularly admired ones, always "she?" Think of the bow as the bosom and the stern as a bottom. Bows should be uplifted and admirably proportioned; sterns, shapely and low. During a beach walk with friends gathered for a wedding on the base of Cape Cod, I fell in love with *Cherry Baron's* tender, a dinghy with a "wine glass stern." It belonged to a Lowell — yes, of *those* Lowells, "who speak only to the Cabots and the Cabots only to God." Our hostess, the mother of the groom, warned that contacting him as a distinctly non-Brahmin, Jewish, Middle-Westerner might not be easy. My hostess misjudged what the shared admiration of hulls can accomplish.

"What was that you said?" asked a secretary, unaccustomed to a name as distinctly un-Yankee as Eisendrath. But I had learned a trick in London while reporting a Beatles story on deadline. Unable to get through to their bankers, I said, in exasperation, "Just tell him it's Sir Charles here." The meeting call sailed through to the boardroom with a jolly, "Righty-ho, then." Mr. Lowell's secretary responded similarly when I mentioned the dinghy. "It's about boats? If it's about boats, it doesn't matter if he knows who you are," she said. "Mr. Lowell is always ready to talk about boats."

Mr. Lowell directed us to a cabin in the mountains of northern Maine. The following winter, with a blizzard coming, we learned we were just in time. Harrison Sylvester made three sizes of the prettiest Whitehall, wineglass-stern sailing dinghies ever seen. He cut spars from the spruce woods out back and lavished centuries of know-how on repeated coats of Maine pink paint and marine varnish. Loving boatwright that he was, something in the news had caused him to unlearn what he had been told in school: that his dyslexia disqualified him for any career requiring more thought than manual arts. Now in his early sixties, he was launching himself on a euphoric new career as a consultant to debunk the stunting message. We bought his last, sprit-rig ten-footer.

Maine breeds Maine. I had *Cherry Baron* fitted so that the mast and sail from the dinghy could double as a "spanker" rig. Ever wondered why you sometimes see lobster boats with a sail that seems too small, wrongly positioned and anyway superfluous on a power craft? They're called spankers and keep the bow headed safely into the wind and oncoming seas without the bother of sea anchors. That's handy for hauling traps, but for me it could thwart disaster in case of engine failure. In a strong wind, lobster boats drift beam to the wind, a most vulnerable position. A spanker could save her.

What to name something lovely and smartly rigged? *Pretty Julia* seemed just right. Alone among thirty years of boats and boating with Julia, Harry Sylvester's sailing dinghy is the only one in which Julia has ever initiated trips. Nevermind that it is the smallest, least comfortable and most apt to get her wet in a fresh wind or stranded in a calm.

FDR JOINS THE MICHIGAN AVENUE CROWD... SORT OF

August, 2016

In the summer of 1943, Allied forces were just emerging from years of World War II setbacks to go on the offensive. President Franklin Delano Roosevelt was exhausted and not at all certain he would succeed in gaining the fourth term that no previous president had even attempted. He needed a change of scene, but American ships were being torpedoed off the coasts, so arrangements had to include the absence of U-boats. Northern Michigan looked ideal.

The locals were respectful, if Republican, and the area lay far from public attention. When journalists were wont to mention the place, the subject was "Hemingway country," the notorious Loeb-Leopold murder case, or fishing, which at that time they described in the glowing terms later reserved for Montana. A boat on the Great Lakes seemed perfect, but who would take FDR fishing, on what boat, and exactly where? Roosevelt loved fishing but was confined to a wheelchair. Resolving all that fell to Lt. Jack Manly, assigned to one of two side-paddlewheel steamboats that had been converted to improvised aircraft carriers for training Navy pilots on Lake Michigan. As he wrote to friend and fellow Chicagoan Lt. Ernest Loeb, then serving aboard a destroyer in the Pacific:

> *...out of a clear sky the Captain of the Carrier Wolverine called me in his cabin and said 'Manly, I have some secret orders for you.' ...The Chief of Staff asked Captain Ross [of Wolverine's*

THE WHITE HOUSE
WASHINGTON

January 12, 1944.

Dear Mr. Uhlmann:

Mr. Early has turned over to me the
letter which you sent to him asking the President to sign the picture of the "Anna H" for
Lt. Ernest G. Loeb. The President has been
very glad to do as you ask and I am enclosing
it herewith.

Please give my very best wishes to
Lt. Manley when you next see him.

Very sincerely yours,

Grace G. Tully

Grace G. Tully
Private Secretary

Richard Uhlmann, Esq.,
1480 Board of Trade Bldg.,
Chicago 4, Illinois.

Borrowed By President Roosevelt

The 38-foot Matthews cruiser
"Anna H," owned by Lt. Ernest
Loeb, U. S. N., of Chicago and
Loeb Farms, Charlevoix, was com-
mandeered recently by the United
States navy to take President
Roosevelt to Canada for a week's
fishing trip. The craft returned
to port here last Thursday. When
the boat was borrowed by navy of-
ficials, the Loebs had no idea that
it was to carry such a famous passenger. Lt. Loeb is now on duty
in the South Pacific, while his
family is at their summer residence
at Loeb Farms, located four miles
south of the city.

STAUNCH REPUBLICANS LIKE MUCH OF
BIG BUSINESS, THE LOEB FAMILY'S LORE
HAS IT THAT THE "ANNA H" WAS
FUMIGATED AFTER FDR'S USE

PHOTO COURTESY OF THE LOEB FAMILY

sister ship, Wilmette, assigned to the Presidential outing] if he knew where there was a small yacht available as he did not like the looks of the motor sailor aboard the Wilmette, he wanted something a little classier. ... The next day about noon, ANNA H was on her way to the great fishing grounds of the North Channel (of Lake Huron) and a few days later was the official 'fishing smack' for the president's only vacation of 1943.

Anna H and a kindred boat, *The Boss,* cut through the waves of memory, defining the elegance of how my grandparents' generation wished to be seen. Long and lean, shaped more like Vanderbilts or Roosevelts than my shorter, stubbier kin, their white hulls and brightwork set off the dresses and jewelry the ladies wore on canasta decks under tan canvas canopies. I see them every time I'm off Loeb Point. *The Boss* is always cutting southward to Horton Bay. The *Anna H*, a thirty-eight-foot Matthews, floats eternally in a slip cut out for her below the ramparts of The Big House —ersatz French chateau it is, but imposing as Norman-like buildings with stone towers high above a lake tend to be. *Anna H* was named for Anna Henrietta Loeb, mother of Ernie and his brother, the ill-fated "Dickie," as my smitten mother and others knew him. Twenty years after the homicidal drama of "The Loeb-Leopold Case," the political drama of the *Anna H*, took center stage, albeit as a tightly-held, military secret.

FDR'S STAFF SIGNED THIS MAP OF HIS SECRET 1943 FISHING TRIP
IN THE ONLY AMERICAN OPEN WATER FREE OF U-BOATS

PHOTO COURTESY OF THE LOEB FAMILY.
THE FDR PRESIDENTIAL LIBRARY HAS RECORDS OF THE TRIP, BUT NO GRAPHICS.

Manly's letter goes on for 1500 admiring words about FDR's grace
and humor and his amazement at being in the company of presidential
insiders including Harry Hopkins, Supreme Court Justice Joseph Byrnes,
Admiral William Healy, General Edwin "Pa" Watson (chief military aide
at a critical moment of the war) and Grace Tully, FDR's longtime private

secretary. For present purposes, however, it is more pertinent to quote notes about fishing and lesser personnel:

> *It is almost unbelievable how good the fishing was. We fished in the Current Bay and waters of MacGregor Bay, across the peninsula and in the uncharted water of white fish bay [sic], all within fifteen to twenty miles north, north easterly of Little Current.*

> *In all sincerity, the meals I had aboard the Presidential Train and the Wilmette can never come up the standard set up for us by one good 'Cookie of de boat,' one Larry Abt.*

The waters mentioned were precisely those *Cherry Baron* visited for pike fishing expeditions with Ben and North Channel cruises with Julia. Each time we passed *Anna H's* old berth at the Loeb estate on the way out. "Cookie" Larry Abt was another young Chicagoan in the Loeb/ Eisendrath circle, but Overlook Farm remembers him for his photography. Larry Abt's black-and-white enlargement of a 1947 picnic scene still holds its position in the living room, a frequent reference for changes made to the house and a base point for much that has gone on and to what effect. Sample: The "old-age tree" isn't there. It was planted much later by my mother, ever the romantic botanist, to trace my parents' life there together. Being a split-leaf maple, it divided into two trunks, one for each of them, with a common base. That seemed perfect…until after forty-three years together, they separated. They should have noted—we all should have—that with age, the trunks had grown farther and farther apart.

MARRIAGE ON A FLOUNDERING, PERHAPS FOUNDERING, BOAT

July, 1999

Expedition is one of those words that a language like English shouldn't need. There's "trip," for example. If it's about water, there's "voyage." To somewhere unfamiliar in any respect, be it geographically to amorously, you're on an "exploration." Leisurely? Use "excursion." Esoteric? Borrow "sortie" from the French, who will give you one of their ironic smirks. The "ex" in expedition means out of or away from, the "ped," to travel by foot. Still, "expedition" is good to have around. In my life it implies a mix of seriousness and whimsy with risk involved and, usually, unusual equipment. We might go to the moon…or just to a huge snag maple out back where a she-coon died facing out of her den hole fifty feet up.

The boys had been instructed early, often and dourly that anything they shot when out by themselves, they would clean, cook and eat. But at nine and eleven such abstractions don't hold up when a large animal lumbers into the iron sights of recently acquired .22 rifles. Up she went, she entered the hole, then, tauntingly, reappeared facing them. Stationary shots were easier. She died in the hole while they ran home to report a mighty deed. This alone was not an expedition…yet.

For boys their ages, it's the spotting, chase, kill and bragging rights that count. Anything later is lesser, if it registers at all. Fortunately, they thought, as I reminded them of the mandatory culinary experience to come, the quarry was irretrievably ensconced beyond the reach

THE DAY WE ALL BECAME HUNTERS

of our ladder, in a tree without climbable branches. Enter, however, Bill Crick. We had never met, but my usual advisors in such situations showed a rare unanimity: Crick was the man for the job, a trimmer young enough to scale with a rope and old enough to imagine such situations with his own children. He also lived close by. Up he went, lasso in hand. Between the time the she-coon died and now, however, her coonness had swelled like the cork in a wine bottle. And it had begun to snow. Leverage beyond what was possible while dangling from a rope would be required—and what better system than a lasso attached from creature neck to trailer hitch? I backed our venerable red-and-white 1965 International Harvester Scout into the woods. To jubilation from some, chagrin from others, dinner began her journey to the table with something audibly between floop and skish, followed by an unmistakable, thirty-pound plop.

This was going to be messy. Gutting took place outside; skinning, by fingers stiffened by cold, in the basement. For coon gourmandize, however, there was no alternative to the kitchen. As a first (sterilizing) step, Julia suggested par boiling. The boys pronounced the gray result inedible. We tried baking what we had boiled. Then sautéing strips with quantities of salt and spices—many spices—but still to howled protest even though the brown looked much more like food. After a couple of hours, it was the chefs, fittingly, who came up the solution—ketchup—turning plates into monotone finger-paint palettes. The boys emptied them quickly, in silence and under close supervision…and thenceforth, at least to my knowledge, they did not kill anything beyond official pests (e.g., crows in the orchard, red squirrels chewing on the house) that they did not eat.

EXPEDITIONS NEED NOT INVOLVE even short travel *per se*, as long as they include travel somehow related. Take the case of Octavio, the stutter-curing octopus. At ten, Ben's jaws often stuck on the beginnings of words before he could get them out; the "st" in stick, for example. The annoyance seemed to exacerbate his shyness and was beginning to worry us. About 100 miles into the 235 between Overlook and Ann Arbor, a small form appeared in the dark between the front seats of our aging Volvo station wagon and Benjamin began a monologue unfailingly smooth for more than an hour. Every flawless word concerned the octopus.

Why the tropical creature after a snowy weekend up north? Why now when never before mentioned? Was it the farm that invited us to encourage the improbable? Ultimately, who cared? The real question was why the very thought of this animal could temporarily lift a speech impediment and what that might imply. I thought I knew.

Because I was teaching Investigative Reporting in the School of Natural Resources, I knew Karl Lagler, the reigning master of ichthyology and, therefore, of related equipment. It would be best, I thought, to present my plan as an experiment to this eminent man of science. With a laugh and a door opened to the store room, he pronounced it no crazier than some research he'd signed off on. He helped me check out a salt water aquarium system and gave me a steer toward ordering live marine creatures. It turned out they had to travel in the main cabin of an airplane, in their own seat. They also had to be met personally at the airport, like a child. We arrived with the Volvo heater cranked up to what might pass for octopus comfort, having left in the basement a tank burbling with ersatz seawater to specifications. There was an octopus bungalow made of Petoskey stones from the farm and a stash of fresh mealworms. As often happens in other adoptions, this new arrival had received a name before being received. He would be Octavio.

Between joyous arrival and ignominious demise, there were many fascinating zoological revelations, like Octavio changing color to match whatever his feeder wore, as if saying, "Bring it on, Bub, I'm ready." Early in the morning he matched my blue bathrobe, later on he turned the red of a flannel shirt. Green and white were in his repertoire, too, and the performances didn't end with this very opposite of the hiding function of camouflage coloration. Entanglement and pounce strategies could be riveting with mealworms and then, when supplies ran out, of crawlers. When they were fresh and wriggling, Octavio performed a truly spectacular flounce, flying up like a ballerina with eight arms a-twist and a-tangled before alighting atop the hapless creature. Ultimately, however, it was the slither that, alas, proved the most dramatic. Octavio demonstrated that octopuses can slide between nearly any surface, even if it means temporarily squishing eyeballs along with a narrow beak, its most 3-D structure. In this case the slither happened between the top and sides of the aquarium and Pity-cat was in the audience, ready. He'd been ready for weeks, eyeing this appetizing new performer near Ben's room, tail a-twitch. For Octavio it was a Houdini debut; for Pity a meal that probably tasted like Kitty Fish.

Interesting and dramatic, all of this, but in my opinion of far lesser import than my findings in octopus speech therapy. Demonstrably, Ben's stammer was fading! I was triumphant, then mystified by the reactions. Professor Lagler seemed only gently amused as he asked when I might return "the research equipment." Julia continued to nurture doubts, even when the stammer disappeared altogether, only admitting, lamely, that the improvement had begun "around that time," i.e. of Octavio's appearance. Ben, who became an accomplished public speaker, does not talk about Octavio at all. Sometimes, the satisfactions of even the most public expeditions must be savored alone.

NEVERMIND MAPS. The first body of water you can't see across remains the biggest for you forever. If the summer nights of your childhood were spent on your grandparents' cedar sleeping porches on a bluff directly above northern Lake Michigan — the scream of a midnight gale; a whole beach of small stones snare-drumming the way a few of them do when shaken together; the boil of surf; the mournful, quintessentially male call of a foghorn hoping to attract company from the lonely gray. All of this reinforces an imprint as distinct as the wave line left after the water drains back: Beware. But the waking hours leave a different message: No matter what the conditions, you've handled them before — wrong speed, misjudged angle, fading light, misread squalls: Proceed.

It became inevitable. I would cross the limitless deep, as alone as I had been all those years on the sleeping porch, dreams floating on the sounds that a Great Lake makes after dark.

My sister Ellen had a new place in Door County, Wisconsin, due west of Overlook. A perfect expedition destination. By then I was fifty-four. You might think preparations would be those of a seasoned adult and responsible husband/father of two who had mastered boating the way mountain children learn to ski. Yes, that part of me knew the crossing was ninety miles and that given decent weather the *Cherry Baron* cruised at twenty-seven MPH. Even allowing for patches of heavy sea, fog or mis-navigation I would be at my sister's dock, or at least in the shelter of Green Bay, within four hours.

But no. Child-me was in command. Only a boy in single digits would have packed a float tube—a flimsy contraption with built-in waders designed for fly-fishing—as a last-hope survival raft. Or enough food for a week and enough extra fuel tanks for a voyage through Wisconsin to Nebraska, had there happened to be a waterway. Let us not even consider blue water navigation beyond sight of shorepoints: A new Loran machine, precursor to GPS, was aboard *Cherry Baron*, but untried beyond the demo program.

Remember, though, all this took place at the farm, and as with so much that happens there, the boybrain leads, manbrain follows...but not always. Because these two entities do not communicate seamlessly, outfitting took forever. Fair weather came and went. My sister asked for an arrival time. I again put it off for a week. Still, conditions didn't seem right. Finally, exasperation ruled. Would my first-gen cell phone work in mid-lake? I didn't check because, I think, I really didn't want to know. On the fourth trial sortie, a grayish morning with haze that could turn to fog, the boat softly burbled past Ward Brother's Boats in Charlevoix harbor and I once again radioed for my guru's reading on what I might face on this epic jaunt, the voyage of my life. Don Ward's expert judgment: "Hell with conditions. Get the fuck gone."

The trip was transcendent. Thirty miles out on flat, lazy swells, I lost sight of the Manitou Islands, the last shoreline. Small thunderstorms appeared; it was possible to steer around them. I throttled down in mid-lake to let one pass, as if opening a door for Julia. Squalls blew up but were easily handled in quartering seas. The phone worked! Ulysses was able to report to his Penelope that all was well. A blip on the Loran screen appeared to indicate I was headed toward Door County. Two hours out, Wisconsin rose ahead, thin and dark, and I laughed out loud with relief, joy, pride.

NOW ADVENTURES WOULD BEGIN from the reassuring calm of our placid mooring in sheltered water. At twenty-two feet, *Cherry Baron* is no yacht, although *in extremis* she sleeps two in excruciating discomfort and provides for bodily functions at the same standard. Not particularly stable, she is admirably seaworthy in a wave-swimming sort of way and, equally important for getting quickly to cover, improbably fast. For an impression of a lobster boat at speed, picture a WWII Jeep at the India-napolis 500, opening the way forward. We would take leisurely cruises in what's called the North Channel, a long strip of water along the northerly Canadian coast of Lake Huron, famously treacherous for hidden rocks and reefs, but protected from the big water by a string of islands.

Julia's approach to the unknown when it's possibly dangerous-at-my-hands hasn't varied. She will pick up and move to new continents, lan-guages and roles, tend to her family in a war zone as if nothing unusual is happening, throw improbable parties featuring porcupine, but only after laying down conditions and after passage of a sufficient time during which nothing is discussed. I've come to know when it's safe to re-broach the topic because, by then, much of it seems to be her idea and what we called "The Marital Deal" had been struck. With cruising: no sleeping aboard and no cooking either; we would find the best accommodations available. And, solemnly sworn to, "If I say no [to weather conditions] we'll stay ashore."

It didn't take long for things to go wrong. Julia wanted no part of anything like my account of returning from my sister's place in weather heavy enough to keep me at the wheel *after* the point of having to answer nature's call down my leg. Although all was calm at the mooring, even at the Charlevoix jetty, the Big Lake's seas were rolling at four feet from the open west and there could be fifty miles of it before we even made the Mackinac Bridge and the mouth of the channel. "No," she said.

In a long marriage, a deal's a deal, but here there were factors beyond the marital, or even meteorological. Again, there had been several false starts and we had run out of farm summer. Alternatives became discussion begot argument resulting in, "I need to do this, so I'll put you ashore and find you a ride back to the farm." While saying this I happened to notice a small fishing lure, a blue Flatfish, floating near the hull and fished it out while Julia weighed factors imagined and real, beyond either of our knowing. Silently, the scales tipped to "Let's go" and I wired the lure to a corner of the windscreen with others. Talismans gathered while underway convert ordinary boats into vessels with stories to tell.

That trip, our first of 200 miles or so, produced two memorable nautical lines. One came a few days into what had become a happy cruise, although certainly not smooth. Julia's reaction: "How come, when we take a trip like this, it's always rough and there's never anybody else around?"

Later that day we were heading through the Whaleback, a narrow passage where lurking slabs of behemoth black granite seem to swim in the swirling seas around them. Others, a few inches below, give no surface warning. Julia, always the navigator, had turned lookout, too. Nobody equals her for maritime guilelessness. It had become damnably rough among the reefs, but what drew her attention was the behavior of birds, a lifetime passion. "How can those gulls stand on the water?" she asked. Ahead, after a dodge to starboard as violent as I could manage to save us, things looked worse, truly trip-ending. Already strong, the wind came up further from dead ahead, pushing one of those thunderheads so full of the dark unknown that they turn the color of puss and burst with lightning. There were no ports and no shelter. Narrowness and confused waves coming from everywhere made turning tail seem unwise. I put *Cherry Baron* into the wind and took green breakers over the windshield. They carried away the wiper blade, leaving me steering from underwater.

But that wasn't the true test it seemed, at least between us. Without realizing it, I had been muttering a commentary about our chances of getting to an island several miles upwind before something truly terrible befell us. At my left, hanging on to a rail and taking splash with each wave, my first mate told me to kindly shut up. This was truly, unimaginably unexpected. Didn't she want my expert reading of the situation, or to know if we might go down? Of course not, she said. Baffled, I agreed, but couldn't resist asking what she *did* want to know.

"Nothing about that we might go down," she shouted above weather-din. "If you've got something to say, save if it for when it's useful!" And when might that be? By now fury had overcome fear: "When we *are* going down."

She was right about the uselessness of talk. Silently, I attached her hands to the wheel, went below and threw out on deck our life preservers and anything else that might float, bunk cushions included. Julia seemed perfectly satisfied. On subsequent cruises we never talked about the weather.

TWO REUNIONS & A HANDICAP

July, 2013

How many ways you go home depends on whether we're only talking about the one with a roof. There are others. The most nourishing, hardest to find—and when you do, the most tangled—is the home with roots. I'd not realized that root-homelessness could be as obvious as a house with a missing roof until young strangers named Eisendrath turned up at the University of Michigan. I make a point of welcoming each. After all, according to family lore, we're all related because "we all left Germany in 1848." Some I could cut from a crowd at twenty-five yards, others not even across a dinner table. So far none has much of an idea of family history; nor, in one case, that Judaism is involved. Their agnostic approach to their heritage jolted me. I realized that opting for homelessness over heritage had defined my path as well, and that produced a full grown flummox. It didn't look right on them. They seemed diminished. Is that how I looked, too?

What happens when you climb out of your pool of family lore, relationships and religion? You lose the status of *belonging*. I could not see my own delusion until these young sharers of the Eisendrath gene pool displayed theirs over lunches in student cafeterias. It was as if they had decided to not remember the city where they were born, even that they were Americans. It was as if I were looking down at them; definitely not from the hereafter, but from another *status*. I had traveled their route, I'd pulled up to a platform without being able to read the name of this new way station, but I would need to exit the comfortable compartment I had occupied so long to explore unfamiliar ethnic and religious territory. With a SHAZAM! moment, chronology brought the signpost into focus — after all, shared genes is one pool from which there is no escaping. I was an "elder." What do elders do? They think about reunions. They gather Eisendraths at some special place because it might be for the last time.

Nobody knows exactly how many genetic Eisendraths there are, not even Clement Bonnell, our in-law/chief genealogist, but we number in the tens of thousands, to be sure. Our branch, however, is manageable. To define it you need only say "Charlevoix" and watch the reaction. To us, Charlevoix is not a town; it is one street and one beach or, alternatively, a state of mind locked in a memory bank to which only we have the combination. Overlook Farm lies within both the sentimental and geographical demographical boundaries, loosely construed.

We billed it "Reunion 2005 for Eisendraths and Their Allies " to include spouses, girl/boyfriends and summer people considered family after four generations of friendship, even if we hadn't actually seen some of them for fifty years. That's the thing about a family place held long enough: It's not just the photos, the furniture and the trees with their initials of forgotten crushes that remind you who you were, are, and might be later. Relationships and states of mind remain scored into family places like the farm until it burns down or somebody else buys it. Intensity matters more than whether you flinch or purr at the recollection. It's the act of remembering that stays pleasurable, the way terrible vacations sometimes make the best recalls because of motel mildew, the bugs, the Mount Arak rain.

What's remembered about the reunion eight years later? That I was deeply happy and calm in a new way. Grandma May Rice's player piano from Michigan Avenue migrated from the "ancestor's room" to the barn, where it wheezed out old sing-alongs like "When the Red, Red Robin Comes Bob-Bob Bobbin' Along." That kind of sound is right up with Proust's madeleine as the sense hard-wired to memory.

Cousin Jeff Rice, a custom cabinetmaker from San Francisco, installed a light in the tower of the garage we'd converted to a guesthouse and it was switched on immediately for the occasion. Ben and Mark grilled salmon we caught right off the Michigan Avenue beach. Stories went everywhere and then vanished. Like the light in the tower, they were meant for the moment, but thereafter turned on at will or at random. It was a first demonstration of what living more rootedly might feel like, even if it were a mere shadow of the passion between the lines of a letter I'd unearthed to present at the gathering.

By their eighty-sixth year in the U.S., the Eisendraths numbered 3,000 as officially tallied by the Eisendraths Cousins Club of Chicago. The organization took itself very, very seriously. So seriously that it fired off a 900-word letter signed by Henry J. Eisendrath and, also, Flora L. Eisendrath, who helpfully added four entire lines under her name to inform Reichs-president Paul von Hindenberg of Germany that she was actually "Mrs. Nathan Eisendrath, Secretary of the Eisendrath Cousin Club, One of the Largest Family Groups of German Descent in America." The letter is dated September 6, 1933, the year in which Hitler assumed power and Nazis burned the Reischtag building, established the SS and opened the first three concentration camps.

Honorable Paul von Hindenberg,
President of the German Reich,
Berlin, Germany

My dear Mr. President:

It is because of my German ancestry of many centuries, and my very deep sympathy and feeling for justice, that I beseech you at this time to come to the rescue of the German Jewish people who are being so maltreated by the political aspirants of your beloved country.

A propaganda of hate has been spread by a few of the present masters of the country, who fully appreciate the influence their malicious lies and abusive articles wield over a small and innocent minority of the people. They are endeavoring in this attack to gain the confidence of many, and especially the younger generation, and thus assure themselves political ascendancy.

This campaign is being waged by people who cover their identity and vulgar intrigue with a cloak of Christianity or German patriotism. They are an insult to both the Christians and the German patriots, neither of whom is responsible for this inane and extremely dangerous, ambitious and tricky political faction. The world has come to realize this and if you do not help to remedy this great injustice you will lose the respect of other nations and the respect of all righteous thinking people.

IT IS RIGHTEOUSNESS THAT EXALTETH A NATION.

I am pleading for the German people and just now for the German people of Jewish belief, who are bearing the brunt of this damnable persecution — the result of a political propaganda spread with the sole purpose of strengthening a faction, who once in power will have no hesitancy in establishing their tyranny over the other peoples of your State and enforcing their unjust and unfair laws upon a liberty-loving population.

Germans, as a nation, love fair play and justice and are cognizant of the splendid qualities of the German Jewish people. Never unmindful as a people to serve their country, the German Jewish people are studious, saving and thrifty — the outstanding qualities for which the German people stood — and they contribute largely to the arts, sciences, professions and business enterprises. As for their philanthropy and social uplift of humanity, that is basic to their religion and surely none is higher or greater. Judaism, the very simplicity of this faith in the One Ever-Living God, hope for the brotherhood of man and its loftiest ideals — aided by the teachings of the Prophets, is indeed a beacon-light to justice, service and humanity.

May I call your attention incidentally to the time when German children were suffering after the war, Julius Rosenwald of our city, who was inspired by his religious teachings for love of justice and humanity, did help and assist to an unusual degree, making and securing generous contributions to the German children, as did others of the Jewish faith in this country, who have always thought of their identity as Germans.

Would it not be a thousand times better if some of the present masters of Germany would study economic recovery on a basis for all its peo-

ple, as our President Roosevelt is doing, instead of battering around trying to match blue eyes and blonde hair, stressing inconsequentials or insane rationalization on the subject of superiority of certain races, and creating ill-will throughout the world, talking maliciously and injuring a portion of its people who should at least be recognized and not condemned for their good qualities?

Of course the people of Jewish faith are as much a part of Germany as the Catholics or Protestants can claim to be, despite the political asininity and vicious propaganda to the contrary. There are no better Germans in Germany than the Germans of Jewish faith if comparisons must be made. Let it be hoped that in the flower garden of Germany there will always be Catholic, Protestant, Jewish and other faiths and creeds, each contributing its part in social welfare and uplift; to the contrary would be a revocation of any religious teaching.

In closing permit me to quote from a great and noted American teacher in Israel and humanity, who was born in Germany, Dr. Emil G. Hirsch — of blessed memory — at whose temple I was privileged to be a member: Love of God has but one interpretation. He who does not love his fellowmen is void of love of God. Therefore let us love one another, and God's kingdom is within us.

A nation that lends itself to injustice, cruelty, intolerance, bigotry, narrow-mindedness, cannot hold respect and is bound to diminish and fall.

In God's name and for the honor of the German people I beg of you your hearty co-operation to stop this great injustice and cruelty and may the Almighty God be with you in this supreme effort to serve humanity and strengthen the leadership of your beloved country.

Very respectfully yours,

(signed) Henry J. Eisendrath
(signed) Flora L. Eisendrath (Mrs. Nathan Eisendrath) (Secretary of the Eisendrath Cousins Club, (One of the Largest Family Groups of German Descent in America)

A second reunion five years later differed in every way. This time I wasn't the host, it wasn't at the farm and there was no "When the Red, Red Robin Comes Bob-Bob-Bobbin." This time there was a dark frame around the light it produced. Afterward, we remembered it simply as "Dorsten," the name of the town the Eisendraths left long ago, the site of the gathering and an embedded message, the way Hiroshima became both an event and a location.

"Dorsten" had been a long time in coming. I told the first part in the *International Herald Tribune*:

AN IDENTITY AND FAMILY HISTORY
THAT ARE INEXTRICABLY LINKED

By Charles R. Eisendrath, June 16, 1999

The letter came from a stranger in a German town I had never heard of. Would I please inform a local history group about my family and an ancestor who had led the Jewish community 160 years ago? It sounded like the sort of study Americans make of long-lost Indian tribes. Bemused with a new status as anthropological curiosity, I complied — and stumbled into a 10-year reconciliation with history.

My reply did not amount to much. Like most Americans, I knew three sentences-worth about where and what I came from.

Anyone named Eisendrath is related because they all—23, lore has it—came to the United States in 1848, bound for Chicago. By the 1930s, their huge numbers had inspired a sociology thesis and the Eisendrath Cousins Club, 3,000 strong, had taken a complaint directly to President Paul von Hindenburg about an upstart named Adolf Hitler. He was, said the club, giving a bad name to good Germans everywhere—Chicago included.

I did not expect much in return. But what arrived was "Jews in Dorsten," a 301-page hardback with an entire chapter on "Die

Eisendrath-Story" and a family tree going back to the 18th century. The progenitor couple, Samson and Julia, had born all the children. German records disputed the number (birth ledgers listed 18, not 23) and also the legend that all had left Europe.

That should have warned me that comfy notions about being completely American, and entirely removed from the Holocaust, were about to dissolve. But for me, denial was a natural extension of a 1940s and '50s upbringing with Christmas instead of Hannukah, Israel as a foreign (unvisited) country and religious training left to the family maid, a Lutheran. Yet we called ourselves Jewish.

If you happen to be a nonpracticing, "assimilated" Jew with a German background, the Holocaust tends to blot out the idea of a single point of origin, as if blood had obliterated your birth certificate. Only gradually did I realize the huge effort going into not knowing something.

Did I have "Jews in Dorsten" translated? No. Yet the book fascinated me. I spent hours with it—the way a child might, looking at the pictures, puzzling out bits of a language, having parts read to me. Equally oddly, I did not look up the town on a map. I had made at least 20 trips through Amsterdam airport between the day I opened the letter postmarked Dorsten 1988 and last spring. Even then, I went only because business called in Düsseldorf, a half-hour away.

At the door of the Jewish Museum of Westphalia stood an Ursuline nun who had founded it and co-authored the book. Her name was outlandish for someone in her position: Eichmann, as in Adolf.

But Sister Johanna bore no genealogical link to the "angel of death" at Auschwitz. After retiring as revered headmistress of the local convent school, she had mustered a platoon of former students and civics buffs in a cause. They would force the town to amend a planned municipal history to include the 30 or so Jewish families that had lived there.

Her personal story partially explained why. A Jewish mother. A father whose Catholicism had protected the family until 1944, when her mother was packed off to a concentration camp, and Johanna, *confirmed Catholic at age 10, was nevertheless drafted into forced labor. At the end of the war, a harrowing escape from the Russians, who detained her as a blonde, blue-eyed Aryan look-alike just as the Nazis had enslaved her because she was Jewish enough.*

We were sudden, kindred spirits. It forced astonished reappraisal of everything, including a face that wore 74 years with neither apology nor excuse. I had had no intention of imparting my distrust of museums of the Holocaust, slavery and other tragedies. The belief that while they inform, they also inspire vengeance is unpopular even in America.

Yet here, in Holocaust heartland, the creator of one of the few Jewish outposts volunteered that she would not permit her center to emphasize how Germany's Jews had been destroyed. Instead, it emphasized how they had lived. And there was something familiar about this nun, particularly the eyes. They were Eisendrath eyes.

Then it happened. Would I please add my children to the family tree? "This is where I come in," she said, pointing. "My grandmother married an Eisendrath. I grew up thinking them special because only one family in the world had that name."

It has taken me a year to absorb all that. Personal history no longer begins in North America. Delusional isolation from the Holocaust has been replaced by something like the angst/relief that haunts children (even some Jewish children) after learning the truth about Santa Claus.

But gone, too, is the paralysis. Out of the vapors stepped my new cousin, the nun, who inspired a sad, strong compulsion to feel more Jewish than I had imagined possible, and more German than seemed permissible.

THE BIGGEST GIFT I had ever made to a nonprofit followed that amazing introduction to my own personal history. And then? And then nothing. I had done my thing. In Dorsten, however, Sister Johanna and the Jewish Museum of Westphalia had other ideas. "Back to the Roots with the Eisendrath Family" in July of 2010 was equal parts reunion and academic conference on the Eisendraths. Three years later, I'm far from over it. Here's how it felt when the memories had been quick-cooked—I'll get to the marinated version later.

A GERMAN NUN INVITES HER JEWISH FAMILY "HOME"

DORSTEN, GERMANY—It started with the usual family re-union surprises: The shock of my long-dead father's face in a woman in her 40's whom I'd never met. The blond hair, tawny complexion, long, thin nose of my sister, 74, in the features of a grand-nephew of thirteen. Everywhere Eisendrath eyes, often blue, but "never so many green eyes in one place," as the newly-met cousin with eyes like mine said, as if just discovering she was not alone on the planet. After a beer or two, the usual family queries about inheritable diseases and the age at which we die.

Usualness, however, quickly ended. Was our event the first of a German Jewish family gathered by choice where the Holocaust began? Or convened by a "family nun?" Possibly IT WAS unique in taking the form of a four-day academic-style conference, complete with professors and footnoted papers, all about ... us? It all seemed unlikely. After all, the Eisendraths haven't produced Einsteins. What has made us worthy of study (including a 1931 master's degree thesis at the University of Chicago) is that we are so easily studied. Like the later Eisendrath admonition to von Hindenberg to mend the ways of Germany, the first recorded example of the world ignoring family wisdom or family wisdom ignoring the world had come in 1845, when Westphalian Jews were required to take Christian surnames. Frederick the Great's government was tired of Jews administratively disappearing for tax and other registry purposes by having only one name, like Samson, when there might be sons, cousins, uncles and any number of in-law Samsons in the same small town. Our Samson and his wife, Julia, chose "Iron Wire," signifying strength and long life and gave it to their seventeen children. Everyone named Eisendrath is related because nobody followed their example.

Fifty-two Eisendraths made the trip to Dorsten from New York and other East Coast cities, California and the Midwest, our American epicenter. The number was remarkable given our collective detachment from the old country, not to mention its gruesome history. Most grew up experiencing Holocaust data as I did, at a remove without the passion of proximity. Early on, we were told that "We all left Germany in 1848." In contrast to our pious Dorsten predecessors, we are overwhelmingly secular—a reunion poll turned up only six practicing Jews. A mere three spoke German. I was not unusual in thinking of Holocaust victims like those condemned to die of terminal cancer: a horrible fate but not immediately about me or mine.

We rallied to a firehouse siren of an invitation from Sister Johanna Eichmann and her Jewish Center of Wesphalia, in Dorsten. Not every Jewish family has its own nun. At 84, she was a contemporary of the eponymous Adolf, "architect of the Holocaust," but no relation. Instead, as the daughter of a Catholic father and Jewish mother related to the Eisendraths, she survived the Holocaust by being converted to Catholicism as a child by her parents. In mid-life, she felt compelled to look back at that. At her insistence, a newly commissioned municipal history added a chapter on its "extinct race," to use the townspeople's term. The experience led her to dream about a study center, about how these, her people, had lived. But not, she is careful to say, how they died.

Sister Johanna headed the Ursuline Convent School for many years, and a former student, an indefatigable organizer named Elizabeth Cosanne Huxel-Schutle, became her assistant. Together they discovered that the Eisendraths had been the leaders of the town's minuscule Jewish community. Elizabeth returned from a trip to the U.S. with the "E" pages she ripped out of Chicago telephone books. The two co-signed letters to those addresses asking for information. One result was a coffee-table book called "Jews in Dorsten," that included a chapter entitled "The Eisendrath Story." With several dozen Eisendraths identified, they began asking us to consider returning "home" for a reunion. What they planned, however, was far from a picnic in a park.

Researchers presented papers to the 52 Eisendraths seated on student chairs. A family tree with 2223 "leaves" reached back 270 years on a print-out 240 feet long, mounted in two tiers to fit on three walls of a conference room. Members of the Center's board, none of them Jewish (Dorsten has no Jews; Westphalia has few, most of them Russian emigrées) drove us to lunches and dinners paid for by the Center. A civil servant dressed up as Julia — our progenitor-mother — showed us where "we" lived on a reconstructed Wiesen strasse and what it was like for Jews to need permission to do just about anything. The Burgomeister himself threw a lunch for us at city hall. There was no official mention of Israel and no request for support. Amazement doesn't describe our reaction as much as being flattered and charmed, educated and compelled.

Some of us knew that despite considerable hype about Hispanics, Germans remain the largest ethnic group in the U.S. In Dorsten we learned why: Massive unemployment in the patchwork of small principalities that became Germany produced a human outflow lasting nearly a century. Conditions were bad for everyone, but worst for Jews, who were excluded by law from most lines of work. By 1848, trains and faster ships made travel easier, more people had friends or relatives in the U.S. and regional emigration "associations" facilitated connections. There was real money in people-moving.

Why Chicago? Our German scholars of ALL things Eisendrath put that together for us, too. Joblessness made densely-populated Westphalia a perfect recruiting ground for the frantic entrepreneurs of the American Middle West. They needed workers — any workers. Jews would do. A decade before the first of nine Eisendrath siblings arrived, Chicago was a swampy settlement of 4,000. Two decades later it had exploded nearly 100-fold to 300,000, making it the fifth largest city in America, a nexus for Great Lakes and railroad shipping, a manufacturing and meat-packing powerhouse. Yes, much of it burned in 1871, but not the unfashionable districts where most Jews lived, and the destruction merely added a building boom atop the general exuberance. The Dorsten researchers referenced Chicago City Hall's mandate for reconstruction with bricks coming from to the new Eisendrath brickyard. There were Eisendrath tanneries, glove makers and Simeon, an architect who worked with Frank Lloyd Wright. His Plymouth Building, which still stands at 417 Dearborn Street in the South loop, is adorned with façade ornaments including a recognizably Eisendrath female face.

The presentation of the family tree on day two was the only session delivered by a relative, and it hit us where big revelations always do—in a region of the psyche that should be called "the tender unexpected." We walked into the conference room to find ourselves suddenly and completely surrounded by us—all of us. On a chart so long that it had to be presented in two tiers on three sides of the room, appeared the names, locations and photos of all 1,662 Eisendraths who could be tracked down. The young man who assembled the chart was just as amazing as his collection. He represented a branch most of us knew nothing about—the Belgian Eisendraths. When I was living in Europe, I heard about an Eisendrath in Belgium, but so strong was the mantra from childhood about "all getting out of Germany," I assumed he had moved back to Europe from the U.S., as I had. In retrospect, my thought process looks like avoidance behavior, because everyone knows that use of fairytales. In fact, one of the children of our Dorsten ancestors had stayed in Europe, and by World War II a sizable number of progeny lived in Belgium and Holland. In Dorsten, we learned the story of our own Anne Frank. Or rather one of them. Forty-three Eisendraths were murdered in the Holocaust. With a single story of one young woman and her family, the "getting out" of Germany, the assimilation in America, the secularism, the separation of a century and a half, all vanished like a belief in tooth fairies.

In 1943, Leonie Eisendrath was 22. She and her two sisters and a brother grew up comfortably in Zaandam, near Amsterdam, supported by the prosperous medical practice that grew out of her father's service in the German Army in World War I. While researching the history of his town, a Dutch civil servant who is neither Jewish, a relative nor a Holocaust scholar came across a letter from Leonie, her last. Leonie's sister, Maja, had fallen for a young man who worked for the anti-Nazi resistance, or so he said. Thinking he could help protect her family, she had given him their various hiding places. Maja's boyfriend, however, worked not for the Resistance, but the Gestapo. "It is nearly impossible for me to imagine that it was me who lived in Zaandam and enjoyed all the comfort and cosiness there," Leonie wrote to friends. "Will all of you enjoy your lives with all your might as long as you are able to do so?" A photo of Leonie and each member of her family accompanied the stories of their fate. With eyes we all recognized, the photographed participants gazed out at the reunion group, transforming it utterly.

THE NUN WITH THE
EISENDRATH EYES

THAT EXPERIENCE changed *me* utterly. Even here, writing at the farm, where I have always felt the very essence of American exceptionalism and its freedom from world complications, I cannot get beyond something new that I carry— not in the woods, not on the boat thirty miles out in Lake Michigan blueness. My Jewishness and German-ness feel like the saddlebags some horses are forced to carry as handicap weight, one on each side, to make them work harder, to slow them down.

And of course it does. That's what makes elders move more slowly, carefully, wistfully and, one hopes, usefully.

A CHAINED DUCK
& A PATENTED GRILL

July, 1987

A strange chapter title, but that's because in the next few thousand words I'll try to explain how some things begin, including the why of them. In this case it's about how and why a book and an invented grill came about, and why both needed something like Overlook Farm.

Passing our orchard on Mountain Road, you would have no reason to associate panic with something so bucolic, although that's what produced both a book and a grill. Property taxes were rocketing. It was 1977. My salary had tanked. Absent the miracle of a cash crop, we would have to sell pieces of the farm, or maybe all of it. The only escape from this road to penury lay far ahead, down a new road, at the exit called Tenure. Thus, a boring book in a deadening jargon and its child of boredom, a patented grill, both produced while looking out the window at the wondrous things going on all around Overlook Farm.

YOU ARE THIRTY-SIX. The career mileposts you wanted to reach by fifty—an age unimaginable at twenty-six, when you married and concurrently emerged from the pupa stage of your life's work—have suddenly, amazingly, whizzed by. So has, somehow, an otherwise gloriously slow year in a roadside rest stop called the Journalists in Residence program, sabbatical fellowships offered courtesy of the University of Michigan and the National Endowment for the Humanities. Ahead, you sense warnings as unmistakable as the whoosh of an eighteen-wheeler as you enter the thruway.

For example, picture having gotten used to semi-celebrity status, like chauffeur service to *Time* assignments; announcements in the *Celebrity News Service* when you arrive somewhere, anywhere; press conference protocols where your question would, *de rigueur*, come right after AP's, i.e. *before* the networks. Not to mention banking nearly all of your generous salary to live on an expense account that included subsidies for rent, children's private schools, language training and virtually unlimited allowances for assignments and entertaining. Abroad, you were regarded as a sort of auxiliary American ambassador. While on the fellowship at Michigan, you were special, too, invited to give lectures and fêted by the area studies people, many of whom had followed your work in *Time*.

Once you decided to *become* one of the faculty, however, that and everything else changed with the speed of falling down a well: pay cut by two-thirds, expense account cut to none and, hardest to take, status cut from correspondent, then Buenos Aires bureau chief, responsible for all coverage for Hispanic South America. I was now a humble adjunct assistant professor in charge of nothing, without tenure or even much prospect of reaching that exalted level, given the lack of a PhD. During the fellowship year, my joking to faculty members that no foreign correspondent would be caught dead with a doctorate because of what it did to people's writing—including theirs—was now a wince-making memory, for it was the writers of unreadable prose who not only had tenure, they *granted* it.

Obviously, the academic version of byline status involved tenure, which had its own rules, not applicable to any other serious career. Ordinarily, you were launched into the process by your professors in a PhD program, professors who wrote the lingo of some particular field in its particular way, lingo that was in turn understood by the editors of particular "peer reviewed" journals, editors who'd had the same particular training, often with the same particular people. It didn't help that the lingo was a dialect of gobbledygook, which I had always loathed and had been trained to destroy on sight as an indicator of either fuzzy thinking, having something to hide and/or having nothing to say. There was no way around this, however. I would need to learn a lingo in order to get anything accepted by the editors of journals with readerships in the four digits, and often three, instead of the seven I was accustomed to.

So in my father's old study on the second floor of the farm, facing east toward morning and a view of our new orchard, I began unlearning the best part of a previous education, where good writing meant clarity, concise judgment and literary appeal. To find these values irrelevant, at best, and possibly even detrimental, seemed akin to ripping out orderly rows of trees so that they could be re-arranged in patterns comprehensible only by the planters.

My fellow tenure-chasers seemed an odd bunch of twenty-somethings. Lacking experience in the real world, they nevertheless knew much more than I of the academic topography we jointly explored. Further disadvantage emerged when I discovered that lacking a scholarly program, I had failed to select that PhD prerequisite, a TFL, or Topic-For-Life. My journalistic specialty over the decades in "general assignment" (or specialization-avoidance) preceded from the notion that I could master enough about everything and that this would be sufficient, could not have been wronger for the navigation at hand. I literally could not determine which way the wind was blowing, let alone set sails to send myself on my way. Instead my goal would be mastering everything about something, even if that ended up being practically everything about practically nothing.

My fellow aspirants also better understood the gravity of the collective challenge. My TFL must be sufficiently scholarly, while also relating to something I already knew about. Experiential expertise, I hoped, might substitute for my competitors' advanced degrees to better position me in the tenure pecking order. About then, too, I discovered something that explained a great deal about why the answers to questions of what to eat, drink and almost everything concerning diseases changed so often "according to the latest studies." These were largely from academe, where tenure depended above all on the novelty of an investigation. In that, it seemed akin to journalism…until I learned that in academia truth was not imperative. In fact, some fields worked on the assumption that there was no ultimate truth, nor objectivity. What the press reported as progress was frequently little more than the latest novel hypothesis; some of my habits changed accordingly.

After much head-scratching, I decided that the French press as a lift-off vehicle was my best bet for the TFL. Through my journalistic version of a graduate program, I knew the French press to be a seriously weird mixture of high principles, reasonable pay, high benefits, high job security, high government subsidies and, for all those reasons, highly self-censored when it wasn't controlled outright by restrictive law and practice. Even better for my purposes, it was a subject that would require trips back to

France—and visits to friends there—to master the intricacies of a press system as different from ours as its cuisine. For me, the idea was not to "publish or perish." The gamble was to publish and *prosper*, and of that I was not confident.

The actual research I found interesting, particularly when it involved a weekly newspaper called *Le Canard Enchaîné*, or *The Chained Duck: canard* meaning duck in French and also meaning something untrue, as it does in English. A drawing of a wacky-looking duck appears in the front-page "ear" position occupied in *The New York Times* by "All the News That's Fit to Print." Foreigners often mistake it for a humor publication, which it pretends to be. In fact, it's deadly serious and for years has uncovered many of the country's most important investigative stories. It's the way it breaks them that provides a key into the workings of an aspect of French society that often baffles outsiders. *Le Canard's* revelations come laden with the puns, *double-entendre*, sarcasm and the pratfall humor practiced by court jesters. For centuries, France's absolutist kings permitted their "fools" to say things that would be intolerable from anyone else. By definition, an official fool was not to be taken seriously. But, of course they were. That was the point. *Le Canard* inherited the tradition, which it practices with glee.[9]

Economic support on this road to prosperity would not come from the journals (magazines, to me) that accepted my work. Anything be-

9   Twenty years after I concluded work on *le Canard* and the French press, I was horrified to realize that our own media had become so weakened by staff cuts and hemmed in by restricted sources and expanded legal entanglements that an American equivalent had emerged: Jon Stewart's "The Daily Show." Like *le Canard*, it became a must-view by kingmakers and vassals, alike.

yond "academic credit" topped out in pennies. No, the serious money would come from the mysterious "research grants" that I was expected to get. However—make that a big, annoying *however*—aside from covering travel expenses, even this secondary pot would merely make money for the Department of Communication. This was because grants to me would replace a portion of my salary so that the Department could hire the graduate student assistants to do the grunt work that freed the exalted ranks of the tenured for more lofty enterprise.

Presenting even my best stuff in language acceptable to the likes of *The Journal of Mass Communication & Journalism* slowed things to a crawl because I hated the forced convolutions and linguistic mangling. Even when I found *The Journal of Contemporary French Civilization*—lesser in prestige, but with an editor willing to overlook clear writing—things progressed at a speed that would have been laughable in my former life. Part of the reason for the sluggishness was that drawings of barbecue grills started appearing where great thoughts about French press freedoms were supposed to be.

These drawings were of singularly awful quality. But there were more of them every day, first at the margins of my reporter's notebooks, then in my research notes and, finally, covering the reverse side pages I was editing for scholarly publication. All were versions and elaborations of the grills I'd seen in the Middle East, North Africa and southwestern France and had used myself, especially in Argentina. What prompted the grill obsession? The main answer was that my ticket to tenure on the French press book was so boring I could hardly stay awake writing it. There was also the summertime view from my study window, memories of Argentine *parillas* and the fact that the old device we had inherited with the farm had finally worn out.

The old grill was a strange thing never encountered before or since. It looked like an abstract sculpture or, with its broad dish punctured by a threaded post sticking up from the center, to which was mounted a circular grate, even a radio telescope for picking up signals from outer space. By rotating the grate on the post, the meat rose or fell away from the coals—a process longer than my patience and also one prone to flinging ribs into flight with centrifugal force. It taught me an important lesson, however. American grills need not look like the ones at the hardware store in Boyne City, which in turn looked like the ones in catalogues and everywhere else—all of them long on marketing and short on thought.

The spherical Weber, for example—a superb smoker but primitive grill—adjusts heat by partially putting out the fire and has no means of changing the distance between coals and burgers. Other grills raised and lowered the coals while leaving the burgers in place, like lowering the campfire instead of lifting the frying pan. None had a system for eliminating flare-ups or recapturing juices for intensifying flavor, which I had found the most intriguing feature of the *parrilla argentina*. Worst of all, none used the best fuel for grilling: wood.

Even a journalist could do better, I thought; even one with no knowledge of design, engineering, metallurgy or, later, when a prototype showed promise, patent law and, later still, business, after a business formed around it.

By the summer of 1977 the doodles were ready. I showed them to a welder in East Jordan, who agreed to take a stab at a prototype on an hourly basis—if I would hang around to explain the drawing that he understandably found unclear. Things were coming along nicely until mid-July when I drove up to his shed to find the grill parts we'd fashioned summarily shoved aside like scrap. A huge machine had parked itself in their place. It was cherry time, when machines broke down at just the wrong moment and had to be welded back in shape right then, overtime included, because picking follows a schedule that determines which orchards make money that year. Disappointment continued when the harvest rush was over, for my welder had lost interest and I had run out of summer.

For me, the take-away from that first effort was a reminder of the difference between a dream and what I was capable of doing myself. With the garden, momentum had arrived in the form of the Gaunts, my octogenarian farm neighbors. To get the grill off the ground, I withdrew $800 in denominations small enough for them to fill a Kroger bag and emptied it on a lathe table in front of a doubting auto-body repair guy in Ann Arbor. As intended, the little pile of cash got him to see me as someone who might help him limp through the recession of 1978. When a friend visiting for a football game asked to see what I'd been up to, I took him to see the two grills—one for Ann Arbor, the other for the farm—and damned if he didn't buy one on the spot. The welder, who had opened up especially for us that Sunday, beamed at the thought of his bumpshop becoming a showroom and manufacturing hub.

The whole idea was "recreational capitalism" because I had no intention of trading a newly-gained tenured professorship for yet another field about which I knew nothing. Really, I'd wanted to patent an invention because of my grandfather. He'd held two: the candle-imitating light bulb and, of all things, a crocus. For me, a grill would do. Plus, some mastery of manufacturing, marketing and business might match the pleasures of the Overlook garden, maybe even the orchard we had just laid out. The pleasure approach went so deep that when a lawyer drew up the paperwork for Grillworks, Inc., I had him insert the disclosure that "Any profit made will be systematically wasted."

Corporate history belongs elsewhere, except for a few light points that are as much a part of Overlook Farm as its view over the South Arm of Lake Charlevoix. For example, a telephone call from the blue that launched the first workable model we produced.

"Hi, this is Jim Beard," said a soft voice that turned out to belong to the most famous chef/critic in the United States of America. Unlike so many other food professionals we came to know, Beard paid full price after answering a blind letter. Response to his syndicated review of "The Grillery" ("Brilliantly thought out and well-constructed") wouldn't fit in our mailbox, located a quarter mile from the house. The East Jordan Post Office delivered it by the boxload for two weeks—hundreds of postcards, letters and personal accounts of astonishing victories and crushing defeats in cooking, inventing, manufacturing—along with more orders than we had ever imagined.

Then a French marine architect with an unusual commission contacted us. A mutual friend had sent him a Grillery in Provence and he wondered if we could adapt it for a "boat" he was refitting in San Diego. The name of his client was a secret, but not the specifications. The custom Grillery would have to burn every possible cooking fuel, fold-down water-tight and contain rotisseries to accommodate lambs "precisely four feet at the shoulder." The client was the owner of *The Golden Odyssey*, a 230-foot yacht which cruised with the hundred-foot tender, *Golden Shadow*. The tender carried additional crew and provisions, including live lambs. The entire crew were RAF veterans and we dealt with the mysterious prince's chief steward, who answered questions with a military clip. "Why precisely four feet at the shoulder?" "Because if that's what His Excellency wants, that's what he shall have, shan't he?" The contrast with the lingo of East Jordan, Michigan, was, um, bracing.

We got help from a nearby unemployed engineer (not an uncommon combination around northern Michigan, a favored refuge for auto industry castoffs) who had turned to operating a mostly-vacant motel, giving him plenty of time to master his newfangled FAX machine and early-model Mac. Our fabricator in Escanaba didn't understand anything newfangled, so we FedExed the plans and somehow met His Excellency's specs. The Grillery passed sea trials, slipped over to the Mediterranean through the Panama Canal and was heard from no more: a good sign, I thought.

Even modest success created storage and shipping problems. Production had long-since moved to the Upper Peninsula of Michigan because when I finally found a fabricator "down below" (south) who would even listen to the idea of the tiny scale I was proposing, he agreed "to make twelve for you"—by which he meant 12,000! Where to put even a few dozen until they were sold?

A barn would be perfect, but we didn't have a barn. So, in the spring of 1990, en route to a meeting of the International Press Institute in Bordeaux, I sketched one of thirty feet by fifty feet with doors on both ends high enough to accommodate eighteen-wheel tractor-trailers. The first delivery backed into a brand-new barn and was unloaded with a castoff forklift that had been lying on its side near the cherry tank building of Sherman Orchards next door.

The farm produced yet another insight into how the real world outside of journalism and academe worked when Grillworks, Inc. (us) began paying storage rent to Overlook Farm (also us). I was amazed.

Then came the largest order in response to a single article: *People* magazine's piece included a three-quarter-page photo of me wearing a decent straw hat and carrying a huge platter of lake trout caught the day before off Charlevoix to a fiery Grillery on the terrace. A picture may not always be worth 10,000 words, but this one translated into the sale of twenty-six grills. A half-year of annual sales in a single week and enough reflected glory to motivate somebody to tape the article to the East Jordan Post Office counter with a big hand-lettered addendum: "East Jordan makes People Magazine!!!!" To me, that was worth a fortune.

ALL THIS EXCITEMENT AT OVERLOOK produced a dawning realization. Striving to master a cherry orchard, an academic specialty and a business was not an aberration: It was me. True, I was unlikely to dominate in any of those endeavors. There would not be a huge agricultural operation in my future, no shelf of books that my PhD friends found so satisfying, nor a major manufacturing enterprise. Fundamentally, what I had learned, what the farm taught me, was the importance of continuing to grow. It's a wasteful process, growth, full of rot and regeneration and unlikely results. Like the birch near the water that died standing, hollowed out to mid-trunk, filled with debris, and then sprouted a cedar, rooted eight feet off the ground.

And the quest for tenure did have its rewards. When researching the legal basis of the French press I discovered that it was as different from our own as my life at Overlook Farm was from Ann Arbor academe. French and American press law had been born of the same spirit (the Enlightenment) and also from fundamental, contemporaneous documents. *The First Amendment* and the French *Declaration of the Rights of Man and Citizen* had been submitted for ratification within a month of one another, in 1789, and were nearly identical except for the *Declaration's* final phrase where it enjoined making laws limiting freedom of expression "except in cases proscribed by law."

Since it isn't obvious what difference this seemingly innocuous verbiage might make, imagine for a moment that you are a journalist accused of reporting something insulting about someone—a not-infrequent situation. In France, you enter the courtroom presumed guilty in both civil and criminal cases. Public figures, who have almost no standing for libel recovery in the U.S., have almost blanket protection in France. Journalism and journalists alike receive generous subsidies and privileges unknown in the U.S., but at the sufferance of boards and committees. This system of surveillance from the inside originated in "Colbertism," the system named for Louis XIV's finance minister Jean Baptiste Col-

REPORTED AND PHOTOGRAPHED AT THE FARM WHILE THE
COMPANY'S PHONE WAS STILL UNLISTED, THIS PIECE SOLD MORE
GRILLS IN A WEEK THAN WE USUALLY MANAGED IN A YEAR
PHOTO CREDIT: PEOPLE MAGAZINE

bert, which sought ways for the crown to maintain control of French economic life indirectly by requiring government representatives in key organizations. After three revolutions and five republics, Colbertism is still alive and well and ready to weigh in about the distribution of newsprint, or who gets a government press card with its income tax break and remarkable vacation provisions. There is freedom, but it's discretionary.

Just as learning how to cope with the mysteries of running a cherry orchard might have led to an entirely different life, forced concentration on Sixteenth Century legal intricacies drove me to develop the sort of novel theory ideally suited to a PhD thesis and, possibly, a life of scholarship. The doctrine of "surplus freedom" I wrote in one of the articles-cum-tenure book chapters concerned the amount of latitude *felt* by journalists to report the news, as distinct from what the law *permitted*. In France there was precious little; in the U.S., a great deal.[10]

---

10   Sadly, dangerously, that surplus freedom in the U.S. media has declined to the point where the recent revelations of government secrecy by Julian Assange and Edward Snowden appeared first in foreign publications.

But, instead of following a single promising line of invention, I chose to combine the ingredients of several. I was a writer, convinced that I needed to serve up the delectable ingredients from France in a literary dish I would never order; so bored by the academic advancement process that I titled my book, *The French Press 1970–78: Abnormal Normalcy.* A writer, further, who loved Argentine grilling and who found himself at a place offering both the time and availability of trained welders. Stir in that dawning realization that an emerging life goal was patenting a creation good enough to sell itself. And that's how a farm and a chained duck produced a manufacturing company. [11]

---

11   The book got done but was never published because individual chapters in stuffy journals sufficed for tenure. In a dark corner of the farm's attic, the manuscript remains in permanent repose because I want to revisit that prose never again.

Son Ben converted Grillworks, Inc. from recreational capitalism to a real business, Grillworks LLC, supplying vastly evolved versions to individuals and serious restaurants in over fifty countries on all non-polar continents. Friends' reports are almost as much fun to receive as orders. Up to twenty-four feet wide, with charcoal makers and self-contained ovens, the grills are still wood-fired and hand-made in a small shop twenty minutes from Overlook Farm.

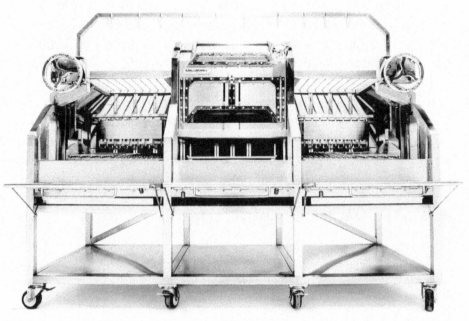

ORCHARDS & CAPITAL

June, 2006

A great friend named Bob Milne visits the farm every August, and when this annual event began he caused three significant fusses. The first subsided when he convinced us that he and his wife, Linda, would really, honest-to-God rather stay in a down-market airport limo they'd converted into a touring musicians' van than anywhere else at a compound that can sleep seventeen indoors. They roll up at night from one of their 275 yearly gigs, park under an apple tree and we see them for breakfast.

Bob caused another disturbance of the normal rhythms at Overlook because he, alone with Jelly Roll Morton, is the only ragtime composer/performer collected *in toto* by the Library of Congress. He plays compulsively, and as spectacularly well as that implies. At first we called a few friends. Then they called their friends. "Bob Night" came to involve a piano out in the orchard under the trees with Bob pounding away and cherries falling onto platters of fried chicken for fifty. It is fuss number three, however, that relates directly to what I call "farmthought."

A team of clinical psychologists from Pennsylvania State University and Davidson College studied Milne's brain to learn how he was able to track three symphonies simultaneously, including the ability to call out, say, the horn section in the Brahms while the Beethoven and the Handel were running concurrently. Only when they tried adding a fourth composition did Bob have to scratch his head. As of this writing they still haven't figured out how he does it, but they have demonstrated — with electrodes and imaging machines — that he *does*, he definitely does.

I have plenty of second thoughts about people judgments, but none whatsoever that Milne is a musical genius. For a long time I didn't apply his tracking system to anything beyond that particular circumstance. Then I began mulling it over in and applying it to farmthought. I realized that what Bob does in music may be quite common, at least at lower levels. Possibly, it is related to creativity itself.

Here's what I mean: while one channel of your brain prevents you from running your all-terrain vehicle into a ditch, or your chainsaw from amputating one of your limbs instead of a tree's, ruminations flow through other mental channels unobstructed. In fact, I'd argue that what might seem a lack of concentration on the job at hand actually facilitates others that are far removed and often more interesting. Perhaps the splitting and multi-channeling of farmthought disconnects mental censors. True, they often edit out outrageous, outlandish and out-of-bounds ideas that can cause trouble. On the other hand, they sometimes lead to the most interesting places, troubles or not. I've known for years that my best thinking happens at the farm. Perhaps that's why.

Bob's musical cue to farmthought made me realize that thoughts most often "piphed"—as in epiphany—while I was doing something unrelated to the subject I thought I was thinking about. Often the prod to piph *(Piph, v.i, to achieve inspiration; n., the state of being inspired; this really should be a word)* is avoidance. Hell, often the *prod* is avoidance. In my case, this includes the founding of a grill company while writing a boring book on the French press. Or planting an orchard to offset alarming farm taxes while plotting the acquisition of the most important map of the Great Lakes and warring with academic administrators. Piph references appear scattered through the notes of these endeavors.

Other piphs involve no more than a dart of fresh thinking, such as how fishing raised the largest endowment grant for the Knight-Wallace Fellowships and revealed the personality of a taciturn BBC war correspondent who had applied to the program. The grant that put "Knight" in the Fellowships title came by cell phone with Foundation President Hodding Carter III — he in his office in Miami and me aboard the *Cherry Baron* with Julia during a lunch/fishing break in Lake Ontario *en route* to cruise the Thousand Islands of the St. Lawrence River. Subject: the most important thing I would do for journalism with five million dollars. Answer: "Teach journalists that they'll be better at journalism if they come at it while doing something like fishing for big salmon on a small boat in the middle of Lake Ontario, like I'm doing right now." Carter, who published his family's famous anti-segregation newspaper in Greenville, Mississippi, and served as State Department spokesman under Jimmy Carter, laughed, but listened. He "got it" — irrelevancies as creative agents — and the foundation gave.

The BBC applicant's call for her admissions interview also came while fishing, this time off North Manitou Island, about twenty miles into Lake Michigan from Sleeping Bear Dunes. The fish were decidedly not biting.

Jill McGivering had been covering grinding warfare in the sweltering deserts of the Middle East for a decade. Ordinarily, there would be no reason to tell an applicant that her call from Bagdad had reached someone who was thinking about fish as well as her professional future, but I thought that I needed to warn her that if she heard me yell "fish on" and the cell phone went dead, she should call back after the time she imagined it might take to land a twenty-pounder — I'm always optimistic — on light tackle. McGivering had just recovered from that shock and was preparing to answer my perennial first question — "Tell me about your professional dreams, because at your level they are likely to come true, and therefore predict to me the journalist you will become" — when I yelled "Fish on!" and left her. She called back just as I got the lines back in the water. A second fish. A third! A fish witch is a woman who knows nothing about fishing but causes men to catch them. As a fish witch, I had never seen the like. Charmed, McGivering softened enough to allow me to figure out her potential for further professional growth.

Sure enough, when her career and personal life broadened after the Fellowship, the fish witch from the Iraqi desert agreed that it had to do with letting herself be surprised at new ways of thinking.

It's not accidental that the grandest application of piphery I know of revealed itself during some of the free-form reading I do at Overlook Farm. Bill Gates had recently bought one of Leonardo da Vinci's three known notebooks, and I thought I'd page through the document to see what all the fuss was about. There it was: While copying out equations to get better at algebra—at which he remained bad—Leonardo had rendered a sketch—at which he is the best of who ever lived. It is of the old man who recurs throughout Leonardo's work, and the luminous portrait emerges from behind the hopeless mathematical scratches, a dream pushing them aside in his—and our—imagination.

WHAT HAS ALL THIS TO DO money-grubbing and the grand enterprise of free expression? In a word, everything. In an orchard, money comes like a drizzle in a drought year. In some ways a few drops are worse than nothing, reminders of what could have been. But—and but and but—if you can get beyond anxiety, like a super-late pregnancy, the little droplets of hope that eventually turn the orange-red of joy are worth a fortune. Not only in the assurance that your investment was not entirely idiotic, but also in the promise that in each successive year, as the trees grow, it will get easier to cover the difference between revenue and operating costs.

This was the happy lesson that I applied to the Knight-Wallace Fellowships for Journalists program. In 1986 the thing was broke. The National Endowment for the Humanities had cut all funding and no angel donor hovered on high. Re-establishing the program on a sustainable basis meant raising all the money for operations while also finding endowment funds. Like a new orchard, this would go on until earnings/crops produced enough to take over. Thanks to Overlook Farm, I was familiar with the practice of starting something with no knowledge nor experience in the field. The endeavor in this case was a mysterious thing called "development." In addition to obvious other problems, a psychological barrier loomed. Like every journalist I knew, the idea of money-grubbing was anathema. In my new situation, however, that attitude was literally unaffordable. My new job depended on grubbing—lots of grubbing—to pay program expenses and, sure, that included my own salary.

Raising endowment is just another version of planting a cherry orchard. The most important part is acquiring the best root stock—root stock that with careful tending will grow, flower, produce. You must have patience because the hardest part comes first—the waiting. Yes, your selection has been suitable for serious investment, but you still won't know the quality of the trees—or the journalists—until you've watched them for a while. With tart cherry trees this is six years; with journalism fellows, about six weeks. In both cases, this is about a quarter of the total time you will spend with them.

During those six weeks or six years, you figure out how to support them and evaluate potential. This is easy with the orchards. Just after the moment of exquisite apprehension, when a frost could easily reduce your crop from 120,000 pounds of cherries to 120 cherries, you venture out among the trees to check blossom uteri. Do most of the stamens show a tiny black dot of fertilization? Those dots will develop the pinhead hardness of a developing cherry; the proportion of embryonic life versus barren flowers provides a rough estimate of the crop. That is, unless there's a late frost or thunderstorms at harvest or any of the other possible plagues, including a sudden drop in price. Evaluating potential is similar with journalism fellows. You look for how energetically, imaginatively and concretely they suck up the intellectual resources of a great research university to grow professional dreams, a task I insist is as measurable as the growth rings of trees.

New trees invariably arrive too soon—when there's too much snow or the ground's too wet or it's too cold. But here they are, so you "toe in" the roots to keep them moist and unfrozen until planting. When the weather's right, the holes need to be wide enough for the roots to spread out and sufficiently deep to put the graft at exactly ground level: All fruit stock involves refined "scion" stems atop a "base" bred to survive hardship. (In academic terms, think of the bases as the resources that keep the lights on in the classroom and the football stadium swept clean after the games. The scions are the rarefied faculty who require special treatment.) Finally, with the ruthlessness of the University of Michigan Law School sloughing off the students who don't measure up, you prune. You get rid of the branches growing at the wrong angle to the trunk or in the wrong direction. You cut off the top to force new growth outward. This can be as painful as discarding flowers that, while gorgeous, are not gorgeous enough.

In the Fellowships for Journalists program, I pruned away the no-go attitude toward development within the first weeks, then realized that pruning the Fellows, themselves, would be next. To realize full potential, journalists often become more, um, *fruitful*, after something shakes up their attitudes. So I questioned the questioners. First off, I asked about their professional dreams because, for the talented, dreams come true. That dreams could actually be operational was a new idea for most, almost as good as cutting off the top of a new tree. But, like a good pruner, one needs to step back and look at the big picture. I have to ask myself, Is whatever they tell me really what they want? Is that really *all* they want? What are they doing to get themselves there? Is that really *all* they're doing? To get the dream right, they need to know what resources they can bring to task. What are talents they can rely on? Who's got their dream job now and how much do they know about how he or she got it? How much does he or she make? How much do their colleagues make? How much money do they have and how much do they need for the dream life? Numbers, please. Few can answer. *Now*, I tell them, is the time to know.

Finally, are their personal lives what they want? A fellowship term a is good time to settle with a partner, decide on a change or realize that for them, loner-ing is best. Any entrepreneurs in the family? Might they have that gene? To maximize the benefits of investing in themselves they should have easy reference to their own capital resources—professional, financial, genetic. This can be stressful. Sometimes it's a sort of lab-induced nervous breakdown.

A visual version of this happens each year at harvest time. Harvesting machines proceed confidently down the rows, the shaker on one side of the trees, apron collector on the other. The shaker's collar reaches out to attach itself to a trunk at about knee-height, the apron extends out to catch the fruit. Whir! The whole tree vibrates like the psyche of a journalism fellow having to review his/her approach to life. Off fly cherries—brilliant red any time, incandescent in bright sun. There is no direction or pattern to their fall—it's just away from the sources of shaking. I've always thought of it like a form of symbolic nervous breakdown-cum-birth event. The apron then gently folds the 200-pound payload and deposits it in a cool water bath that retains the cherry's color and shape as they head for market.

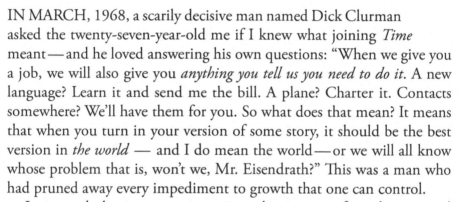

That cherry harvesting image became the core of my mentoring technique for each journalism fellow.

IN MARCH, 1968, a scarily decisive man named Dick Clurman asked the twenty-seven-year-old me if I knew what joining *Time* meant—and he loved answering his own questions: "When we give you a job, we will also give you *anything you tell us you need to do it.* A new language? Learn it and send me the bill. A plane? Charter it. Contacts somewhere? We'll have them for you. So what does that mean? It means that when you turn in your version of some story, it should be the best version in *the world* — and I do mean the world—or we will all know whose problem that is, won't we, Mr. Eisendrath?" This was a man who had pruned away every impediment to growth that one can control.

I repeated that story to incoming classes to preface the essential assignment for which they were being paid and encouraged. It was to grow, to grow professionally, and personally, too, because the two go together. And, *in loco Clurman*, I would clear away all impediments to getting what eight months of sabbatical time at a great university can provide. For most, competition had always been easily defined as who got the story first, or best. In comparison, "Grow!" was vague beyond normal measure. After a few months, however, they could detect it in others—a new kind of comparison with no model other than what they, themselves, put forward. It's exhilarating and terrifying, just as Clurman intended.

MOST OF MY PROFESSIONAL CAREER was foreign reporting, and when I came home I was shocked to witness what I'd only heard about before—that the amount of international news reaching American audiences had declined from marginal to terrifyingly inadequate. Didn't everyone know that we were a superpower whose passenger-citizens were flying blind in world affairs? Naturally, I thought high-talent journalists like the Fellows would like to know more. Sadly, no. They reflected their audiences. And these best and brightest were unlikely to reflect more than a dim light.

So I invited study. I brought in speakers. I lectured. I hectored. All to dismal effect. Finally, since nobody else was providing answers, I asked myself what would goad *me* in the right direction. The answer was simple, but became obvious only after implementation. Instead of trying to *tell* journalists what to do—which almost never works—I would invite them somewhere. Volunteers, please, for a free trip to Argentina? The resulting Buenos Aires news tour, which included encounters with politicians, terrorists, academics, journalists, film directors, etc., later expanded to Brazil, Turkey and Russia. The trips were always optional, but within short order nearly everyone signed up, often with spouses.

The same trick worked when raising money for the endowment. Since people weren't interested in what I wanted, I would find out what interested them. I stopped trying to assemble money for "high quality journalism"—which everyone liked the sound of, but not enough to give the millions I needed—and began offering opportunities to improve the coverage of donors' interests, be that business, law, medicine, education, public policy, foreign affairs or minority communities.

In some ways, knowing nothing about building an endowment made it possible to see how the whole process worked from the outside before trying to actually do it from the inside, like watching an instructional video. However, after struggling to raise money for the whole project—without reference to instructions—I came to my senses. When building an endowed program, finishing any part of it—for example, suggesting to Mike Wallace that he invest in his passion for investigative reporting—makes the whole of it easier. Approaching donors with the same basic, overarching need eventually signals a hopeless case, and they'll walk away like one does from a panhandler. (Yes, you might give loose change or even a ten-dollar bill, but not the thousands actually needed to turn around someone's life.) If the whole project number fails to walk in the door—and it seldom walks in the door—dividing the project into sub-projects works wonders.

Another counter-intuitive lesson from fund-raising is that hate, or at least dislike, is often the strongest motivator. Do you hate the way medicine is covered in the news? Why not improve upon it instead of bitching? Do you think Americans are woefully uninformed about South America? How about helping send eighteen of the most talented mid-career journalists to Argentina and Brazil? Think the health care system broken or badly reported? Money to upgrade coverage will definitely improve things, one talented journalist at a time.

In my experience, the need for money was never a powerful motivator for large donors. If this sounds odd, ask yourself how many times you've given a hundred dollars to the guy asking for handouts on the street. Yes, it's nice to feel virtuous, but it's so much more exciting to be involved with a winner or something that identifies you as a winner, too. If this became the first law of endowment development, the second is, *Never ask the potential giver directly*. Big donors are generally well-practiced in deflecting advances from strangers. Do a little journalistic digging. Find a friend or two they trust and make your pitch to them—to be passed along.

Finally, law number three: *Eternity sells*. Because of one widow's sadness and outrage about cutbacks at *Time* and the dissolution of her and her husband's love of foreign news, the Fellowships program received the largest endowment gift in the history of the University of Michigan from an African American. And this, even after I urged her not to because the gift was a significant percentage of her net worth. She went ahead anyway, because we could guarantee training for both aspiring and seasoned foreign correspondents in perpetuity.

You don't enter the life of a cherry tree or a working journalist until circumstances make you a pruner/mentor. And you are only there to edit the life, never to create it. Was it accidental that I was not producing a shelf of books like academic colleagues or amassing far greater wealth by selling land instead of planting trees? I think not. The Fellows, themselves, are my legacy and the individual trees are, too. Not a permanent one perhaps, but close enough.

PART THREE

THE MAN WHO
CUT OFF HIS FOOT

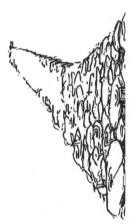

WOODSMOKE, SOUR MILK
& WHETTING OIL

August, 1993

Judd Hardy smelled like sawdust and oil; the light machine oil that hand tools need to work better and resist rusting longer. A whole generation of the workmen I knew carried a sub-scent of oil, I suppose because nearly everything in those days, when most things didn't have ball bearings, had to be oiled continuously from cans that leaked and long spouts that dribbled. Judd's smell and one visual memory in black-and-white is what I carry around sixty years later, and only because the image comes second-hand, via scrapbook.

Proust was right about the nose being hardwired to memory and, God knows, he's French for finding memory in food. But what's stuck in my olfactory system is how the men in northern Michigan smelled. Maybe it's because the men in my everyday non-summer existence — I'm not talking about my father; all fathers have distinct smells and we all remember them even if we don't know we do — didn't have smells, or at least not their own. Talc and aftershave don't count. Around Overlook Farm, there was usually an oily rag in a pocket or on a seat or surface nearby. The men were always sharpening pocket knives, too, and those who didn't prefer spit, dabbed on a droplet of light oil to fine-up the cutting edge. Oil did much of the job now outsourced to electricity — it was the means to cut back on the required amount of muscle power.

Judd was around for years and the joke was that we only knew it was lunchtime when he opened the buckle on his tin box with silver scratches showing through the paint. He was always friendly enough, but never accepted the invitation to eat with the rest of us at the big pine table out-front, with its spectacular view of the lake 500 feet below and a quarter mile down the bluff. Here's the one image I have: It's lunchtime (was I sent to repeat the hopeless invitation?) and Judd is out back, taking down the "summer kitchen" made of barn boards that houses had here-abouts for coolness during canning season. Summer kitchens were early necessities in farmhouses that did without plumbing or electricity until the late 1940s. They reduced the risk of burning the entire house down from accidents in the wood stoves and, most usefully judging by the as-tonishing variety of stuff found in them, they provided storage that didn't require cellar stairs. In the photo, Judd is wearing what I knew would be his workman green with a railroad engineer's cap. There are sweat stains and places where oil has been partially washed out. He's looking down at a board across two saw horses that were still in the basement a few years ago, but I hadn't yet connected them with the image and committed them to the burn pile — a mistake. His arm is cocked, holding the wood-en saw handle in a stroke registered for the length of memory.

ART RANGER SMELLED OF LAKE, and when he didn't smell like lake he smelled of varnish and marine motors. Which is, in a way, just like *The Boss*, a forty-two-foot power cruiser commissioned by Uncle Al Goldman for three purposes that I know of. First, to be the fastest big boat in Round Lake, which it was. Then, to please its namesake, the white-haired Auntie Blanche, who demanded a stately, smooth ride for the canasta table set-up under the aft canopy as she, my grandmother and other ladies glided the twelve miles from the Round Lake "City" boat-house to "the cabin," a rustic retreat-from-retreat where Horton Creek flows into Lake Charlevoix — by chance, the exact spot where locals set out in a rowboat to teach beginners fishing to little Ernie Hemingway, at that point just another Little Lord Fauntleroy from the cottage people. *The Boss* accomplished this, too, easily, as well as goal number three: the ability to pass beneath the swing bridges across both channels between Round Lake, where it berthed, and the open waters to the east and west.

Truth be told, this great, white mechanical swan couldn't actually clear

ALWAYS REGAL AND, UNLIKE MOST OF THE CHARLEVOIX GRAND
FLOTILLA OF HER ERA, THE BOSS SURVIVED INTO CELEBRATED OLD AGE

either bridge without Art folding down the mahogany pennant mast on its heavy brass hinge. To me, this was serious ceremony. Then, to be truly underway, Art would push a bright knob forward and the huge engine would lift *The Boss's* bow upward, just enough to show the waterline, like a long skirt revealing an alluring amount of ankle.

The Boss was Art Ranger's livelihood, preoccupation, love-object and identity as well as occasional quarters and conveyance. His title of Boatman fit as well as his jaunty anchor-braid cap. The hat still evokes his memory with a sniff, which was the first thing I did when his son Alvie showed it to me a year or so ago. No need for Alvie's warning actually: putting on that hat would have been like putting jam on a madeleine.

On sunny days, the water glowed so brightly in the dark inside of the boathouse, between the deck and *The Boss's* white flank, that it seemed to have a smell of its own—one sense just wasn't enough to process that ethereal, undulating green. And then, presto! The clean, sharp breeze as *The Boss* struck out through the channel and into the Big Lake for fishing trips. Or north to the Straits of Mackinac and the North Channel; Lake Huron to the east, Lake Superior's Bachawana Bay to the west. All of these images invented because I was never included on those, to me, Jules

Verne-like voyages. The outings I did witness — the ladies' canasta parties and the men's poker sessions with bourbon and cigars — live in my memory under fresh, tan canvas that, to a boy, and so soon after World War II, smelled like the heroic U.S. Navy, forever victoriously bombarding tropical atolls.

Art Ranger could supply, remedy or doctor anything *The Boss* needed, and did so without being asked and usually before anyone else noticed, which was what Uncle Al needed most. Art was born to do what he did, with one exception that went happily untested. He could not swim "except with a stick in my belt." He told me that one day (I've spent the rest of my life pondering how this might look/work) when our ever-needy outboard had stranded me once again. Art wasn't tall, but he had the head of a giant and features to match. Would any kind of stick through any belt float 225 pounds of sinkable human? That puzzle by far outlasted the mysteries of female anatomy. The best image I've ever conjured of him came the day of that conversation, maybe in a dream soon after — an Easter Island head kept afloat by an unseen section of telephone pole, somehow fastened out of sight in the deep down somewhere.

WHEN HENRY HOWARD didn't reek of silage, various manures or fresh cut hay, he smelled like woodsmoke; specifically, as I learned later when I occasionally smelled the same way, of sugar maple and ash. It wasn't strange that the smoke attached itself to him that way, or that it had the distinctive scent of those two trees, for they were the most common source for heating the large number of homes that relied on cookstoves, heat stoves and wood furnaces. But that the smoke smell should overpower the competition was beyond imagination.

Worst among the bad was the semi-liquid silage at the bottom of the silo, a brewery of stink powerful enough for fainting. It was so awful that Henry took the liberty of leaving his youngest son and me the hateful task of disposing of it. The top was the easiest to remove, as it was the last layer of straw for winter livestock bedding. Since it leaked, the bottom several feet was stuff converting itself into liquid noxiousness through the same fermentation that produces wine and vinegar and methane. Nevermind chemistry — the fumes can kill if you pass out alone. Getting drunk on that stuff somehow wasn't fun, so the frequent gastric eruptions had no countervailing pleasures. Then there was mucking. The accretions, or "bedding" of a dozen animals cooped up during a northern Michigan winter resembles kitty litter the way a clean garbage can resembles a municipal dump. The approved way of mucking, as with silage removal, was with a pitchfork and wheelbarrow. Jeans might recover; boots, never.

FOR SYLVIA GAUNT, A GINGHAM DRESS AND SUNBONNET SERVED FOR CHORES, SUNDAY AND EVERYTHING BETWEEN

SYLVIA GAUNT'S COMBINATION added up to woodsmoke and gingham. (I swear smells *can* add up to colors and the other way around.) Sylvia's gingham smell came from the cool, sour milk house, the only whitewashed structure on the farm housing the only spotless implement, the chrome-topped milk/cream separator. The milk house was a sort of cave of lightness, with whole nations of blue-green bottle flies glittering like noisy beads where something delicious spilled. The rest was maple smoke. It was Sylvia who did the splitting and kept the fires burning, her false teeth clattering in a monologue that didn't require the presence of another human being because the cats and dogs were there and Bill had heard it all before anyway. She is the only person I ever saw wear a gingham cap of covered wagon-style. She wore it every day until she could no longer go outside.

We inherited our farm during the "back-to-the-land" movement of the 1970s, heavily weighted with well-heeled urban intellectuals seeking "something real." After a few seasons of reality, most of them insulated, re-plumbed and centrally heated the old places, eliminating an important part of their initial attraction. Why did we keep a drafty old farmhouse pretty much the way it was? Partly because it's wisest to leave old love affairs alone. Even more, I think, because efficiency doesn't have a smell, and the house having one suited us. Finally, everything on such a place requires tending, tightening, oil and the kinds of tools that you can keep in your pocket. Keeping warm, or even alive this way in the northern Michigan climate means dealing with wood in every season. Pretty soon you acquire the scents, yourself.

WITH MY BACKGROUND I wasn't surprised to find that whole countries have smells. Put me down blindfolded somewhere familiar and I will be as sure of where I am as a sommelier singing out where the bottle came from. After knowing France, who can't smell the sunlight in Van Gogh's summerscapes or Monet's lily ponds or the flowers in his garden at Giverny? For that matter, who can't smell a sour / foul / black mood? Unless you declare a time-out for chemical or mathematical breakdown, sensation, in the literal sense of incoming data from one of our five instruments for experiencing the physical world, function by comparison. Try describing "blue" without reference to something.

I wasn't really aware of all this until fairly recently, when a new generation joined the family and began visiting Overlook Farm. In them I saw me at their age. I watched them exploring how everything looked, felt—smelled. Theirs is a post-mechanical age, the way mine was the beginning of the post-metal age that dawned around the time Murray Hamilton takes Dustin Hoffman aside in "The Graduate" to tell him that, young man, "There's a great future in plastics."

Also, I don't think it's my imagination: I'm positive that among the sensations registering on my grandsons as they explore the barn and come along on my little missions is how I smell.

MOSES MOMENTS

July, 1982 / July, 1985 / November, 2018

L ike many lucky enough to have a second home, I didn't realize that offloading the stuff from the shelves, drawers and closets of one place into the appointed shelves, drawers and closets of another is just a beginning. If you do it right, the most important item of transfer occupies no space at all in the car, but considerable volume in your psyche. That is, the expectations you bring from one place to the other about the people around you.

It takes a while to look for unfamiliar credentials. For example: Within three miles of Overlook Farm live three men who symbolize what you don't see until something takes your consciousness by the elbow and gently leads you to another world located inside your mental planet. Picture the flames signaling Moses that this was no ordinary bush. Extraordinary existences camouflaged inside the ordinary people you encounter on the side of routine paths can be Moses Moments. You look at neighbors differently, you listen for a special voice.

I'll start with Glen Seagraves, who charged $10 an hour for designing a little part that went into several million GM cars and trucks manufactured during the 1970s and into the 1990s. It was the small plastic gizmo on steering columns that activated trouble blinkers. Doesn't look like much, but legions of high priced, fancily educated engineers of the (then) biggest corporation in the world reached out to somebody in overalls whose sole engineering credential was a pinstripe cap. Sometimes, in rare moments, mammon's endless pinching of pennies for profit looks hilarious; this time there was no last laugh on the good guys. Seagraves didn't give a thought to asking for a percentage royalty, which would have meant big money no matter how small the sliver. "Nah," he said. "I'm paid by the hour." Happily, and with modest pride, he added, "Things like that don't take long."

Seagraves identifies with geriatric machinery, particularly the steam powered, as if each item were an ancestor dependent on him for immortality. This suits him perfectly as the unofficially official chief mechanic of the belching, tooting star attractions of the annual historical agricultural show that covers one hundred acres near Buckley, Michigan, just south of Traverse City. Tens of thousands attend. Strolling the lines, Seagraves works his tobacco chaw, carries his long-spout brass oiling can like a stethoscope and hoists kids to bottom rungs of black iron ladders so they can feel hugeness by climbing it.

I go to him after exhausting all possibilities and he resolves the impossible. Once it was getting a huge old tank out of the basement. I couldn't think of enough men I knew well enough to haul it up the steep, narrow stairs. Complete technical requisition: "Got a towrope?" One end around the tank, the other looped over a trailer hitch, out it comes with the steel-on-concrete screeches that are a kind of background music for his projects. Then there was the roof for a boat hoist down at the lake. There's no electricity there for assembly and no way to deliver by land what amounted to the top of a good-sized metal shed. He asked to see the hoist, but told me to put the tape measure away. All dimensions would be taken by eyeball. A couple of weeks later he phoned (a rarity) to tell me to meet him at the lake in about three hours.

I waited. No Seagraves. About a half-hour later (remember, he wears a pinstripe cap always, but never a watch), I began to make out an oddly configured something approaching very, very slowly from the south. The rowboat with a shed strapped to the hull looked like a mini-ark. As the striped-cap Noah pulled ashore I noted that he actually looked a little nervous, the way the Biblical figure may have as all the world's creatures prepared to board, two by two. In this case, too, the fit was demanding: not only did the smaller pipes supporting the roof need to slide into only slightly larger ones at the base, the whole contraption had to be just high enough for the top to be mounted with no additional lifting—all from a sixteen-foot steel rowboat pulled up on shore.

It fit.

WHEN THE TIME CAME for me to have something to do at the farm, at age fourteen or so, my parents came up with a novel idea that I think explains a great deal about my attachment to the place. They literally farmed me out to a nearby farmer, paying Henry Howard to pay me to do whatever needed doing around his place up on Mountain Road. Sometimes this was clearing acreage, sometimes building fences. There was the milking of cows, hauling hay into barns and shoveling silage and manure out. Henry's youngest son, Lyall, shared my duties on his father's farm. Older son Bob was entrusted with more sophisticated tasks, like fixing the equipment that a fellow city-boy pal and I had incapacitated. Bob thus escaped experiments, such as my theory that if you were scared enough *you would get up* on water skis for the first time and you'd damned well *stay up* because, like most farm boys at the time, you couldn't swim. (A life preserver, my fellow theorist and I thought, would have reduced fear and thus nixed the experimental result.) Lyall Howard, his farmer's tanned face and forearms seemingly from a different body than the white rest of him, did stay up.

I lost track of Lyall, but Bob Howard eventually settled in a ranch house on what had been the family property after the rest was sold off. In the Navy, he'd found an adult outlet for the kind of engineering you learn as a child on a farm. And while Seagraves could fix anything, Bob, in a unique moment of expressing what I knew to be an amazing gift, once answered a query about miniaturizing a Bogdan salmon reel, the most complex (and desired) ever devised. "I can make anything," he said in a tone you might reserve for telling somebody you can ride a bike.

So here I was, outside the door of Bob's basement workshop with a project of the ilk I brought to him. It was hard for me to see. For Bob it must have been worse because of thick bifocals perpetually smogged. Bob smoked pretty much continually, heated his house with a leaky wood furnace and illuminated his desk with a single sixty-watt bulb hanging from a cord. All sorts of drafting documents—all of them smudged— covered one another to some degree on the desk and the nearby floor. The last job he had done for me was a double-block pulley to raise a bug screen and weather hatch separately, so that lines located in the attic could turn a corner before going through the floor of the lookout tower to its ceiling without getting hung up on sharp edges. Complicated, but his solution made it look simple: twin tracks like in a dentist's drill or the controls of old airplanes. Those WWI airplanes were in mind, which is probably why I noticed the improbable letterheads on the floor: *Aerospatiale* and *Dassault*.

Bob was famous along our road for machining the metal banks for a salmon/lake trout lure called "The Stinger," which others then festooned with all sorts of bright colors that, improbably, did indeed attract fish. Until then, however, none of us knew that the same machines were routing out aluminum circuit boards for advanced airliners and the most lethal bombers in the world. Someone from his Navy days had remembered the uncanny skills of a farm boy and tracked him down. "I guess they couldn't find anyone over there," he said, meaning Toulouse, France. Not at Bob's hourly fee of $15, that's for sure.

WHILE SEAGRAVES CAN REPAIR ANYTHING mechanical and Bob Howard, who continued smoking after a lung cancer diagnosis ("Why stop now?"), could design and fabricate it, Glen McCune concentrates on the fleeting creative moment between conception and creation. His medium can be a crippled bird's broken limb or a neighbor's demented dream of converting a handsome old runabout into an exuberantly atrocious motorboat sculpted into a twenty-foot-long duck. McCune restores shotgun stocks and canoes, carves 300-pound deer doors, 600-pound bear bedsteads and gorgeous cherrywood platters. He once constructed a dainty tabletop dragonfly that buzzed a carved lily pad by means of a crank, for no utility whatever. He fashioned the most beautiful mahogany kayak ever conceived, and likely the only one, ever, anywhere, with all of the hardware fashioned from deer antler.

Unlike Seagraves, with his barnful of beloved body parts amputated from tractors, or Howard, with blueprints from unlikely places, McCune's interest departs with the object, leaving only a scrapbook reflecting the admiration of others. His masterpiece? It is a lifestyle framed by a homestead that reflects it all in peacocks squawking from roofs, cages for recovering raptors, a rescued printing press from the 1890s and road kill hanging from trees before being fed to his various winged creatures and the peregrine falcons and red-tailed hawks used for hunting. How do you decide which bird to take hunting? Ask either McCune or his wife, Cindy—also a former teacher and present master of whatever-needs-creating—about any of this and the answer will be disarmingly simple, while also displaying an uncompromising mind-set. "Depends on what you want for dinner," she says. "Redtails like rabbit and will keep getting them for you as long as you leave them the parts they like to eat first—legs. With a peregrine you may end up with a robin or a chipmunk or even a fish." Don't they ever fly away? The McCunes don't take an occasional departure personally, although it means the loss of months of training, often after nursing the wounded bird back to flight. "Sometimes they get way up there where they can see around," she went on with a set of knuckles on one hip, "and just decide they'd rather live in Traverse City."

In service to their lifestyle the McCunes have mastered the art of agnosticism in their clients' tastes. In addition to the duckboat for the misdirected but valued neighbor, they produced at least twenty fiberglass bears for the Red Cross, each likeness progressively a worse offense against the McCunes' dedication to the natural world. At the direction of various Chapters, they covered the bears with bright stones and flags, leaving not even one looking right. This is full of irony: The McCunes regularly win competitions for these commissions, all of them based on the artistic merit—in this case, the bear-ness of the original. There is, however, no anger. "We set our artistic eyes aside," as Glen puts it, "and proceed on auto-pilot."

The transformations from purity to travesty at client instruction proceeded with an equanimity paralleled only in successful child-rearing, with its inevitable loss of control over the finished product. Their two daughters are a few years younger than our two boys, but close enough for us to take careful notes on contrasting styles. To us, it was essential that Ben and Mark had separate bedrooms; we never asked ourselves why. Tanner and Rainey slept in bunks hung from the ceiling in the laun-

GLEN MCCUNE CAN MAKE ANYTHING…AND USUALLY DOES
PHOTO CREDIT: IIJA HERB

dry room/closet off the kitchen of a 1912, four-room fieldstone house with a one-floor footprint the size of a classroom. In education, our efforts centered on living in the right districts with the best public schools and coughing up tuition for private equivalents. The McCunes provided the schools—kindergarten, grade school, junior high, high school. True, they had both been teachers, but I don't think that was the point. Their girls were just other young living things growing up under their tutelage and, like the others, they required some skills more than others. Before knowing the McCunes, we had associated home schooling with religions and cults, but here, right down the road, was a thoroughly secular example, and as far as we could tell, one producing results indistinguishable in academic achievement and social acculturation. Chicks grew up, laid eggs and were eaten. Puppies learned to gather eggs scattered around the yard with a soft mouth, then to retrieve hunted birds the same way.

Orphaned furred creatures were loved, fed with eyedroppers until weaning and thereafter with road kill matching what they would be hunting for themselves, then allowed to wander away. Baby birds got the warmth they needed and some sort of ersatz nest. Most gave a furtive look back as they departed; a few actually returned a few times. Eventually, both girls went off to college on basketball scholarships.

The sign on Ferry Road hints of this, but only if you pause to consider the vast unlikelinesses implied: *Yellow Dog Gallery. Fine Art and Wooden Boats.* The dog part reflects the reality of ubiquitous golden retrievers. The rest doesn't tell the half of it. Notice the photo on the facing page, taken by a pro who was supposed to record the drama of our new maple sugar operation at the farm, but instead focused his myriad lenses and all of his attention at the McCune establishment. There are three main buildings. Each has a coating of interesting stuff dangling from ceilings, mounted on walls and cluttering every surface. The coat endlessly molts as discarded projects, or parts of them, become décor. I'd give you a list, but if I've done a decent job with this verbal sketch, you can do the picturing all by yourself. It might even spark a Moses Moment.

WOODS

July 21, 2011

The decision I thought I was making was whether to attend a fiftieth high school reunion or encounter a new way of looking at the world. Truth be told, I hadn't stayed close to my old classmates, or the school, and the competing invitation promised a whole new group of people somewhere where the fishing was supposed to be terrific. It seemed a no-brainer. And, like some no-brainers, not using the brain to make a decision made dealing with the consequences more complicated. In this case, what happened at the reunion in Missouri while I was in Montana.

The Big Sky resort is close to the Gallatin River, famous for cutthroat trout. My host was the Liberty Foundation, the money pot for Libertarian theorists. My fellow panelists, assembled by old friend and fellow trouter Tom Bray, a *Wall Street Journal* editorial writer who had moved to take over the page at the *Detroit News*, were an engaging bunch from the *Washington Post*, the Libertarian *Reason Magazine*, *The Journal*, other think tanks and academe. The assigned readings were spectacular, so good that after debating the main points—after only skimming the summaries, my usual pattern—I found myself fascinated by the main line of thought and read my homework on the way home. All of it.

The Liberty people told us they were merely observers, and remained true to their word. Tom had researched and selected the readings to debate a question I had never heard mentioned in print: whether diagnos-

134

ing the human causes of climate change and dealing with them ASAP was more reasonable—as in the magazine's title—than husbanding the resources to deal with the effects as they appeared. We were enjoined to leave out of the conversation Al Gore, whose Nobel Prize had been awarded for *An Inconvenient Truth*.

That debate alone would have justified skipping a high school reunion. The other draw involved fishing, but not for the usual reasons. My enjoyment fishing the Gallatin that year was centered on confirming the prejudice that trout fishing in the western U.S. is 1) over rated, 2) sterile, and 3) overpopulated…which leads to 4) don't bother. What luck! Every fish I caught acted like it had been caught before. Plus, I couldn't tune out the SUVs whizzing by—mountain country roads often follow rivers—nor that the water flow over the bottom reminded me of fishing in a flooded gravel road—no moss, no muddy, life-sustaining muck. In short, it was way too simple. Tom, who was moving full time from Michigan to Montana, taking his fishing with him, had no such reservations. Watching him—and the others who, seeing us identify a promising stretch, waded in for themselves—I discovered another east-west difference, or at least one of old school / new school. Next to their sleek, quick-dry outfits and systematic trout regalia, my clunky chest waders and other gear looked like something improvised over decades of last-minute decisions, which was, of course, true.

While there was no slacking in the enjoyment, I did begin to notice a flow of thoughts leading back to John Burroughs School and its class of 1958. Maybe because, as mid-summer overtakes me, I slack off fishing at Overlook Farm. By then the sizable brook trout in the small rivers I favor have been taken and there are enough lake trout and salmon in the freezer for the winter—a strong signal to stop. I found myself re-visiting the no-brainer: How, really, could I miss seeing the people who, in their teens, formed concepts I've carried and applied all my life? One of them always called me "Charlie Rice," without having the slightest idea how much I liked hearing my worshipped maternal grandfather's name applied to me. For my part, I called him "Woods."

Woods (I don't remember ever adding John) was the oldest boy in our class. He was a full year older than me and had physically matured on a schedule even more advanced. He could drive before anyone. He had the body and experience of using it with girls before some of us even knew the names and locations of the key parts of female anatomy. He was also tall, slim, blond, rich and full of zany plans.

He outlined "cherry bomb dodg'em," for example, during a two-car expedition to Overlook Farm with two other friends after the end of our junior year, in June, 1957. More the size of walnuts than the namesake fruit, these cherry bombs were the largest firecrackers then made, red with green fuses that hissed fire when ignited with a cigarette lighter. The idea was to break up the tedium of the thirteen-hour drive from St. Louis by trying to get the bombs to explode under whichever car was in the rear. In our sedans—loosely-sprung and painted the bird-egg pastels of the 1950s—dodging was a colorful mix of high-speed blur and the dust from when we left the shoulders of two-lane roads and zigzagged across center lines with their ignored warnings about passing.

The week also included the first-in-a-lifetime attempt to pick up a girl. We found her in Charlevoix and, at fifteen, she was everything a nubile blonde could be… and more, given her willingness to come with us to the farm for water skiing. Yes, that was all we had in mind—that and looking at her in a bathing suit and hoping something mighty might happen. Only Woods might have known what that could be. And it nearly did happen, although not with her. Lolita's mother, thirty-something and comely in way we thought maternal, explained that she was divorced, without any of us understanding what that might imply. The definition of divorced became clear soon enough. She liked the look of Bill Bascom, one of the friends along the for ride. Equally clearly, unlike us, she knew exactly what to do should circumstances permit. This, however, terrified Bascom and left the rest of us so mystified we didn't egg him on. Except for Woods, of course, but neither Lolita nor her mother—who still had much of her daughter's Junior Miss beauty—seemed at all interested in the lanky kid with a twinkle for everything.

One of which was explosives far beyond cherry bombs. The Woods family maintained a turkey ranch near Steelville, Missouri, about two hours southwest of St. Louis. It was the first house with a name that I'd encountered, which is probably why the name stuck: La Chaumière, or "little thatched roof cottage." Well, hardly. The view from this sprawling establishment swept from the swimming pool down a broad valley between limestone outcroppings. Thousands of white turkeys, floating against the green background like foam on a calm bay, pecked at feed, bugs and each other. It was the ridges above that so tempted Woods. Their ledges over narrow crevices, he explained, were perfect for dynamite. Even better if there were a few loose boulders nearby.

Only Woods could cut the fuses just the right length for a getaway, and only he would light them. To the rest of us, that was just fine, particularly after we saw what happened when Woods yelled "Fire in the hole!" for the first time. Huge projectiles soared in miraculous, slow-motion arcs as we slid, bled, fled straight down the rocky, brambly slope to one of the farm's World War II Jeeps. They didn't always start right away. Over our shoulders, the missiles sailed like the giant German guns blown to heaven in "The Guns of Navarone."

It was never clear why the turkey farm had so much dynamite on hand. It was nothing short of ridiculous that Woods also had access to it at his other named home, "Warson Road," the family's ranch house set on sufficient acreage in the St. Louis suburbs to have its own valley out back. The property sloped down to a little creek which, like the ledges, provided an irresistible temptation. What happened there has defined courage for me ever since. Woods decided that a half-stick of dynamite in a pool would not only show what fish and other creatures might — or rather *might have* — been present, but would also produce a worthy geyser. As usual, we others were swept along like Huck Finns enchanted with each of Tom Sawyer's schemes.

But so was NoName, Woods' clueless English Setter. Spewing the usual exciting sparks from its short fuse, the half-stick — "Not loud enough to bring the cops," Woods explained with characteristic assurance — flew end-over-end toward the pool … followed closely by NoName. Untrained to any command, she raced to the pond, swam out to the stick and, in a heartbeat, was on the bank, shaking herself. Was it time for a game of bring-the-stick-close, but not too close? The immediate prospects shorted out whatever thought process might have replaced the preceding idiocy. I only remember that I needed to be as far away from NoName as possible. Not so Woods. Calmly and kindly, with the sort of smile particularly effective when training puppies, he stooped low, calling gently to the dog. She came slowly, indirectly, but came nonetheless, shaking her head to tease us, tail wagging her whole rear end with pleasure. One lunge got the stick. Woods threw it and then himself on the ground on top of NoName. The explosion deafened us all.

Ever since, that moment has defined for me the sort of reaction that wins Medals of Honor. Bravery of a kind that's only considered so afterwards because, to that person in that singular second, it's no more stoppable than kicking a knee when the doctor strikes his rubber mallet. To me that that kind of hard wiring makes the individual all the more admirable.

At our fortieth reunion, I had gone over that story with Woods and the survivors of those exploits, while at the same time wondering why our friendship, backed by so much admiration on my part, hadn't remained active. I learned that Woods and his wife Judy, also a classmate, had been summering "forever" in Sutton's Bay, no more than ninety minutes away from Overlook by boat and not much more by car. Why hadn't I known that before? More to the point and ten years later, what stopped me from arranging visits afterwards?

For the fiftieth reunion, Woods invited our class to the turkey farm where he had installed a scale model, working steam train complete with passenger cars, miniature station and miles of track. Photos showed him in a railroad outfit, playing engineer, everyone following into his fantasy world as "child leader-in-chief." Even those who hadn't known Woods well came away from the La Chaumière visit suffused in his charm and ability to not only handle family money—and multiply it in the stock market—but to make magical things happen. "A sort of genius," one said, "who had never done well in school." I had obviously missed a lot, and had just begun balancing that against the Liberty Foundation seminar when classmate Bill Bascom sent an email report, dated Oct. 18, 2008:

> *Thursday was a spectacularly beautiful fall day here. Temperatures were in the mid 60's. After the reunion, John and Dave [another classmate, a doctor] had ridden their motorcycles down to have lunch with a friend in Eminence. The road was one of those narrow, twisty, roller-coaster kind of stretches so typical of highways in that part of the Ozarks. Dave was riding lead about a half mile ahead but out of sight. I guess that's the safest way to ride as a pair*

so as not to get tangled up with your partner. Dave kept checking his rear-view mirror to be sure John had not had any mechanical problems, and he told me that a semi which was speeding and crowding the center line passed him going in the opposite direction. He did not think too much about that until he noticed that he could no longer see John behind him.

Dave rendered what first aid he could and short time later a medi-vac helicopter flew John to the emergency room at Barnes Hospital (St. Louis), a 40 minute flight. John died in the operating room.

Woods had briefly regained consciousness—his wide blue eyes, the kind with white swirls as if to include not only a clear sky, but the faint clouds that sometimes accentuate it—were my first "mental flash." I pictured him staring up with that face of an aging boy to report, as he always did in fake-adult terms, what had happened. I am an eye person. I remember more irises than names of people and get seasick-queasy when eyes are injured within my sight. As I imagined John's that day, they remained perfect, gazing up from the spattered pavement to the blues and clouds of an Ozark sky.

BILL & SYLVIA

March, 1993

W hile Bill Gaunt was cutting hay in his eighty-second summer, the sickle bar on his sun-faded red International Harvester tractor cut off his left foot. That was in July, 1978. He'd kept his IH Model A going since 1953, when he brought it home new as the proudest man alive. He'd kept his body in repair since 1892, when his mother produced him right on the Gaunt homestead across Mountain Road from us. To Bill, a body wasn't much different from a tractor. Something always "got broke." So he and his wife Sylvia gathered up the parts needing fixing—mess and all—and they left for Little Traverse Hospital thirty miles away. Bill drove himself. Sylvia's removable teeth would start clicking even at the mention of "machines," as she called automobiles. Never drove them. Luckily, this machine only needed one foot, the right one.

Bill arrived in the emergency room the same way he showed up at the Farm Coop garage—without notice, expecting to be taken care of when his turn came. The doctor, who was younger than Bill's grandchildren, looked to him "like he never saw many legs." In fact, the tendons were gone, some of the bone, too. The ends had been smashed rather than broken and his shin looked like a sapling after the brush hog goes through. Only a strip of hide held that part of him to the others.

"Don't worry about this," the doctor said. "We're going to take this one off and give you a new one."

Bill had heard mechanics say things like that for years at the Coop. "Young feller," Bill said, I imagine in the tone reserved for common assumptions he knew to be wrong, "if I'd wanted it off, I wouldn't of needed you. Could of done that at home and saved us the drive."

Bill's foot healed usably, which surprised no one who knew him. He and Sylvia returned to the rhythms of lives unchanged appreciably since they took over the house from his parents in 1920, different only in the substitution of engines for horses and party-line phones for gossip bees.

Our place and theirs had been linked from the start. Bill's father, Dave, had helped his uncle, Doug Cater, clear the place, and Bill had watched as they put up the house in 1900 from Sears-Roebuck plans. He had been there when the Caters topped the huge maples out back, remnants of the original forest, so they would bush out to shade the horses. They did the same to the beech at the corner of the drive for when neighbors came "to set a while."

"Setting a while" — always on a Sunday, after church — could mean all afternoon. The scrapbook my mother kept illustrates the event in black and white. There is Bill, in his engineer's hat and overalls, and his father Dave, at eighty-six. My mother never looked at the picture without noting how handsome Dave was, with a shock of white hair and mustache. The Gaunts look content; the Eisendraths, impatient to get on with a weekend and unsure of what to do with "tomato-juice bread." Sylvia brought this as a special treat for these "new kind of people" in a neighborhood where the Caters had been kin to the Gaunts, the Gaunts to the Myers, the Myers to the Schelenbergers, Shelenbergers to Mac-Donalds and all of them neighbors to the Brickers, Howards and Adamses. That was it; there weren't any more.

That the Eisendraths really were "a new kind of people" — Jews — I don't think completely registered. The explanation for this assumption became clear during the first year Julia and I visited as the new owners of Overlook. We were on a home leave coinciding with the Israeli-Arab war of 1973. The generational changeover at the farm signaled the need for several niceties we hadn't expected, beginning with the first ritual visit from the county snowplow crew. Conversation drifted to certain expectations, such as acceptable currency would not be money. From the likes of us "seasonable people" at the end of a public road, a bottle of bourbon was in order, specifically Jim Beam.

JULIA'S PARIS FRIENDS
COULDN'T BELIEVE IT

Doug Coblentz not only headed the local crew, but was married to Eleanor, who helped us out with housework. After scrambling in the basement for something that would do, I leaned over the hood of Doug's pickup and turned the conversation from plowing to politics, unable to resist using Eveline Township as a sounding board for how rural America processed the events I was covering for *Time*. "So," I asked, "what about the war?"

"Them Israels and Arabs (Eyes-rAY-als and A-rabs) sure do a lot of fighting," Doug observed.

Doug's deputy plowman and I nodded agreement.

Unable to resist a little light probing, I asked, "But what kind of people are the Eyes-RAY-als, anyway?"

Doug wasn't sure, but he felt confident enough to pass on the consensus of our township: "I hear they're a bunch of Jews," he said, producing more nodding agreement.

I decided to push into what I already knew to be beyond where Doug usually ventured: "So what about Jews? Who are they?"

Doug looked away without any particular focus. "I think it's some different kind of Baptist," he said. "That's what they tell me, anyway."

Foreign correspondents will often tell you that they learn most about their own country when covering the affairs of others, and that conversation is one of the very few that fundamentally changed how I look at America. Even though my life's work has been informing the public as a reporter and professor, I am convinced that America's great, never-admitted strength is its widespread, casual ignorance of history. It isn't tolerance that makes us united; more that as a people we are so interbred, with so many historic hatreds mooted, that we often can't sort out which of the ancient invocations to hate we should activate. When we do so, we behave as though the melting pot has boiled over. Doug Coblentz was a fine man and atypical in no important way. When reporting, and then teaching thereafter, I kept him in mind as part of the test audience we all carry around for communication purposes.

MY FATHER NEVER SAID WHY he didn't hire Bill Gaunt to look after the place. Bill clearly thought it his rightful position and was still trying out for the job thirty years later when the decision became mine. It's probable that my father couldn't handle Bill's open-ended idea of human discourse every time Dad wanted mowing done. I turned away as well when a first conversation drifted from winter plowing to the second-growth maples that needed thinning to what to do with the big field and, after that, the small one. Julia and I needed instruction about every-

THE BEAM ABOVE THAT TOOL SHED DOOR HELD BILL GAUNT'S SIPPIN' JUG, AN EASY REACH

thing, at every turn, after we decided to put in a garden. I had written about first gardens for Associated Press News Features and elsewhere as a way of filling in the financial gap left by the two-thirds pay cut taken with the job as assistant professor. But we still wouldn't be the Gaunts' employers and, thus, victims of a logorrhea that while charming afterwards was tedious in the moment. Instead, we figured out a way to benefit from nonstop advice: we would become their students. Without their hands-on tutelage, the lessons the garden taught us would have been merely botanical.

Julia is the family's natural scholar. She read up on gardening. Steeped in organic lore and the wisdom of a shelf of new books, armed with stainless steel implements and wearing a chic jacket from Buenos Aires, she marked off a neat rectangle twenty by forty feet in the big field east of the house. The rows were as straight as her taut twine guides, neatly marked with seed packages over the stakes exactly one foot apart, as instructed. At the time, I couldn't find the words, let alone the ways, to express my reaction in a maritally acceptable fashion. To me her layout looked like a patio. We had inherited a *farm*. A farm meant bigness. Fecund messiness. A place to haul machinery through, nevermind that we had none. I didn't know all of that, exactly, but my gut sensed the scale was wrong. At the time, all I was sure of was that the neat little scratches wouldn't do. Since it was still early in the season, Bob Sherman could and did disc up an acre or so north of the house. As with many of my decisions—which tend to be ruled by intuition, the good among them based on unconscious knowledge—this one hit the garden equivalent of a gold mine. We re-seeded a much longer rows, much farther apart, smack in the middle of what had been the Cater barnyard. Powered by decades of natural fertilizer, stuff rocketed out of the ground.

That was in 1976. By 1987 we were seeing a marriage counselor and came closer than the rows in Julia's garden to putting permanent space between us. The issues seemed far more complex than they do now, of course, but they centered around the growing of other things. Our two sons had developed all the weeds of adolescence and we had staked out two quite different plots. We needed to find a way to grow things differently, but together, and the farm experience helped.

But the Gaunts' forte wasn't psychiatry. It was nematodes. Bill liked to convene class before dawn, roaring instructions from the terrace at our bedroom window as if addressing an auditorium without a microphone. Then he'd be out in the garden delivering grades, frequently "F's" at decibelage we could hear from there, too. "Where was the dishwater?" "Where was the laundry water?" "By gol', how can you expect to control them dang things without soap?"

Unlike Bill and Sylvia, we weren't in the habit of keeping gray-water around. We had to manufacture it, meaning something else to forget doing. Courses on squash worms came the same way. We had admired the Gaunts' own hybrid gold-and-green winter squashes; the Gaunts produced seeds from a coffee can. The worms loved the stems as much as we relished the *carbonara* Julia made with them from an Argentine recipe. But just as the fruit would form behind the incredible orange flowers, the broad leaves would droop like green parachutes on the ground. Lectures followed, delivered by a bowlegged agricultural drill sergeant storming down the ranks of vegetables in a uniform that included a seed catalogue hat and the Bermuda shorts he suddenly and unaccountably took up in his eighties. "Nematodes? Cut 'em out with a paring knife, one by one. Tomorrow's too late! Just look at what them leaves is telling you."

Later that year, the Gaunts demystified frontier winters in the north. Frankly, I had never understood how people who couldn't get around for weeks on end because of the snow could put anything fresh on the table. The answer came one fall weekend while digging up our carrots, rutabagas, parsnips and turnips. What were we doing, Bill asked? For once we had an answer: We're getting everything in before the ground freezes, that's what, we said, delighted to be confidently ahead of the game. Hardly. For this, mere words wouldn't suffice. Our instructors ordered an immediate field trip to their garden across Mountain Road. The remedial tour revealed all, without being much to look at after repeated early frosts. Here, the earth was mounded where late cabbage had been. Tall stakes marked the ends of root-crop rows. Before us was an Eveline Township refrigerator with zero electrical consumption and still in use since the area was settled. From then on, we shopped with snow shovels. It was something of an amazement to locate carrots by the few inches of a three-foot stake sticking up out of a drift. It was an epiphany to dig down through brilliant, blinding white to find bright green and neon orange! The soil remained sweet as at planting time, a quilt of snow trapping enough earth-heat to keep the temperature hovering just above 32°F.

Then there were the basics to be left to grow wild near a respectable garden, but not actually in it. These plants weren't gifts so much as commentary—unusually gentle—on our agronomical judgment. To Bill and Sylvia, kitchen gardens unadorned with clumps of horseradish, comfrey and Jerusalem artichoke were unthinkable. We dutifully planted them, although only the former spent much time in our kitchen. Comfrey, a frontier staple with pulpy leaves that felt like a two-day beard, was to be used for abrasions, compresses, tea and…fresh greens! We never got our heads around hairy salads, however, nor green bandages, and found it nearly impossible to eradicate. As for Jerusalem "artichokes" (botanically unrelated), after repeated boiling to reduce their production of truly theatrical flatulence, they weren't bad when sliced thin and sautéed with plenteous garlic. Then again, they weren't good enough to cancel out the nasty habit of mass invasion shared with comfrey.

SOME OF THE BEST TEACHING goes on without the teacher knowing it, and so it was with Bill. From him, I first learned the merciful side of age and the complexity of friendship, neither included in his monologues. We had been taking notes on each other—I just hadn't read mine as well as he had.

My mother had always thought of the Gaunts' basement as a museum. Stocked with produce "put by," it was, indeed, a glimpse of how settlers turned Jefferson's Eighteenth Century theories of prosperity on 160 acres into accomplished facts. Pickles, honey, carrots, tomatoes and tomato juice, apples, applesauce and apple juice. Asparagus ("asperee-grass" to Bill), dandelion wine, potatoes, peas, beans, corn and combinations of things I could neither identify nor read from mildewed labels. There was venison, too, and fish. Twice each summer, Bill would launch a rowboat with his tractor and a small farm trailer, trap minnows and sit with Sylvia in exactly the same place midway across the South Arm off the south point of Holy Island. In my forty-five years' involvement with this place, I have never seen anyone else fish there. Water-skiers rushed by; sailors waved. Sylvia wore a sunbonnet that made the little craft look like a floating covered wagon. One day, I paddled a canoe out to visit. From their anchorage the sunset was in full view; on their stringer, three northern pike, fanning slowly as they awaited their fate in canning jars stacked in a basement at the top of the hill.

We watched Bill make maple syrup. On one of those suddenly warm days in early March, I rode out to his sugarbush, standing on the hitch bar of his tractor as the big wheels churned through the drifts like riverboat sidewheels and a late sun turned the snow shadows blue and the trees amber against the sky. His rick had been burning all week, Bill interrupting other chores to keep boiling the huge, black pan filled by the sap buckets he and Sylvia brought in on snowshoes. There's a scene in *Moby Dick*, maybe the best scene, in which the Pequod's crew renders whale blubber using the whale's own oil as fuel. There's something infernal about it; a midnight thunderstorm turns the topmasts to hellfire as the ship crashes through the sea that will eventually claim it. Boiling maple sap over its own wood, I thought, awaits its Melville.

Unlike the maple syrup industry, or at least its marketing people, Bill liked his syrup dark. I was an instant convert. The glowing jars brought back the co-mingling of woodsmoke and burning sugar. Like ours and all the area farmhouses built before World War I, the Gaunts' had a "Michigan basement," meaning stone foundation walls high enough to keep the structural wood and siding above the late snow line so the melt wouldn't rot it like lumber left at the shoreline. Those walls permit windows, and the shelving stretched from the light to a dark syrup corner. I asked how much he kept on hand. By that time, Bill no longer spent his early springs in the sugarbush, a concession, he wanted me to know, that had nothing to do with his severed foot. "Just as much as I'll ever need," he said. He was eighty-four. I was thirty-nine and I date my imaginings of the permissions of age from that moment in that dark basement. One chore less.

Bill gave me a quart jar of syrup for Christmas that year. Once, while delivering a trailer-load of stove-wood to the Gaunts after cutting was getting beyond them, I noted the pint jug of syrup-colored whiskey Bill kept on a toolshed rafter for nipping throughout the afternoon. "To keep the spirits up," he said. Bourbon costs real money in a subsistence budget and I took to presenting him with a bottle of Jim Beam, which came in a gift box. My present from him came wrapped in a quilt of dozens of tiny pieces of paper taped together. For years, maybe forever, the Gaunts had saved Christmas paper from people who inhabited a world that included store-bought wrapping; I recognized the mistletoe pattern my mother  always kept on hand. I wasn't old enough then, or wise enough, or maybe both, to understand the nature of what Bill gave me. Of my many Gaunt embarrassments, burning that wrapping in a Christmas fire lingers among the worst. Like the cuttings from sewing projects farm women made into wedding quilts for their girls, Bill had given me a record of the way he lived that outlived him. Winter breakfasts came and went, and the syrup was gone.

THE PLEASURE OF SURVIVAL

July, 2006

"You got to take 'em out, by gol, you got to take 'em." With a shake of the head, that was Bill Gaunt's pronouncement on the maples and ashes in the long, gentle valley leading from the east side of the property to the swamp close to its center. He had something specific in mind. When a forest is cut, stumps from some species send up multiple shoots. Most get crowded out or devoured by deer, but what survives is a forest of trees in pairs (sugar maple), several pairs of twins (red maple), or even dozens (black ash). This kind of growth tells you you're in cut-over territory, no matter how undisturbed it looks. Although several shoots produce more wood, each shoot grows more slowly because they use a root system designed for one. Upshot: more and smaller trunks mean more kindling but less lumber, the forestry cash-crop. Bill waxed enraged that "them doubles" hadn't been thinned.

At that point Bill Gaunt knew our trees far better than we did—not only the species, but the *communities* of species (the ones that like to grow

together) and the hills and runs where they live. He carried the memory of old growth around in his head like a photo of a love mishandled. As we watched him advance from a seventh to a ninth decade, some of the trees were as big around at waist height as he was. Wistfulness became obsession.

I admit to having been tone deaf to the music of how my new, local friends spoke. I should have known that the words, as they spoke them, had far different meanings than I was used to, even if spelled and — usually, but not always — pronounced the same. Theirs was an idiom of saying nothing in a mist. For example, when a used washing machine was delivered from Boyne City, I'd responded to the dud appliance the same way I would have in Paris or Buenos Aires: *Please remove this defective piece of junk and bring me something that works.* In either of those latter home towns, directness was accepted; prevarication suggested weakness. In Eveline Township, by contrast, the man who had rebuilt and delivered the washer reacted as though he had been felled by a sucker punch to the gut. I had provided straight gin when the situation called for linguistic Wonder Bread. Something like, "You know, I think there may have been something wrong with this machine."

I was equally unaware of how our attitude toward the woods sounded to Bill. My saying, "Don't touch those trees, leave nature alone!" was a slap against everything he'd learned in a life just one generation removed from pioneer farming. Using everything available was the only means to survive. To us, as part of the middle class, play-farmers of the 1970s — and part-time at that — the imperative was nature rescue: *Use as little as possible of each thing in order to save the whole, to save the world.* After all, if all else failed, we could go back to the comfort we'd come from.

A decade into our pioneering experiments, Sylvia Gaunt was too sick to tend the cookstove that kept them warm and fed all year. By that point in their lives, everything they did took several times longer than in the past, and even in the best years "everything" took every minute of an eighteen-hour day. Bill asked for some help: a load of wood. It had to be branch wood, he said. A little scouting for where wood the right size for a cookstove might come from easily and accessibly led me to the valley. It had been so long since the last cutting that there was plenty of dead, dry stuff already on the ground and as least as much standing.

Within an hour, Bill and Sylvia were quietly acknowledging an appreciated service. That didn't take long either, but it contained one of those morsels that you save for digestion later. The nugget was that Bill, himself, had logged that valley, maybe for the previous owners, maybe for himself. Was Bill's blustering about the doubles actually a cover for guilt? For having poached a little timber? Was he making amends by insisting on thinning the stand? Or was he eliminating the evidence before we, the new owners, caught on? Maybe he calculated that the thinning would guarantee more wood for us. Maybe all those extra trunks just made the valley appear "not looked after?" I guessed most of the above.

Mental chewing on possible ponderables leaves a residue. In this case, an insidious mental aftertaste demanding palette cleansing. At the time I called it "a sudden need to thin the hardwoods" and associated it only in the vaguest way with Bill Gaunt's maneuvering, aesthetics or whatever. Sure enough, though, I went straight to the valley to implement my self-diagnosed forestry uplift. For several summers I felled, winched out and cut so much that the two-tracks were lined with green wood stacked for drying. The piles looked oddly estate-like and very un-Overlook Farm, but they were satisfying, too, in the manner of many works-in-progress. I'd look at the different lengths, sorted and neatly resting on long runners to lessen ground rot, and imagine winter fires—fireplace, furnace and cookstove—each with its signature scent, burn pattern, heat-throw: birch, ironwood, maple, ash. Although Julia denigrated my passion for re-creating the French allées along East Jordan byways, she admired the stacks. After a few years, I'd thinned so much that the stacks doubled and I was filling the Suburban with wood for Ann Arbor.

All of this came to an abrupt, violent end on August 2, 2002. I was off on an assignment as unrelated to the Overlook world as anything in the rest of my life—explaining the career-advancing possibilities of journalism fellowships to the National Association of Black Journalists. I got the call from Julia at their Milwaukee convention, just after speaking about how time off for self-reflection is the most important lesson because it helps journalists grow.

"Something terrible happened in the woods," she said. "I went in as far as I could, and then there was a wall of tree trunks. Just a wall! And explosions everywhere. They kept going for hours."

Julia knew about explosions and shooting. At the start of the Marxist guerrilla terrorism in Buenos Aires that triggered the "Dirty War," there had been gunfights in the park in front of our apartment, and occasional bombs in the neighborhood. People whom the military considered suspiciously leftist were "disappeared" into the maw of a judicial system that gave cover to the bloody tracks left by right-wing squads and their military masters. On the other side, Marxist guerrilla groups targeted journalists. I spent every day reporting, analyzing, writing and recounting to Julia this full-blown terrorism—state and anti-state —all around us. By some unconscious process she managed to tune out every bit of it. She even pooh-poohed being shadowed by a man who mysteriously turned up at the market and at the kids' model boat basin in the park. To her, my hiring a private security agent was ludicrous. Sometimes I'd doubted her survival instincts, but this time she was right. When our guard confronted the suspected kidnapper, it turned out he was merely an Argentine with the good taste to be smitten with her.

Back to the farm: The three small tornadoes that had rocked the house and destroyed much of our timber thirty years later felt to us like the terror in Buenos Aires—unpredictable and indefensible. Although the house, outbuildings and barn were intact—even the plantings around them — Julia was lucky to be alive. The explosions were still going off when I got back late the next day. When you fire a deer rifle in a thick forest, you get more than just a bang. The sound echoes off saplings, twigs and bark and, as the lead behind the copper tip deforms, its edges whine. All over the parts of our woods that were hit by the bullet winds, trees had been uprooted, slammed down and rammed into each other. They were contorted, splintered, mangled. Where some of the big beeches had been snapped at mid-height—about forty feet up—wooden sprays of splinters jabbed upwards in a frozen still-shot of quick destruction.

If the sound put us most immediately in Argentina, those tableaux called up France. The previous year we had been blown away—the metaphor we used at the time— by watercolors of the Battle of the Marne, dashed off by artists commissioned by the French Army to record the Great War. To those artists, the mayhem appeared heroic, but they'd found it impossible to express that scale in terms of human physiognomy—perhaps because the bones, skin, guts, hair and blood of any single body just aren't big enough to visually register the oceanic agony felt by one person's wounds through another person's eyeballs. As a pain communication device, the artist/war correspondents had settled on the trees. In their shattered forms, you could *hear* what had hit them. Juxtaposing what a force could do to something as solid as an oak—stripped of its bark at midpoint and showing the color of tree insides—and wounded men—lost limbs and spattered body fluids—demonstrated pain.

Many—most, perhaps—think that comparing human pain to animal pain is a stretch and, where plants are concerned, ridiculous. I am not one of them. Not after planting, nurturing, pruning, felling and burning them for years at the farm. Not after listening carefully to people who dedicated lives to them. Not after seeing with my own eyes plant responses to what would cause pain, human or animal.

We went about dealing with our shattered woods the way the French approached Verdun. First, we looked for particular individuals—climbing over, under and between the giant trunks that the whirlwind had slapped across the hillsides and our little two-tracks. When I made the reconnaissance trips alone, I was spooked by the rifle shots of trees cracking under unbearable strain, just as the hunched figures in a watercolor called "The Graves Detail" must have flinched with the detonation of a delayed artillery fuse or a land mine. Our "Eagle beech" was the easiest, old friend tree to reach. For several years when the boys were young a bald eagle couple had built one of their huge, inelegant nests in a high crotch. Having them close to us as landlords made us feel, well, chosen. Protective, too. The boys competed to limit who would be told about these extraordinary beings. Next-to-nobody, they decided, then fewer still.

The Eagle beech had lost a major limb, but survived. As did by some miracle a remnant nest. The "Balinese dancer," also a beech, still stood as well, but no longer had the sinuous shape that inspired her name. One of her arms had been torn out at the shoulder, taking part of her trunk with it. When I realized how quickly her special distinction as an individual leached out of our attention, I thought I had a clue about how the French must have felt about veterans blinded by poison gas, dismembered by explosions or both. How deep the wounds among the healthy must have been as that shrieking of loss and grief flooded the Metro, the sidewalks, parks and kitchens of their consciousness.

A lumberman we called understood the dangers of our shattered valley as well as Marshal Philippe Pétain, directing grave details, knew the valley of Verdun. Our land mines were roots ready to snap when great weights were lifted; our unexploded ordinance of twisted trunks 80-feet long ready to launch splinters as the recovery process shifted tremendous pressures. The salvageable were removed as individuals. The rest, as at Verdun, were collectively bulldozed.

THE STORM HAPPENED within a year of the terrorist attacks of 2001 and I felt compelled to seal off the searing images of New York from the memory mix of Verdun, Bill Gaunt and their respective valleys. Not that they seemed more personally important; quite the contrary. September 11, 2011, merely changed the world *around me*; the whirlwind changed *me*. For months, I avoided the valley and felt a sense of impotence when I couldn't. The woods, it turned out, had been part of what made us feel impregnable when at the farm. They were the outer layer in a place surrounded by so much of ourselves that nothing un-us could enter without permission. Two hundred, thirty-four point eight miles from our house in Ann Arbor, Ridge Road crossed Mountain Road and the zipper began to seal off the non-us behind the car. Ridge Road peters out after two houses; when we turned in toward ours, the zipper zipped.

The storm tore it open. Woods vast, unbroken and dark in our psyches, had been cut in three. The missing crowns of trees were as notable as broken prongs in a royal crown, with the same suggestion of a reign upended. From the house we could see unaccustomed light through the north tree line to the hill beyond. Sunlight sliced through the cuts and the solitude, too. It had been the darkness that permitted our imaginings of infiniteness and a collective family dream.

Commercial loggers Lee Miller and Lee Eckstrom, for thirty years our foresters, both depended on woods like ours. On the job, Miller stays in the cab of his truck — at 350 pounds, he's too heavy to heave himself around in the timber. Every Saturday and Sunday he's in church all day. I picture him eating snowmobile club breakfasts followed by Lions Club lunches with Twinkies in the afternoon and a barbecue at night, all of it while seated. As far as I know, he makes no connection between God and the forests he levels, preferring clear-cuts (taking everything) and prizing speed above all. He's good at what he does; honest and straightforward about what he will do and won't.

In contrast, Eckstrom, blue-eyed and lean, spends his free time in the woods—keeping tabs on tree growth and spiritualizing in equal parts. He's a fisherman, a furniture builder, and he likes to leave den trees standing "for the critters." He's a timber "cruiser," walking every acre, sizing up each tree before marking it with orange spray paint just above the root flare—where it should be felled—and again at chest height for easy spotting in the snow. When the tree's down and removed, he verifies the right cut at the right height. One day while marking trees to come out for a lake view, we traded songs about the woods. I sang "The Frozen Logger," a tall-tale ballad about an ill-fated Michigan axman who stirs his coffee with his thumb and fatally forgets his Mackinaw jacket in a storm. Eckstrom Lee sang "Nearer My God to Thee." He knew every verse.

Taut and bulgy, the two Lee's agreed completely and emphatically about what I should do with the storm's killing fields. Leave them alone, they said, the cut-over will come back with a fury no human regeneration could match. In a forest like ours, never converted to agriculture, an infinity of time leaves an infinity of seeds to sprout when there's suddenly more sunlight reaching the ground.

But, of course, I couldn't leave things alone. What general forsakes his dead or their remains? Casualties require decent markers. For humans, that means stones, often particular kinds, like granite and marble. For trees, it's more trees, special trees. I chose red oak, black cherry and black walnut for their beauty, relative local scarcity, resistance to blights ... and something else, but that's for a bit later in the story.

On a sleeting knife-wind of an April weekend the next year, José Ambrosio, his wife Rosa, their adolescent daughter and two small sons began planting trees with me. They are from the Yucatan and live on the next hill to the east in a house trailer they converted the northern Michigan way: replaced wheels with blocks, added skirt to make it easier to keep the floor warm, then put roofing here and there and finally siding until the original metal disappeared. José and I speak bad English and bad Spanish together because his first language is Mayan. He stands about five-foot, one inch, with fingers as least one whole joint shorter than mine and feet that make sense of the narrow steps of Yucatan pyramids. Deployed along the tangled hillsides with bundles of leafing tree whips in one hand and froes in the other, we planted "grandchildren trees." My choices grow slowly but keep their value as lumber and resist the plagues that have swept North American forests with the finality of smallpox among the Indians. Above all, they would be beautiful for me to think about and look at, compensation for the certainly of my not being around at their maturity. Hundreds more followed the next spring.

I also had an order from the grave. One of the top generals of my life introduced me to the iconography of trees by first establishing himself as a man who produced miracles. One day when I was seven or eight my grandfather Pops introduced me to Superman. Superman had come to the Missouri Ozarks because my grandfather had invited him. There would be a program just like the ones I had heard on the Philco radio, "broadcast from right here in Leesburg, Missouri!" That the whole thing was a publicity stunt to steer tourists from Route 66 to Onondaga Cave—in which he had installed fancy lighting and even an underground boat trip—only added another dimension to the glory.

Nor was Onondaga Pops' only miracle cave. At "The Lodge"—his weekend place closer to St. Louis—he fashioned what we called "the cool room" until air conditioning came along to give us new terminology. In the 1940s, Ozark summers raised questions about why anyone would live in the unpleasant duality of being soggy and roasting concurrently. Pops' solution was to capture unlimited cool air. An opening at the foot of the mountain gushed pure spring water and exhaled the steady breeze that flowed with the water—both at 52°F, no matter how hot the summer. Stone walls built head-high trapped delicious air; you could put your hand above your head in the roofless enclosure to feel the sweltering misery you were avoiding. After burbling over a little waterfall—with drinking ladles always handy—the current ran under decking that supported a picnic table and then fell first into to two trout ponds, then continued on to a huge swimming pool. We were told with great pride that it was the first reinforced concrete structure in the state of Missouri. I was more influenced, however, by reports of giant snapping turtles and water moccasins.

Significantly, it was the exhibition, "From Picasso to Fontana: Collecting Modern and Postwar Art in the Eisendrath Years, 1960–1968," honoring my father's contributions to Washington University's museum, that brought me to my old home town of St. Louis in January, 2015. After two days living with my father—now dead thirty-two years—and the lifelong avocation that became his vocation from midlife onwards, I decided to try to find The Lodge. Thirty miles and whole planets divided St. Louis from Pops' masterpiece, about the same distance that separated those two seminal males, and also my expectations. I imagined having to deal with taupe-colored suburbanization sprawling over beloved Ozark landmarks. I even invited my oldest friend, who had tramped the place with me in high school, to join the search. What we found was what I began thinking of as "The Miracle of Antonia, MO."

Near that unchanged little town, Pops had converted a gravel-choked gulley into two miles of dams and ponds by scraping the lime-slab creek bed clean to reveal the flow. He loved showing that Ozark creeks didn't disappear in summer, they just hid, flowing low under gravel.

Where cliffs crowded in too close, the trail escaped to the gentler side on dainty stone arches, opportunities taken for wildflower plantings. In another six weeks, overgrown forsythia would bloom bright foreign yellow amidst the native dogwood white and the redbuds. Ditches along roads leading to the place, including one named for Pops, were choked with bottles, broken toys, socks, McDonalds boxes. But here, along a pathway he'd actually built, there was not a single bottle cap, as if an army of groomers had been on duty day and night for more than a half-century. Where the creek gardens valleyed out at the cave, coolroom, trout ponds and swimming pool, the wonder of it all brightened into a sort of spiritual tingle, the kind shivers are made of. I knew I wouldn't see any of this again and, soon, I'm certain, nobody else will, either. Eventually, miracles succumb to the ordinary and nothing is more predictable than subdivisions.

It may be, too, that trespassing added excitement. Only emotionally did I have any right to be there. The place had been sold and resold and the present owners, according to a man living in a trailer nearby who helped discern a driveway amidst a tangle, warned that they "did not take kindly" to those who entered. But you hardly ever get caught trespassing and there's no more exciting way to explore. Landmarks mean more because you'll need them going home and they can be psychic as well as directional pointers. If you need to trespass into your own history, you never actually *do* get back to where you started, not as the same person.

I guess I should think of that few days as Progenitors' Weekend because of how obvious it made the previously unconscious. No, I hadn't entered business first but, like my father, I did have a second career as academic entrepreneur and my collection of maps follows the tight focus he advised for art. Like Pops, I went to law school, then dropped out. Ever since, though, I've looked over my shoulder as, one after another, his passions catch up with me, including the passion for concurrent passions.

I HAD BEEN HAPPILY PUT to the planting of walnut trees in furtherance of Pops' pioneering theory of inheritance: He calculated that in less than two hundred years, the timber he'd planted at The Lodge would make his grand- and great-grandchildren rich! Of course, things didn't work out that way. The Lodge and its adolescent black walnut grove were sold. But did that give pause as my little crew planted hundreds of seedlings of the same species along the ridges at Overlook Farm? None, whatsoever. Some of our trees are thirty feet tall now, about the size of the walnuts at The Lodge when my cousin sold it. Even the smallest will reach that height by the time I see them for the last time. They could be a significant monument if you knew what they were about, which isn't likely. No matter. It's the *dream* that counts.

Stumbling through the hillside tangles there was plenty of time to let thoughts float, a farmthought process as integral as the seepage of spring water into the lake along the shoreline. I had spent the last few years thinning the woods in precisely the places that haunted Bill Gaunt—in the way he would have, should have, gone about it. Then the three small tornadoes touched down and thinned it another way; knocked most of it over, ruined it all and blew away a whole

memory structure. If I had believed in God, the tornados might have represented His furious breath and the bolts-of-lightning messages that sent Job onto his ash heap to weep forever. But I didn't need God to understand fragility, the tiny scope of human endeavor and the laughableness of my re-forestation project. I had to love that part, too—no ash heap of repentance that the Biblical Job required. A fool in the right cause is a happy fool.

As both Lees predicted, the woods responded furiously to insult. The creepers didn't just creep —full sun made racers and booby trappers of them as they slithered up the few remaining trees and outlined the crisscross of log carcasses on the ground. Mullein by the thousand lunged eight feet above the creeper green like saguaro cactus after a downpour in the desert, their fuzzy arms yellow with tiny flowers. The next year burdock took over, likewise growing taller than I'd thought possible. I tried killing it with spray to reduce our de-burring time: socks, pants, shirts and Mose, Mark's big chocolate Labrador. Silly me, but some impossible missions are irresistible.

In complexity and fascination, these compulsive missions grew with the new trees. Major discovery: Deer generally prefer cherry trees, but the sudden availability of springtime oak leaf salad with its delectable sap as dressing equaled adding milkshakes to a menu limited to milk. The electric fence was no deterrent. Deer repellent worked, but had to be sprayed on each tree individually and again after heavy rains. Pruning side branches indeed speeded vertical growth—to get the tops to grow above browse level—but also put them off-kilter. The saplings shot up like teenagers and behaved accordingly: they turned gangly and askew, sometimes enough to require forcible return to the straight and narrow with the aid of stakes, braces and twine. Their immature bark made them look naked, and not only to me. Just before the rut, when feeling "horny" could not be more literal, the bucks found the cherry's polished skin irresistibly inviting for removing the fuzzy sheath from their antlers.

Then there was the bramble conundrum. We had purposefully planted the whips randomly, to avoid the look of row-reforestation. At the tip of each we tied bits of torn bedsheet soaked in Deer-Away, the commercial high-concentration of putrescent egg. The white flags also made the whips easy to locate ... until the raspberry onslaught. Suddenly we found ourselves with acres, whole ravines of them. Blackberries, too, some of them eight feet tall. So many, so thick, so tall as to turn a confirmed berry lover sour. Meanwhile, the predicted comeback of maple, ash, ironwood and elderberry had been making up for whiling away years, decades, who-knows-how-long in the shade, awaiting their main chance in the sun.

Other strange perceptions: in the remaining mature woods, the forest floor stays brown all year because crowns block most of the sunlight. The tornado gashes bandaged themselves in brilliant light green speckled with flowers and berries and thick with insects, many of them of the non-blood sucking, beautiful varieties. They register life—determined, even furious new life—and with it new twists in old trade-offs. When we built the electric fence around the orchard, the deer quickly adjusted their diet, stripping the trillium that had turned the valley's south facing slope a nodding white. Now, with so much additional browse, the flowers are coming back and bringing yellow trout lilies with them.

In a favorite recent book, *A Woman in Berlin*, an anonymous (later identified as Marta Hillers) German journalist tells of being young and female when the Russians crashed through Nazi defenses at the end of World War II. Was her repeated rape pleasant? Of course not. But by attaching herself to one Russian officer she gained food, shelter and protection from his marauding troops. Biggest surprise: in an out-of-body moment, she casts herself as a fictional poltergeist, writing in the third person:

> *For three heartbeats her body became one with the unfamiliar body on top of her. Her nails dug into the stranger's hair. She heard the cries coming from her own throat and the stranger's voice whispering words she couldn't understand. Fifteen minutes later she was all alone.*

Ask whether I feel raped by tornadoes and I'll say, of course, in the sense that crime victims often describe themselves as "violated." But there's no doubt about the pleasure—the pleasure, not just relief—of survival. Recovery is another matter.

ON THE WAY TO THE BEACH, Julia and I stop the ATV dead because of something very young and tiny. A ruffed grouse chick has jumped up on a tangle pile bulldozed to clear the road through the blowdown. We hadn't seen a grouse in years. This one was clearly from the present year's hatch, an adolescent with that know-all/know-nothing expression all creatures share at that stage. It had probably spent all three months of life in the raspberries that had taken over what had been the deepest and darkest part of the woods, the home of the biggest trees. Since nothing as bizarre as us had ever passed its way, it turns its head to one side to ponder us the way our sons did when considering major new phenomena. In any species, this particular size-up pose suggests nonchalance; really, it masks a bottomless bog of ignorance, some of it dangerous. To us — two duffers in our sixties — delight and a little wonder descend. Surprise, too, because destruction suppresses hope, not to mention the knowledge that grouse are indifferent to majestic trees like the ones we spend so much time mourning. No underbrush, no food. These aristocrats of game birds love tangles.

ELSIE AND THE OTHER TREES [12]

August, 1999

Optimists plant orchards. Ironists maintain them. While just as chancy an investment as anything else in agriculture, orchards take longer to pay off, even if everything goes perfectly (which it never does), goes well (seldom), or so-so (the most farmers can hope for). Thus, the sane orchardist feels insane, or at least suspects internal disorder as soon as the enormity of reality comes into focus. When the fruit comes in, when you think manna will flow your way forever — paltry as it may be — the mist of unsettled psychic weather is replaced by a thunderbolt. It's not the death of trees that's so bad, but the realization that outliving the trees you planted as tiny whips makes you very, very old. Orchards are not for everyone.

Yet one of George Washington's first entries in his horticultural diary reported the receipt of cherry tree whips from a neighbor. Thomas Jefferson planted 1,200 fruit trees at Monticello, grafting limbs on peaches as well as branches on governments. In addition to becoming France's most famous dramatist of the eighteenth century — and chief literary tormen-

---

12   A note about the title: to understand it without explanation you must have been a child in the 1940s or early 1950s when "Elsie, the Contented Cow" was the poster female for Borden's condensed milk. While the test of the herd might be agitated by milking schedules, errant bulls or whatever, Elsie was shown on every red-and-white can, dreamily gazing back from an endless recline, the picture of contentment with things just as — permanently as — they were.

161

tor of both monarchy and religion—François-Marie Arouet (aka Voltaire) was admired for the peaches he planted at his estate at Ferney. The orchard was also noted for lying a mere four miles from the Swiss border. Imprisoned once by his countrymen, he had no intention of repeating the experience. More recently, author John Fowles kept a few fruit trees in the garden of his house overlooking the sea in Lyme Regis, Devon. He wrote *The French Lieutenant's Woman* there, but more germane to present purposes, he also produced a little book in honor of trees, inspired by a pathetic backyard grove his father—whom he thought missed the big things in life—doted upon in lieu of his wordy son.

Orchards make large impressions on those who tend them. I think this is because, while they look straightforward enough, they are full of surprises. Effortlessly, they blend aspects of human perception that otherwise stay apart, un-combinable, like oil and water: economics and predictability; economics and unpredictability; wisdom and folly; utility and frivolity, whim and plan. As an example, there won't be any commercial return on your investment for five to seven years, a period during which any decent stockbroker can double your money. Meanwhile, you pay taxes. Then there are the monumental costs of "planting," a serious misnomer.

Let's talk about planting. There's lots to do before anything that might produce money comes anywhere near your ground. First, you deep-plow to kill weeds, break up the soil and remix its ingredients. Next comes fumigation against mold and microbes, as if your acres were hospital wards. Cultivate again to invite worms, one of only two welcome tenants (the other is bees) among the dozens you will try to evict until they simply outlive you. Finally, you lime to balance soil chemistry. Only then, after a mere twelve months of preparations, may you lay out the rows.

At this point you encounter one of the orchardist's great imponderables: Who decides where trees get planted? Given your obvious commitment to the enterprise, your sensitivities to the ecology and aesthetics involved, you might think this too obvious to mention. But only in a general way do you or your topography have a say. In fact, the decision rests with the people in Oregon or California or Japan who build the harvesting machines. The size and turning radius of these behemoths predicate where the fence lines, rows and the trees themselves will go.

Making matters even more unpredictable, every ten years or so machine builders change their minds.

So, let's say your trees live fifty years. That length of time has brought us from implements the width of a horse-drawn wagon loaded with step-ladders and the housewives and kid-pickers who climbed them to the quarter-million-dollar harvesters that come in two self-propelled pieces the length of small yachts. These cherry shaking machines require two separate rows to operate and an open ocean of room for turning around. Your job, new orchard owner, is to predict the future. In the probable case that you are proved wrong over the next several decades, you'll have to start over ... and remember how long that takes. Everyone around you with a soybean field will have taken six crops to market. A fecund future will be what you dream about, and also what you'll discuss endlessly at Darlene's, or whatever the name of the cafe is in the little town near your place, where everyone harvests the misfortunes of others over breakfast coffee.

But back to getting those trees into rows. Orchards are basically forests laid out for economic convenience. This means density: one hundred tart cherry trees to the acre. Even if you've laid out the commercial minimum of twenty acres, you're going to need little whips—each a little over a half-inch thick and about four feet tall—by the thousand. And you'll need hired hands to plant and water them, which will probably get you into the intricacies of migrant labor. Then, there's the fertilizer formula to nurse the little darlings; the seed for erosion-control sod strips between their rows; showers of herbicides to kill the weeds; and the pesticide and fungicide treatments to keep away the creatures that munch in the night.

As for the things that go *bump* in the night, you wire the entire perimeter with a twelve-foot stalag through which runs a 7,000-volt alternating current. This deters most of the deer, but never all. Your compound will keep out the crawlers, but not the jumpers. This quickly comes down to individuals: crawlers get zapped—and deterred—because their feet act as a ground and the current goes through their bodies like lightening. Without the necessary ground, jumpers don't notice anything except the occasional scrape of the wires, indistinguishable from the branches they encounter every day. They develop no natural deterrent against repeating their crimes and so, to eliminate or at least control the jumping gene in the DNA of the local herd, you shoot the offenders. Your family is going to be more concerned—and more whiny—about "Bambi" than you ever imagined.

You're going to have other mendicants: raccoons, opossums and porcupines too heavy for fruit-laden limbs, which break; squirrels happy to find soft, red "nuts" they don't have to crack open; and, of course, the flocks of birds. But all of these merely maim and rob your investment; they don't kill it. And so, although they are all impervious to the fence you have installed at considerable cost and a hike in your liability insurance payments, you let them have their way, mostly from exhaustion. Only a few of our neighbors resort to cherry "cannons," which fire noisy blank shots at timed intervals. After the first couple of explosions of the season this causes no more interruption of mealtime than the moment it takes a few hundred birds to look up from their devouring and, maybe, cock heads or flutter up a foot or two.

Yet, somehow, perhaps because of the length of peacefulness induced by the long winters at our latitude, halfway between the equator and the north pole—at a precise moment in May, it all seems unaccountably worth it. A blooming orchard captivates every one of your senses. It buzzes, chirps and smells. It feels velvety. Above dark red trunks, a cloud of white floats between a brilliant first-growth green speckled gold with dandelion and a sky never again to be so brilliant a blue. Four months of snow cover prevent dust from softening the color and the line of the horizon. In May, the sky is as distinctly blue as a baby's eye. It is a day you just do not miss. After six of them, you'll know if you have an Elsie.

Elsies shame all the others at budding-out time. My Elsie loved flowering so much that had she been able to speak words—in addition to her other expressive behaviors—it would have been irrelevant. What luscious blooms! Orchards are full of sex and Elsie was up for the pleasures. Bees loved her to pieces. Pollen grains festooned her pistils in their hundreds of thousands. I know that it sounds a little odd to phrase things so directly in an age of euphemism, but it is the intimacy of my first official orchard interaction of the year that must be understood, and I have discovered that political correctness only applies to everyday speech. Completely different rules govern clinical talk and visual images.

So, let's get clinical. What we perform in the orchard at this time of year is a sort of pregnancy test. With exquisitely intimate examination, we determine what proportion of tiny black dots of the male principal have made it past a Montmorency flower's very recognizable yellow labia and into a translucent uterus of exquisite tenderness on its way to its ultimate rendezvous in an ovary. I return a day or so later to feel the ovaries themselves: swelling means cherry. This OBGYN-behavior is how you predict your crop.

By age nineteen, Elsie stood out. She was a couple of feet taller and at least that much broader all around her crown, towering over neighbors and shading the alleys between her row and those on either side. From the observation tower atop our house, there was a sea of trees ... and there was Elsie. However, all her strength had gone into bodybuilding. She had never been picked, because there was never anything *to* pick. Nothing. Never a single cherry after all those millions of gorgeous flowers. Elsie's idea of planned parenthood was promiscuity on a scale to shame anything the animal kingdom might nominate for comparison, and then to sit the rest of the whole thing gloriously, contentedly, ostentatiously, out. She rewarded all the purest appetites for growth, beauty and health, but would have no part of that base pursuit, production.

Elsie herself was tree No. 5 in row No. 7 of a 163-row, 2,200-tree plantation of Montmorencies, the variety of tart cherry dominant in our district. In a good year, the orange-red of their fruit—it's the color that determines their value—makes the branches glisten. A late afternoon sun can turn a row neon. In a great year, every bit of wood on the trees bow under a weight that is eighty percent water and can come close to 200 pounds. That's quite a lot for a tree that never grows taller than fifteen feet. If the fruit were allowed to ripen, then drop naturally, the roots could make up the difference from groundwater. But a harvest is like childbirth, beginning with the violent breaking of the water. And, while a human picker might strip a tree in an hour, mechanical shakers do it in under ten seconds. Call it an induction. Within minutes, the leaves twist and shrivel. Branches abruptly droop. The tree looks, well, *post-partum*. It is a dangerous time. If a particularly heavy crop is followed by a prolonged dry spell, the tree may have reproduced itself to death by dehydration. Even in a good season there are risks. If the cherry shaker's mechanical coupling that fits around the trunk "barks" the tree—meaning cracks open the skin—the result can also be fatal. Deadly white fungus attacks exposed veins and the tree often dies after the second season.

Somehow, the Elsies of the world know all of this and take appropriate action. I loved her for her beauty, to be sure. But she was a great teacher, too. In a population seemingly of one mind about the prime business of the community, Elsie proved an outlier. Is the goal of multiculturalism really to assure variety? There is as much variety in any one variety as you care to look for, at least after learning how to look. Aberrant reproductive patterns aren't the only variations from what cherry trees ought to be—are thought to be—ought to be thought to be—and Elsie wasn't the only instructor. Some trees think—know—that they were meant to be bushes, no matter what efforts are made to shape them. I took this particular class at a time when national attention was focused on the proclivity part of the gender wars. If some trees/people needed to be different, why should we expect them to change merely because we tried to prune away behavior not in line with how we wanted our rows/population to look in school, church, wherever?

But back to the trees. You start with whips about four feet high. If they have branches, you learn to lop them off immediately, along with at least one foot of height. Since whips are priced by height (a four-footer Montmorency costs twenty-five percent more than a three-footer, being one year older) and your goal is to have them reach bearing height (about eight feet) as quickly as possible, this is a painful act requiring the discipline of dieting. This is drastic medicine. You've got to equalize the leaf area, which loses water, with the root area, which takes it in and which any transplanting drastically reduces. Otherwise trees hyperventilate. To some this means dying of thirst. Others go into a kind of shock that takes more years of recovery than the initial surgery.

Trees in "shock"? Shock and more. Beyond ER amputation—I'd call it circumcision, but the metaphor would invite delusionary machismo—cutting off the fast-growing tip of the whip also forces the tree to strengthen its main shaft. This is not aesthetic; it's industrial. Without four feet of clear, branchless trunk, a tree cannot be mechanically harvested. Some trees, however, just don't care. I have two that insist on being bushes and a few more that grow back into slingshots no matter how many times I discipline them with lopping shears.

And that's just the start. Pruning goes on for the life of the tree. True, these days, that's only half the sixty years of productive life they had before mechanical shaking came along, but thirty years is still a long time. (Just think of a stalk of corn; almost as tall as an adolescent Montmorency and dead by October.) A good pruner starts with the theory of "the fruit basket," even though while being a descriptive term it describes the wrong thing. It should be called a "sunshine basket," but somehow I can't picture anyone I know who works in or owns orchards using such a term. The fruit basket is a hollow place sculpted out of the center of the tree by removing any and all branches that grow inwards. The idea is to let in maximum sunlight so that the cherries on the lower branches ripen along with the ones on top—which would otherwise be shaded. This is all very well for personkind, particularly the sort that hangs out in college "Hort." departments. But not all trees want to behave or even comply. They don't want basketry. It's density they're after, and they simply flat out refuse the alternatives.

Nor, necessarily, does the orchardist's discovery and discipline progress in a predictable, linear fashion. At about year four, when the whips are maybe eight feet tall but still largely unbranched—just as we want them to be—they are discovered by the young bucks of the neighborhood. Yes, I mean the animal. Bucks need resistance to scrape the velvet from their antlers. A big tree is no good because antlers aren't straight; they need a spring action to maintain pressure along the curves, forks and tight places. To do this properly, you've got to get your antlers in close to the trunk. It's tedious work in the best of circumstances, like sharpening kitchen knives to prepare the vegetables after the dinner guests have already arrived and the power party of the year is about to begin. Maybe that's not the right metaphor. Antler-sharpening coincides with a towering horniness—ever wonder where *that* expression came from?—a horniness that comes (this keeps getting worse) but once a year. You can't concentrate on anything else but urge. Something like a little twig jabbing you in the nose or poking you in the eye when you've got to get going to do your thing with all the girls you can find because they're only in the mood once a year—but I mean *really* in the mood *right now*—and when nearly anything with antlers will do. Any little irritant at a moment like that might cause you an outburst. Like bashing down the goddamned little whip of a tree. Or chomping its top off. You do a little of that. But mostly you look for a place where there are lots of small trees with just the right amount of spring in the trunk and no lower branches. One year, an entire plantation of 350 trees had to be replaced because of its discovery by a herd of deer as spring salad greens and the next fall as filing tools for antlers.

THIS YEAR, I CUT ELSIE DOWN. Rather, I didn't move to save her when her row was marked for the bulldozer. Was I through with her? Are we ever through with our favorites? Like the best secrets, the ones that nobody ever discovers, Elsie's was more precious than any revelation. Whatever lie I told to save her would risk just the sort of tear in the mutual respect that someone who owns land, but tends it only part-time, cannot risk. The best things about orchards are secret. You can't easily admit to the guys on the tractors that the reason you want to keep a non-bearing tree like Elsie is that she's gorgeous in bloom and that you like her obstinance. Or, that you've named her and occasionally talk to her. Or that you have speculated whether trees can be lesbians—let alone admit that she's a muse. Better not talk about muses at all. In America, success at gentleman farming permits you to be a little odd—after all, it's expected—but dictates strict limits on *how* odd. Too odd and the mowing waits, the picking's late, the fences sag. The only way I could think of to protect Elsie was to not mention her existence, or at least her strange proclivity. It's not unusual for single trees, or small groups of them, to behave oddly in a given year. Frost may have lingered around them a critical few minutes. A disease or insect attack may have weakened them. Men working dawn (5 AM) to dusk (10:30 PM) during harvest at our latitude are not in a mood to ponder the likes of Elsie's inner motivations. Not having to shake that particular tree lets them through the row a little quicker, to a cold, foaming "roady" in a bouncing pickup and home.

Along with the bill for removing Elsie and the other trees came a scribble announcing that the 'dozers had spared "the party trees." I had no idea we had something called "party trees," but I knew what it meant:

the four trees under which we move the grills and tables for an annual high harvest barbecue just before shaking. The bill came from the crew foreman—not the sort to respect a fool. Risk adding "a mistress tree" to the "party trees" already in the folklore? Certainly not. The bugs, fungi, weeds, freezes, deer, porcupines and markets—all of which conspire to make orchardry an optimist's game—remind you with each chomp, blight, kill and glut that what you've got most of in your inventory is risk. No need for more.

Before learning this principle, I was less careful. We—all of us, including the tiny boys and Irene, the Buenos Aires *au pair* who came home with us—used to parade around our disregard for local standards in gaucho sombreros and burgundy *panchos Saltanos*—uppity even for a tolerant place like East Jordan. Small wonder that when I inspected our brand-new orchard in the spring of 1977, it was impossible not to notice a sign of rather eloquent contempt. Near the gate, where I couldn't miss it, a single tree had been planted upside-down, roots in the air. Did it say "ignorant fool" because I wouldn't know the difference, or care, or both? You bet. Did I also have my head "where the sun don't shine?" Some gestures need no translation. In a very, very old way, we were being told that we should behave ourselves. That with our fancy educations, a house we didn't really need and orchard we worked only when we wanted to, we were setting ourselves up as examples. The expectation was that we would be decent examples. Remembering Hervé de Carmoy's pungent summary of the periodically murderous relationship of the landed French with their neighbors, I replanted the tree without comment. And the Argentine costumery was quietly retired to the closets.

ELSIE'S SINGULARITY didn't change the way I looked at the world, but it did open up a whole side of it that I hadn't been able to see before. Suddenly, any group was a collection of individuals; any species, an aggregation of personalities. It's common to joke about "(fill-in-blank) all looking alike." But what about other things?

I'm a fisherman. All of a sudden, the well-known differences in the way rainbows and brook trout fight, for example, were only half the story. Each individual fish has a survival strategy which, like our own,

reveals itself only in survival situations. Finding, suddenly, that a food bug is attached to something that thinks *you* are the food is surely one of them. Some fish throw everything into an instant frenzy, ending quickly in freedom or exhaustion. Others wait, or hide, or jump, maybe to take the measure of the tormentor. What is my survival singularity? Do I run downstream with the current like most rainbows, or hopelessly swim against it like a brook trout? Am I a rainbow with the strategy of a brookie? What about the President? The country? The human race or a single cancer cell? Would I have left Nazi Germany ahead of a round-up for the death camps? Vietnam provided a dry-run test case early on, and I recognized the impulse that would have saved me had I been alone. But I also saw my life with a wife and children, they who would link my survival with theirs, possibly fatally. Like all aspects of familiar landscapes, orchards are memory banks. To me, it seems natural for an individual cherry tree to help probe the past of life, even run reality checks on brainstem survival reflexes patterned with heredity in the genes.

The spring preceding Elsie's unceremonious—and unwitnessed—bulldozing, I photographed her in full bloom. I was out to capture the contrast between her branches and those of lesser rowmates around her. Some difference was still visible to the eye, but not much. Her distinctions—and distinctiveness—were by then in me, not her. Elsie had become part of what I'm becoming, here in my row, year after year.

LIFE POWER AND ESCAPE TECHNIQUES

July, 1998

Post-9/11, the Empire State building is again the tallest in New York. It's 1,254 feet high, counting the spire that famously failed its intended purpose. Okay, so nobody even tried mooring a Zeppelin there, but all agreed that the cloud-scratcher looked great. Even greater though, the shaft earned forever-status as a movie hang-from-bar for King Kong. All to the point in an essay about the unlikely, beginning with basics: The perimeter of the Empire State's base is 1,222 feet. That makes a height-to-base ratio of a little more than 1:1. Dubai's Burj Khalifa, more than twice as tall at 2,722 feet, has a more impressive height-to-base ratio, but only by an order or two of magnitude. Construction time for the Empire State, three years; Burj Khalifa, four. Big deal.

Every year, the unmown, big bluestem grass between the orchard and the east lawn produces a living structural marvel when compared to the modest achievements of steel, bricks and glass. In the two months between May sprout and June flowering, bluestem builds to seven feet on a base so economical that envy must be the only response by those interested in construction footprints. The height-to-base ratio I measured this morning is seven feet by one-eighth of an inch, or about 1:420. That means that a King Kong atop something 420 times higher than the Empire State's mast would need a space suit: he'd be at the low end of Sputnik's orbit in space.

That's just the beginning. Most inanimate structures taper to avoid top-heavy vulnerability to hostile forces. In the earliest human experi-

171

ence, this would have involved gods like Zeus, who threw thunderbolts, or Yahweh, who smote the tower of Babel—a gesture so eloquently mighty that it shattered the one-tongue monopoly, too. Picture the Eiffel Tower with its swoop to 985 feet on those gracefully curved legs over a base 1,312 feet around. Ratio: an uninspiring 1:1.3. Now imagine structures like grass stem leaves, sprouting from the sides of the tower and made of the same material (steel). On the scale of the bluestem, they would extend beyond the limits of the *Champ de Mars* to the banks of the Seine. Finally, consider that leaves on a stem of grass only grow on the sides of the stem facing sunlight; so to mimic that, imagine adding giant steel sheets on only one side. Result: a tower so imbalanced that the most paltry of gods would have no trouble toppling it, if anyone managed to construct it in the first place.

There's more. Even before the first frost, life begins receding from the living tower, flowing downward into the leaves at its base, then into the roots. Without the life force, the tower possesses no magic: Dormancy demands that the structure obey the rules of mechanical engineering. Come the first strong wind of fall—of the same or even less velocity than it has withstood all summer—and the towers blow down. What was in the stem to hold it upright? What was in its roots to anchor it?

We'll start with roots. Chances are, gentle reader, your normal references do not include what's available at Overlook Farm — not only the notes on what a season does to big bluestem architecture, but also exercises involving bushes. It's impossible to contrast the relative efforts of pulling living and dead honeysuckle bushes out of the ground with a power winch. Or how a perfectly ordinary device with a 7,000-pound pulling capacity mounted on the back of the farm's Suburban provides a positively religious experience. Lo, an ingot-like rootball it would take hundreds of muscle spasms to dig up glides toward you in the clutches of a collar of chain. Live or dead, an uprooted lilac that spent the last hundred years making sure its ever-spreading, underground mountain of a foundation would anchor it forever creates a chill when winched slowly, root by root, from the earth. Its obedient approach makes a Mohammed of you. But there's a huge difference between raising the living and the dead. A dead bush comes out of the ground with a lack of struggle that makes the vanquishing small and your deification correspondingly modest. But a *live* bush! It holds onto the earth like, well, dear life itself. As if every cell, capillary and tendril knew that its existence depended on maintaining its grip, as indeed it does. Your difficulties overpowering the life force are of a geometrically higher order, the difference between putting a dead cat where you want it and making a live one go there.

Yes, I'm aware that science can explain all of this in terms of the effect of water on organic materials and how it gets to them. But why? Science does not answer the ultimate *whys*, which are the things of ultimate interest. To understand the *why* of mechanical engineering and the inexplicable strength that living — indulge me just for a minute for calling it "spirit" — imparts to a bunch of molecules, it helps to experience both the winching of honeysuckle and the contemplation of serious human design. For this sort of thing, a small farm in northern Michigan is ideal.

Life strategies have inspired warehouses of books supporting and debunking the theory of evolution. My subject is narrower, but assuredly not smaller: wonder. I am thrilled to be sharing a patch of earth and, concurrently, a separate existence with nearby white ash and cutleaf maple trees. I neither pretend nor want to know them in taxonomical detail any more than I do our neighbors. For one thing, our interactions are more violent than the law permits among humans, in that they include amputation-by-chainsaw. I am more attentive, too, beginning with the appreciation of their beauty. I spend more time contemplating the size and comeliness of their various parts than would be seemly among individuals of my own kind. But I didn't mention perfection; even the most gorgeous can do with little more here — or more often, a little less. Let us talk post-amputation survival strategies.

Cut the top off an ash and the next year it grows six, eight, dozens — on a big one, hundreds — of replacement trunklets, some of them shooting up four feet in a single growing season. Ash strategy goes for height. A topped ash almost never opts for lateral branching if a side limb is pruned; the wound simply heals with no replacement. Duly noted, all of this, by people long ago who domesticated the ash and some other hardwoods as the sort of cooking fire equivalent to a milk cow. Because they are narrow, the top shoots dry quickly into light, easily-handled kindling. Even with woodstoves long replaced, trees all over the French and northern Italian countryside echo a previous utility in shapes that look "Thalidomided" (Julia's term) to American sensibilities, with sturdy trunk bases distinctly out of proportion to the spindly tops and at heights convenient to a man with a hatchet.

Hydra-heads work for ashes, but some trees have alternative ideas. All apple-pruners know what happens when you trim a side branch. Unlike ash, another sprout — usually several sprouts — grow from the same spot again, and again, and again, even though you'd think the repeated message from shears or saw would communicate, *Not here, please.* A few years ago, I went to work on a big cutleaf maple whose lower branches blocked the straight-line view from my writing table to the orchard. Off they went. I expected re-growth, but not *that* re-growth. Instead of sprouting outward from the trunk — as had the original limb, and indeed all others on that and every other tree I've surgeoned — the prosthesis limbs grew tightly against the trunk. And I do mean tightly. As tight as two fingers pressed together. When the leaves were gone, they camouflaged themselves perfectly with the trunk's bark ridges that also ran vertically. Two years on, it took quite a tussle to get a pole-pruner saw blade past the defenses of these young offshoots.

White (or paper, or canoe) birches are the most poignant of trees, with their delicate bark, their link to the lost ways of the Indians, their beautiful shapes and their leaves that register a breeze before most others. The striking beauty of a big birch at the northwest corner of our clearing invited me to remove the large ash that had matured as its inter-rooted life companion. The result was gorgeous, but still imperfect. A long, low horizontal branch was painfully colliding with my head while mowing, brush-whacking or ambulatory daydreaming. The effect on the tree, however, of the loss of its leg-sized limb was nearly as immediate, certainly more dramatic and infinitely longer lasting. Within days the leaves on that side of the tree drooped. Temporary, I thought — I hoped. Not so. The wilt lasted right into autumn leaf-drop. Nor did things end there. The following spring the leaves that had gone limp the year before grew back healthily stiff, but half the normal size and decidedly smaller than on the side of the tree unaffected by pruning. This imbalance persisted throughout a full three years of mourning, something akin to the many reports of amputees continuing to feel real pain from a phantom limb. I don't mean to suggest a botanical nervous system, or plant consciousness — not quite, anyway. But failing to appreciate life strategies where you live amounts to travel without noticing the different languages being spoken.[13]

AT TWENTY-FOUR, OUR YOUNGER SON Mark called to say, "Hi, Dad. I have a brain tumor." It was May, 1995. He was in Providence, studying painting and sculpture at Rhode Island School of Design. I had been doing Saturday don't-know-whats at my desk in Ann Arbor. After the expectable questions and screaming uncertainties of the answers, my conscious self left where it usually lives to crawl into the darkest place. I was sitting where I had been, where to anyone else I would have looked like someone doing Saturday don't-know-whats, but in fact the tissues and body electricity I had relied on all my life had been lopped off. Amputation of a psychic limb? Maybe I'd been topped.

Loss — but not fear, yet, or even loneliness — spread through the empty house, a home that suddenly felt huge and haunted. (Julia was visiting her parents in Washington, D.C.) I felt no imperative, or even temptation, to see or say anything out loud, to anyone. All I could control, at least temporarily, was time. I could make it stand still for as long as nobody else knew how my life path had been chain-sawed. And, in those first hours, standing still seemed like the most important thing I could do.

I don't know how long I sat staring at the notes I'd made from what Mark told me in the same tone reserved for reporting complications with art school "crits" (critiques). I wasn't seeing paper with ballpoint scribble. Whatever I was looking at — carefully, carefully — was behind my eyes in the dark place.

If he should die, what would it mean? What chances had I missed with him, with what consequences to be regretted? Who needed to be

---

13   Of the several books on the unexpectedly animal-like features of a plant's behavior, the inimitable Peter Wohlleben's *The Hidden Life of Trees* stands out. His subtitle doesn't come near saying it all, but suffices for present purposes: *What They Feel, How They Communicate.* Not that his scientific mastery supplies the magic — quite the contrary. It's that he allows a lifetime of caring for a single forest to inform when science rests mute.

notified? What could be done to help? In the dark place there is no order or hierarchy of importance. Those considerations took on an absurd
artificiality, like the sentence meted out to the living in punishment for
leaving someone you love dead. When I went out for the walk I thought
might clear my thinking, it did: I would sort things out at the farm. Not
so my vision, though, hopelessly blurred by tears. I ran into a tree.

Mark lived. The *polycitic astrocytoma* we came to call "Mr. T." (for
tumor), was the size of a lemon and growing too close to the brain stem
for conventional surgery. It wasn't cancerous; it didn't need to be. Mr.
T., all by himself, was filling a sack with fluid. With no place to drain,
he would expand like a balloon, gradually—or not gradually, one of the
many unknown aspects of his personality—squishing brain tissue into
non-function. This seemed to begin with the electrical circuitry, as the
left quadrant of Mark's vision had begun fading after a second seizure.

FROM THE TIME he could hold a pencil, Mark drew. He was a natural talent of the type incomprehensible to the rest of us. When tiny, his
crayoned stick figures fell in ways that severed their limbs. Later, it was
soldiers dying in splats of gore, football pile-ups, then more sophisticated
war destruction. Nearly all done without color, an afterthought to the
violence of line. Action was all.

Picture the Sistine Chapel ceiling and the finger of God nearly touch-
ing the finger of Adam. Michelangelo allegedly began the drawing at
the tip of God's forefinger, and until I watched my eight-year-old do the
same, I considered it the province of major genius and careful training.
Nope, just talent. Having none, I always started with, say, an oval for a
face. Mark's miraculous gift of line seemed like enough to sustain a life's
work. A professor friend once let me take him to an undergraduate still-
life class where a teaching assistant leaned over for a better look at my
small artist's rendition. As he did so, Mark sketched his profile. "Break
that kid's pencils," whispered the instructor.

In art school Mark continued the concentration on line right up to
the moment in his sophomore year when he made his call about the
tumor. We were twenty-three and fifty-four: Mark too old to be told
what to do and me old enough to recognize a gap that would complicate
a delicate calculation. At minimum, whatever came next would risk an

impaired life. Whatever happened would change everything for all of us. None had confronted anything of the like.

During the exploratory biopsy we learned that things were actually worse. The harmless-sounding phrase in this situation meant full-scale brain surgery to sink a probe through the brain's speech, sight and thinking centers to extract a test piece of what Mr. T. might be made of. Before we had quite

AT EIGHT, MARK DREW NOTHING BUT VIOLENCE. WHO WON? WE ALL DID

processed this—our previous understanding of biopsies involved shallow tests and pap smears—we were invited into the operating room. Our son / brother / fishing buddy / family / artist lay strapped to a table looking ready for execution. Screwed into his skull, a modern surgical equivalent to the medieval torture devices that "put the screws" to victims. The probe required motionlessness. Mark was sedated but awake. Fear screamed in his eyes, the only movement in his head that was possible. Each of us clutched a hand or a foot—anything to keep him with us—too terrified for tears.

Hulking, Germanic, commanding, the surgeon appeared after the procedure. Scalpel work was not recommended. That left two somethings called a laser knife and conventional radiation. While he worked up a formal report, I felt an old and trusted instinct click on in this most unfamiliar setting—journalism. Something in this man's tone sounded familiar—a note not quite true. Afterwards, I replayed the exchange as a sort of out-of-body experience, in which a David-size journalist with no medical training turns himself loose on a six-foot, four-inch Goliath surgeon whose blondness and Austrian accent somehow increased his authority... and my suspicion of it.

Surgeon: The gamma knife has a one-hundred percent effectiveness in killing such tumors and killing them immediately. Mark's tumor would stop making fluid, and the existing volume would be drained. The laser would not harm intervening tissue. This is the obvious way to go, and we are lucky to be at one of the few hospitals in America that have made the wise commitment to buy such an expensive device, imported from Sweden.

Reporter: What are the downsides? None? Everything has downsides. Ah. So intervening tissue would not be harmed, but there's a chance that tissue adjoining the tumor might be? Tiny capillaries that feed other parts of the brain? Necrosis? The damage might register only after three years? Oh, it was you who made the pitch to the hospital to buy the expensive laser knife?

Metaphorically filling a reporter's notebook convinced me that my "source" was selling self-interest and Mark was just another case to justify his hospital's large investment. The "story" quickly took shape. Following laser knifing, Mr. T. would be pronounced dead. Mark would be out of danger and we would all rejoice—except when we remembered that somewhere deep inside Mark's brain, tiny blood vessels might be atrophying. More of the left quadrant of his vision—already damaged—would be the first to fade. Then more seizures. Speech would go next. And we wouldn't really know the surgery was a success until it was too late to do anything else!

Get rid of Mr. T. Now. Kill it. Take it out. Get me off the hook so I go on with my life. That's all Mark said, and who could argue with any of it? But I needed to think clearly. That meant the farm, where the pros are best dealt with the cons of difficult problems.

Every alarm bell clanged my psychic belfry to deaf numbness. In reporting business failures, awful crimes and politics from local to presidential, my journalistic instincts had not failed me. What I saw in the surgeon was a man who had staked his career—or a good part of it—on persuading the board of a middle-size hospital to buy a device with a king-size price and the paying customers to justify it. I didn't need medical expertise any more than I had needed to know everything about Chile to peg Augusto Pinochet as a ruthless killer. But it wasn't my brain Mr. T. was squishing.

Mark was between panic and the cold calculation of endgame. His age straddled the rim of adulthood, where doubt and fear begin to counterbalance perceived invulnerability. It's the stage where you still go out on the South Arm ice, but only after considering that it might not take your weight. It's when soldiers still volunteer for particularly dangerous patrols, but not thoughtlessly, as they would have a few years earlier. Being Dad wouldn't work, so I shifted to the other familiar role of fishing buddy. Together, Mark and I had sized up outfitters in the familiar unpredictability of the Ungava territory, where an overloaded seaplane, a pilot with booze on his breath or a guide who didn't know the terrain have consequences we understood. We should at least have a look at another doctor, another hospital. Someplace where, I silently hoped, the considerations could be purely medical and all about my son, not a cost/benefit analysis of a machine and a doctor's career.

Mark made the call I hoped he would and it worked. Mr. T. remained a tenant-for-life in his brain, but a quiet one, unable to cause further damage by refilling a lethal sack with fluid. Six months later, he invited us to an exhibition of his first post-radiation paintings. I would not have recognized them as having anything to do with my son's work, which I had tracked since he was two: they were huge, abstract and all color. There was no drawing, whatsoever. Nor, I marveled, any link to past work. He wouldn't discuss whether or not Mr. T.—who might have moved in recently or been with him from birth, we never learned—had somehow restricted him to line. Or, whether the black strokes explosively set off by orange flashes celebrated goodbye to Mr. T. All he would say was, "Don't you remember the treasure board?"

Our theory of summers at Overlook Farm was that if 146 acres of bugs, butterflies, flowers, ferns, forest, mushrooms, songbirds, game birds, reptiles, deer, raccoons and eagles on the shore of a lake containing equivalent marvels in aquatic form couldn't occupy the minds and spirits of young boys, well, then, nothing else was likely to interest them, either. Understanding what Ben had done with those thousands of hours of unstructured summer was easy; Mark's internalization wasn't so obvious. Very few birds, bucks or fish appeared in hundreds of pages of large pad drawings. Overwhelmingly, their subject was the violence of scrums so thick that the struggling bodies formed a solid mass. Or soldiers dismembering foes, bleeding profusely, falling to their deaths from cliffs, the sky, or just plain falling. At the same time, however, "treasures" — old bits of farm implements and farm life from the last hundred years — were emerging from the former barnyard that became our unmanageably huge organic garden and were being wired to a peg board at the door leading to the terrace. Mark passed the board every time he carried a plate out to the picnic table where we ate most summer meals. The red evening light intensified the rust color of every edge: the saddle leather punch, the lynch pin, the hay rake tine. Now, in Mark's Providence studio, in a flood of the colorless, cut glass light of a New England morning, I tried to see what these paintings had to do with that board. Maybe how the black strokes separated items of other interest in color and shape? Maybe that shade of rust color so predominant in several? "Maybe," Mark said.

THINKING SPORTSMEN can't escape noticing escape strategies. In fact, producing, bearing witness and being part of death struggles is probably the most fascinating — and most deeply sublimated — aspect of all hunting, catch-and-release included. Fishermen relish the "fight," which is really how a particular species goes about the business of remaining alive. Fishermen mourn "the big one that got away," but more often that not, that is the fish not forgotten.

Without really trying, I could tell you about "Lumber Lips," the outsized smallmouth bass that said goodbye to me off Hemingway Point while my two sons and brother-in-law witnessed how it bent the rod double and broke my heart. Or the mighty tarpon that a hammerhead shark ate all of but the head before I could land and release it off Bahia Honda in the Florida Keys. Not to mention the brown trout, way too big for a stream as small as the headwaters of the Pigeon River, that exploded out from under a snag and broke Ben's bamboo rod just after we spotted its nose in a shaft of light between shadows. We knew what would happen, but Ben couldn't resist trying and neither of us regretted anything.

Death struggles don't take as many forms as there are fish because basic escape patterns are hard-wired by species. Anyone experienced on the cold-water streams of North America knows that if a fish stays put or dashes upstream, no matter how exhausting and self-defeating that is, it's likely a brook trout. If the fish takes advantage of the current by running downstream with it, jumping all the way, it's probably a rainbow. If there's no discernible upstream/downstream pattern, think brown trout.

In escape mode I'm a salmon and Julia's a pike. Male salmon react to the hook with a lunging, all-heart run. If that fails, they will jump with quick, desperate headshakes to throw off the thing holding them. Only as a last resort will they dive—and only then if there's sufficient depth—or "sulk" in place, exerting just enough pressure to resist the pull. By the time they're at the net, they're on their side in the water, done. Pike, on the other hand, never run. At first these top-predators don't do much beyond making minor adjustments to a new situation that seems more baffling than possibly mortal. Pike are used to having their way. But, as the line shortens, they dive for the weed beds that define their restaurants, food markets and neighborhoods. This is all going-home behavior, except for the parking maneuver. Instead of straight-ahead, they roll face down, twisting themselves (and the line) in a tangle that uses the weight and rooting of the weeds to resist what's pulling them upward. The crisscross of line and plant can strap the gills shut, suffocating them. But somewhere between rarely and occasionally, the increased pressure on the hook pulls it out and frees them. Mostly though, pike reserve their energy for last-minute thrashing at the boat. By that time, the net is in the water and it's already too late.

Individual struggles can vary wildly by size, sex, circumstance and personality, but the "by-and-large" rule holds for fish, as it does for any creature. The ones that surprise you are often the ones that escape in the stream, but not from memory. And when you've lived with somebody as long as Julia and I have, and have spent as much time at a place like Overlook Farm, where survival strategies are on intimate display, you come to understand where your differences come from and consider the consequences. We lived in Europe in the 1970s. Had that been a few decades earlier, as the Nazis closed in on Jews like us, would she have insisted on hiding in the weeds? I think so.

Mark, hunted by Mr. T., got off the hook, true to species, by running downstream with the current of the best medical care available. His unbreakable, unshakable silence on how it changed his art, however, seemed to me the equivalent of a salmon behaving like a pike. Maybe that was his point: to leave Mr. T. wondering while he rejoined the currents of his life.

THREE INDIANS

June, 2002

John Racine materialized at my shoulder the way suddenly the buck is right *there*, exactly where you've been looking all along without seeing, plenty close enough to hear but not hearing. More recently than hunting, I'd been to an exhibition of Rembrandt drawings and, in one, a young girl's face emerges from the paper the same way. A faint line makes you look again, then you work with a hunter's squint to bring her out of the paper to where you can concentrate on her features. Indians, at least the ones who haven't been repurposed as domesticated "native Americans," can be like that. Racine, a Chippewa, soundlessly walked the softly carpeted cedar tangle instead of crunching down the old gravel road. He wasn't trying to be stealthy. We'd met at the shore to discuss building a dock, and when we returned back up the hill together, I couldn't help but notice that I was the only one making noise. Sometimes you manage to recognize secret doors that open into different world. This door led to one that's vanishing, for sure, but still there if you bother to ask yourself what a stranger might be besides a dock builder who drifts through the woods like a column of mist.

About Racine I never learned more. He vanished from my life as silently as he had visited, leaving no dock behind. Perhaps something came up. With Indians who still live most of their lives outdoors, I learned the flow of life often overrules well ... rules. Soon thereafter I broke one of my own. *The New York Times* was putting out a section called "Sophisticated Traveler" that I'd disdained as insufficiently *researché* for world travelers like us. "Better read this one," Julia said. It was a story by a

182

TOM TOOSHKENIG, OUR "MIGHTY POTAWATOMI" TAUGHT THREE
GENERATIONS OF US TO LOVE HIS TEASING AND THE MARSH

journalist about my age with two sons about the ages of Ben and Mark. They had gone to a place called Ungava in sub-Arctic Quebec where, he reported, they had routinely caught huge brook trout in nameless streams that nobody had fished before. I actually called the telephone number listed. One trip and we were hooked for a decade. Initial returns were guided by white men who knew more than we did, but had learned it from the outside, as we had. Then, suddenly, there was Henri Boivin, a Cree with a profile that belonged on a coin and a life from the other side of the door, the door that had seemed so enchanted at the farm, but that I had not opened.

Coming home one day from grade school, he told us, his father said, "Henri, let's go for a walk." Without changing out of short pants and T-shirt—he was ten—he followed his father into the woods around Mashteviatsch, a tiny place sufficiently north of everything else for the Quebec bush to begin at their door. His father carried nothing more than a knife and fish hook at the end of a coil of line. They emerged four months later. Henri had mastered much of what he began showing us without saying a word, most emphatically after we—mostly me— asked for some kind of explanation. Henri's father hadn't liked questions; someone else's answers don't stick like what you come up with yourself.

Sure enough, no questions necessary to learn how to carry trout without a stringer. Do you have two for lunch, or four? Then your spruce branch—dead, without resin—needs that many prongs to put through the gills. Need dry wood on the third wet day in a row? Forget chopping it up Scout-style and walking back and forth with armfuls. Eliminate all but a single trip by carrying a whole length of long-dead trunk to camp. No need to cut lengths at the fire, either. Instead, split the whole thing to expose the heartwood that's always dry, then slide it into the flames as needed. Bigger fire? Use two trunks. The list lengthened each trip, even each day. Gales like Ungava's often fling sleet; ignore the instinct to huddle behind the nearest boulder. Henri built us fires *in front* of the windbreak so we'd take the punishment on our back; mere pings and bluster that we could—almost—ignore, in thankfulness for the warmth reflecting on our faces and hands. And the wind blew away the smoke.

Some things, however, lay beyond my ability to fathom wordlessly. Ungava wilderness is impressive, but not beautiful, in equal parts granite hills, inter-connected lakes, streams and rivers with oozy muskeg between. You sink to the knee in caribou trails. The weather is terrible: the too-hots dividing the brief intervals between the too-colds. We kept returning, I think, for the beauty of being together at first light, sardined together in an overloaded Zodiac with an Indian full of magic at the outboard; shotguns, rifles and bamboo fly rods up front and all of us ready to let the day determine what we'd do with it. I began thinking of those situations as "the Indian dimension," even when I was back at the farm, nosing a boat still slick with dew through the Charlevoix channel, the water so slack that you could watch the miller moths flutter to a surface made of green breathlessness, then burble out onto Lake Michigan, its dark blue rollers so slow and smooth that they seemed to be not quite awake yet, either.

As for Ungava, its visual glory comes either at ground level in a weaving of tiny flowers, lichens and fungi; in the eye level glory of its creatures; or, zooming all the way out, to northern lights so spectacular you think that you can hear them. I wrote up one display for *The New York Times* op-ed page:

THE LIGHT FANTASTIC

By Charles R. Eisendrath, Oct. 6, 1998

About 10 AM, my fishing companions and I were roused by a slapping on tent canvas and a rush of English from our French-Canadian guide: "Quickly! Come, it's starting." Nobody around our campfire, nor the rest of the world for that matter, knew what was about to appear in the night sky. …

It was Aug. 27, and we were a bit south of the Arctic Circle in a place called the Ungava Peninsula, which begins 800 miles north of Montreal and goes to the straits above the Hudson Bay and the Labrador Sea. In summer, you get around by seaplane and boat; in winter, beyond a few tiny settlements, nobody's there to need to get around.

People go there for giant brook trout, caribou, ptarmigan and maybe salmon and bear. But that night we were also given the gift of a tremendous gamma and X-ray bombardment from a magnetar—a collapsed star that is believed to have a greater mass than the Sun, compressed in a sphere only 12 miles in diameter. The force of the blast shut down scientific instruments, yet ordinary eyes recorded what God and/or physics could do with a celestial light show.

It started with a Rothko-like vertical glow in the north, in the manner of many northern lights. But within a minute or two, a shimmer of the palest green appeared in the east. Then someone noticed that the same thing was happening in the southeast, where northern lights don't normally appear.

A cloud overhead covered the eastern half of the sky. Suddenly, a gigantic bridge of light crossed the horizon, linking north with southeast. The cloud began glowing an ice blue and turned silver

185

at the edges, where it began to ripple gently, like fur fringes on a parka with the sun behind it.

Within 10 minutes the sky was writhing, as if some huge thing might fall out of it. The light bursts reminded me of nuclear tests in old Army films. My ears strained because it seemed impossible for something so violent and so immediate to be so silent. The event seemed to call for explosions, or maybe Beethoven.

Something about it intimidated the wolves. We were quiet, too — until as if with a switch, the theater went dark. What else was appropriate? We applauded.

Scientists have now explained what happened that night. But to calibrate it, they had to be where they couldn't see what they were describing. That role falls to a group of fishermen who had traveled far to worship the constellations of spots on the flanks of brook trout — and caught a glimpse of the astral competition.

It's ominously known as "The land God gave to Cain," a term coined by explorer Jacques Cartier in 1534 to describe the untillable Labrador/ Ungava coast seen from his ship. And it's easy to get lost there. Hilltops provide clear views but there are no human landmarks to distinguish one gray-green vista from the rest. Down below is where the snaggle of stunted spruce and alders is the most interwoven, the only tracks are made by migrating caribou, sometimes augmented by the foxes, wolves and bears that follow them on a circular path leading north, all of them seeking the relief that a frost provides in killing off the marauding stingflies, biteflies, suckbugs and no-see-ums that can turn eyelids into a black, maddening insanity-inducing crust. None of their paths lead to human comfort, even if you happen to survive making the loop. When the killer cold freezes and /or buries their forage, the insects disappear, too.

Yet even when in territory as new to him as to us, Henri did not use a compass, a fact I noticed on the sort of trudge between streams that makes you doubt that any fishing, no matter how spectacular, could be worth *this*. Finally, I couldn't help asking why. "Too dangerous," said this man, leading a small band of the inexperienced through honest-to-God wilderness, packing no food, no radio and limited ammunition. This time exasperation—and perhaps a bit of panic—pressed me on.

FIRST LIGHT AND NO IDEA WHAT THE DAY MIGHT BRING
IN ADDITION TO EXCITEMENT AND SURPRISE

So, in short strokes, the way a watercolorist expresses a landscape, Henri explained that if you're looking at the face of a compass you do not record the passing face of the territory you're traveling. Those are the features—and the different ways they look in light or shadow—that will get you back where you came from. Also, trying to follow a straight compass line in country where that's impossible is ridiculous. "You'll miss that broke tree," Henri said, "or the way that bear [track] cuts around it." I kept carrying my compass, but I stopped looking at it.

In extreme circumstances, Henri called on the Spirits. Mark had brought his fiancée along on one trip and, by the last day, he still hadn't taken a caribou. Packing up my fly rod, hanging with the others on the tent frame, I noticed that a ptarmigan feather had been worked into Mark's line at the reel. Odd, I thought, and no accident. The float plane was already circling when Henri raced up with Mark's rifle, unpacked and loaded for him. We heard the shots in just the time it took them to scramble up the ridge behind us. Henri couldn't bear that a young man

187

he favored fell short in the eyes of his woman. I didn't ask whether it had been he who'd summoned the juju with a feather. There was no need.

We didn't go to Ungava to hunt caribou, but caribou were Henri's lifetime—generations of lifetimes—preoccupation. Any cast-off scrap of time had him scanning the ridgelines for the moving dead bushes that turned out to be antlers outlined against the sky. No matter what else we were doing—eating, fishing, hunting ptarmigan—not joining one of his stalks was as unthinkable as marking a trail with surveying tape, standard practice around the trackless places near the farm.

Once, in the gravel of a dry pond on high ground, away from most of the bugs, we killed two nice bulls. In this surgical arena, Henri went to work. Indians—Henri's Cree people, anyway—don't clean animals the way hunters around the farm dress their deer. Virtually all recoverable meat is on the legs and lower neck. They field-strip the carcass the way I'd watched "my" Puerto Rican gang in the summer of 1965 remove the similarly valuable parts of outsiders' cars parked along East Fourth Street in the East Village. Carefully sparing those belonging to us locals, they took no longer with wrenches than Henri with his knife. It was the meat-dressing equivalent of his firewood technique, both of which I've used ever since. We had what we would eat. We had the antlers we would show. Why, then, did he gut it?

I hadn't considered the Spirits. Meticulously aligning each organ on a clean stone, as if arranging an anatomy lecture, he then plucked puffs of wiry gray caribou moss, wetted them in a stream a quarter mile downhill, and returned with Ungava-sterile cleaning pads. He might as well have been wearing surgical greens and latex gloves. Cavities propped open with sticks, he scoured the insides and assumed the additional role of priest, preparing a sacred vessel. "Otherwise the Spirits can't get free," he said, shrugging at the obvious answer to an unnecessary question, and turned his back.

The wind happened to be screaming on that rare clear day, which made me wonder how an ordinary carrion fly had found—and flown—to this pop-up buffet. I paused. Amazingly, undetected, other insects arrived—the kind that feed on dead things, not us—followed shortly by a couple of whiskey jack jays. Above, a hawk awaited its moment. The site happened to lie on a slope open to the river we were using daily. When I scoped it through the rifle sight the next afternoon, rodents, foxes, wolves and bears had consumed everything soft, even removing most of the bones for more convenient dining elsewhere, perhaps closer to a den.

THE RECENT DEATH of my father released impulses I hadn't even known as repressed. Being part of the hunt-kill-consumer cycle made me crave it closer to home. At a cocktail party soon after moving back to the U.S., a man I'd just met began talking about duck hunting with his dad and I found myself confessing my loss and the inability to find a substitute experience—you don't see many wild ducks around Ann Arbor. "That's because they're all on the main runway of the Great Lakes Flyway, just east of here," said my new best friend. "The Walpole Island Indian Reservation has some of the best duck hunting in the world."

Walpole is a marsh about twice the size of Manhattan on the Canadian north shore of Lake St. Clair, a sanctuary for a mixed band of Chippewa, Algonquin Huron and Potawatomi refugees from the Iroquois wars of the Seventeenth Century. Present inhabitants proclaim it "Unceded Territory," never taken by Whites. I liked that the Indians required you to hire one of their own as guides. Which Indian, however, defied usual rules. I found I had no say in whom the head guide might assign from among the several available.

My chief was Wilfred Laleen, who had ruled his section of the island's hunt for decades with a squint, a grinning tangle of teeth and a straightforward reputation as the very best. From his sons and various others, I was introduced to the rudiments of duck hunting; from other clients the basics about Indian guides. Here are the cardinal rules for each: *Hunch down and don't move from the moment you see or hear an incoming bird because they will flare in unpredictable directions; hunch close to the guide before hunting with him and don't go if you smell beer on his breath. If you do, enjoyment will elude you with same unfathomable predictability of alarmed ducks scattering.* But it wasn't so much the skills or sobriety of the men I set off with—what I couldn't abide was not getting to know any of them. Recalling my loss of Racine at the farm and the psychic bonanza with Henri Boivin in Ungava, I wanted to go to school—I wanted to learn about Walpole's humanity, along with the birds.

In my office, Wednesdays had become "duck emergency days." Calls were deflected with "He's out of the office," or "He's in a meeting"—the latter particularly effective because, in academe, everyone is always in a meeting, and the higher your rank, the more the endless appointments earn you respect, all by themselves. On a couple of those Wednesdays, myself and Tom Tooshkenig—a man about ten years younger than me who seemed to need glasses and was among the least experienced of guides—seemed to hit it off. I decided to ask Chief Wilfred for a dispensation. Tom and I were having a good time together, I explained. Clearly he wasn't among the most in-demand of guides, so why couldn't we be paired up regularly? I'd committed to season-long regularity—meaning predictable revenue. Results? A grunt followed by a not-Tom guide the following week, and again the next, and the one after that.

That last day had been so empty we came in early. There was time for more leisurely conversation. Chief Wilfred and I faced each other across the hood of my truck, arms extended toward one another, but hands not too close. Dusk summoned its mosquitoes and did nothing to dissuade flies and hornets from feasting on the duck innards nearby. Two hours later we were still at it. The chief won. I had no right to ask him for special treatment. He would not agree to assign me Tom. Yet the next Wednesday, Tom loaded decoys and a gas can into the back of my truck without explanation and we've hunted together ever since. Unknowingly, I had taken part in a sweat lodge experience, where unspeakable amounts of time somehow distill resolution from unspoken vapors.

I had no way of calibrating Tom's hunting skills. It was hard not to note, however, that his spotting improved markedly when he finally succumbed to wearing glasses and that his calls gradually had more effect on the birds we were trying to lure. He came up with new ideas about which decoys went where in a layout and how many were enough. Able to hear birds at uncanny distances, he knew more about what their vocalizations meant. He learned more places to try first, even when it was still too dark to mark flight patterns for that day. Not that we often stayed put. After getting started early enough and gauging the wind, the tertiary rule seemed to be that the first blind out was always wrong. That meant picking up twenty or so decoys, winding their anchor strings and setting off to find another place to run the boat into tall covering weeds. When I ventured a suggestion, it was invariably dismissed. Often we ended up there anyway, always, a-la-Wilfred, without comment.

Tom was guiding every day and got steadily more expert, maybe the new best on the Island. I became merely adequate and stuck there, as far as downing birds was concerned. My learning ran more to other things, beginning with getting to know another man in the intimate language of hunting. Crumpled below the line of sight, long before the birds arrived, I came to recognize species, range and number from the pitch, timbre and pace of Tom's calls and the shuffle of his feet on the aluminum floor of the boat. Before opening his conversations with the birds—generally the females, who lead the flights—Tom's face and manner were what you would expect during hours—hours!—of scanning empty skies. Locked onto potential prey converted him from a dozing house cat to a panther about to spring. It was the moment of the *possibility* of death that brought peak life. Decoying ducks lock their wings and present their breasts. Calling stops. In an exquisite procession of seconds between silence and the shot I could feel the high wattage of his expectation. He cared less about the result. A flash of possibility bright as a gunblast faded into an echo of predictability. His features and body language slumped back into a man dealing with time by the hour.

At first I was called "Eyes-in-Draft," pronounced, I thought, like "Rain-in-the-Face." I became "Charles" about the time I realized I was beginning to understand Indian humor—when directed at me, for sure, but also among Tom and his friends. I found it light-hearted, surprising among a people so often described in the dark tones of tragedy, cruelty and guilt. Most of it was based on teasing, and it never concerned bathroom humor, sex or God. Mistakes ruled. Ready at hand, his quiver held a tease-shaft for my every horrible mistake or unimaginable miss.

We also shared the blunders you smile about afterwards: gushing through above-wader-level muck to retrieve ducks and having to pull each other out; a friend blowing a hole in the bottom of the boat, and me—not the guide—jumping overboard to save the trip with a handkerchief. Most of all, being left standing in waist-high water in 20°F near darkness. Tom had disappeared to break off shelves of ice to open water for landing ducks. He hadn't bothered to tell me — he'd just wandered off in the gloom until I couldn't hear his splashing. I had no idea how to get anywhere—even just to land—nor when he might return. I would not be able to remain standing motionless much longer in the cold. Worst, there was this eerie, metallic jangle out there somewhere, dry as death, with no apparent cause. Of all adult apprehensions, that night was the absolute, unqualified weirdest and transported me back to childhood's "things-that-go-bump-in-the-night." The light of sanity didn't go back on until the dark form of Tom emerged, hand-hauling our boat. He had forgotten his flashlight. (Like the nothing under the bed, the tinkling of a strangler's chain turned out to be riffle wavelets clinking the necklace of ice at the shore.)

I brought the boys along, singly and together. First meeting, invariably in darkness, couldn't help but unsettle a twelve-year-old. Tom's was a face too like the illustrations of Indians bursting through frontier cabin doors — his string of duck leg bands hung where scalps had been worn. But they came to love this man with a bandanna around his forehead, long black braid down his back and a house that, inside, seemed as much like a tepee as anything with clapboard walls could be. At the kitchen table his tiny, lovely wife, Elaine, made sweetgrass baskets and teased by pretending to have cleaned the wrong birds.

Still, a discoloration in our friendship persisted like a stain on a favorite shirt you're going to wear anyway. Early on I had developed a habit of hefty tips for special guides I wanted to nurture as endangered human subspecies. Tom became the most regular beneficiary, but I never got a thank-you. Nor a handshake. When I'd held out my hand in a congratulatory way during one of our first outings, the limp, awkward result discouraged other gestures. An explanation suggested itself one evening in a familiar situation. The only birds showing any interest in our layout passed us en-route to one of the private clubs nearby. When the club members took their shots, clouds of mallards and black ducks would rise, wheel, then return to those club waters strewn with feed corn to attract and hold them. The club people had, in effect, colonized the marsh and its natural game. They were on the inside of a new, foreign Walpole; we were locked out.

Tom's profile was a dark outline against a horizon only a couple of shades lighter. The features of a people who had been excluded from all but the scraps of their own continent in transactions followed by the odd custom of clasping a white man's hand. What was there, exactly, to thank any one of us for?

I've reported elsewhere about the fear of losing the wild parts of the farm, a gradual but inexorable shriveling of psychological space that rides behind the mechanization of landscape called "development." At Walpole, a horizon clear to where tall, waving weeds swept against sky has been chopped up by giant windmill generators turning, blinking red, distracting, remind-

HENRI BOIVIN

ing one of what's coming and what has already gone. Our last Ungava trip with Henri raised similar thoughts. His wife had come to tend the base camp and had brought along their son, Anthony, eleven. They could not have children of their own, so the Crees applied traditional ways. As Henri put it, "Others had too many, so they gave us this one." His adoption was the only example we saw in Anthony of the old ways. In most others he was more like the windmills around Walpole marsh, existing in a world that had already eclipsed the wild parts that Henri and Tom were so gracefully part of. Anthony snacked sugary things nonstop, candy that his surrogate parents supplied but would not touch themselves, doting on the appetite of a developing warrior even though he was well past pudgy and into pre-adolescent obesity. Unlike Henri, he spoke perfect English, less French and no Cree. When Henri brought up binoculars to sweep ridgelines for migrating herds, Anthony's hands also had an automatic pattern, but around the buttons that activated Pokemon games. Henri admired that. He never took Anthony into the woods.

PART FOUR

A GRANDSON NAMED CRASH

PLANT TIME

July 21, 2009

It wasn't meant as a party wrecker. My dinner partner and hostess had recently taken up fly fishing because in catch-and-release "you don't hurt the fish." I merely suggested that she test that hypothesis by having herself dragged upstream by a hook through her lip, tongue, eye, or maybe all three. I was so impressed with her huff, which spread around the table like a sneeze, that I submitted a piece about it to *The Chronicle of Higher Education*. It became the first article on hunting (fishing is hunting with a hook) in the magazine's history. After syndication and inclusion in a collection of opinion writing arguing that catch and release is serial torture, it seemed I might be on to something broader: I would begin thinking about the perception of all kinds of living things as sentient beings, including plants.

Yes, the pain of plants is another party wrecker observation, but this time deliberate and aimed at the conventionally self-satisfied people who eat only fruits, roots and leaves because they "don't want to kill anything." Or those who oppose the use of animals in research because they can't bear the personal pain that the animals' pain causes *them*, a less altruistic position. Like the creatures they grieve for, these human defenders have a complex taxonomy, although not in the abstract Linnaean sense. Their categories are all about classification based on how much the creatures concerned resemble, um, us. My dinner partner had proudly demonstrated her broad-minded extension from household pets and look-alike apes to lowly fish, but after years of raising, admiring and killing a wide

variety of living things at the farm, feel-good frippery seemed dangerously delusional. Life is life no matter what it animates. Taking it is literally
the most natural thing in the world, and for that reason should never be
taken lightly... nor graded on supposed merit.[14]

Until quite recently the population, even in developed countries, was
mostly rural. You grew up knowing where your food came from and how
it got from a field or a barn to your plate. Often, you had a hand in the
process. Although science disdains this sort of personal observation as
"merely anecdotal," to many of us it trumps "data" handily for believ-
ability. Just as those in widget factory towns know what it takes to make
widgets, people living on and around farms understand that harvesting
crops is not so different from slaughtering livestock.

Curiously, none of the animal-love groups give the slightest thought
to life—divine or merely miraculous—as it animates plants. Here it's
worth pausing to note that we don't even have a way of expressing life
and liveliness in plants without referring to animals. For example, what
better demonstrates millennia of prejudice among English speakers than
the lack of a word like "animate" to pair with plants. Milkweed seeds
are said to fly "like feathers," vines "snake" their way into an arbor. Our
language thus relegates an entire biological kingdom to also-ran status
in everyday speech and perception. Few wonder whether, or under what
circumstances, plant life may be taken "humanely," or taken at all, with
a narrow exception for endangered species. Nor do they consider the carnage wrought upon plants (again, requiring reference to animal needs)
just about everywhere, including what gets trampled every time you walk
on your lawn or decapitate it—often weekly!—with your mower. Imagine a set of whirring blades tearing off the heads of an entire herd. Compared to that, what happens to a calf, killed for veal before the chance to
wander verdant meadows, is mild stuff indeed. Anti-cruelty arguments
are concurrently obvious to anyone who isn't a sadist and anthropomor-
phically idiotic when evaluated on the cuddliness scale. No matter. Re-

---

14   I give a pass to people who don't eat meat because they don't like the taste, they
want to lose weight or flesh doesn't like their digestive tract. Slightly less realistic: those
who abstain because of how domestic animals are treated. That's true more often than
not, but the alternatives are anything but gentle, whether or not "natural."

cently, hunting became "harvesting" among "sensitive" hunters and critics alike in order to make the killing involved merely plant-like.

Urbanization removed the link between the population from its food base and with it the awareness of how much death is involved in keeping humans alive. Farm kids in 4-H programs like the McCune girls down the road are not insensitive when they lead the pigs they raised (whose ribs and hams ended up in our freezer) to the county fair and subsequent slaughter. No doubt feeding, naming and often conversing with them from birth reveals each as a distinct being with individual looks and personality. Small wonder. Humans like Rainey and Tanner McCune share seventy percent of their genes with pigs. That's far less than the ninety-nine percent commonality with chimpanzees for sure, but it's only halfway between our genetic relationship to the "highest" ape and a daffodil. Pause for a moment, please, to consider that you share one-third of your genes with daffodils.

Only a tolerant few among us blur the distinction between man and the rest of planetary life, as in the belief system practiced by the Cree and Potawatomi hunters who taught me much more than technique. Their spiritual approach was like a bespoke suit at final tailoring—comfort, texture and color—all mutually complementary. The One God approach, however, with its elevation of man as master of all else? To me, it feels anti-nature. More to the point, belief in that sort of God seems irrelevant to a deepening awe, or what I somehow sense beyond the five senses recognized by science. The freedom of this sort of internal expression, undertaken with a minimum of guilt baggage, is one of the joys of the spiritual atheism I practice most intensely at the farm.

"Atheism?" A hateful word that runs us gobsmack into God and another linguistic prejudice, which in this case can best be taken literally—as in judgment-before-anything-else—including direct observation and common sense. Try to describe being an ordinarily spiritual person whose admiration for the universe does not involve an old man in white who lives on a cloud somewhere. English, French and Spanish—the languages I know best—herd you into a linguistic prison with all exits blocked to the positive expression of a non-God universe. You are not allowed to say what you are; you are only permitted to say what you are not: atheist (without God), non-believer (as if there were nothing else but God to believe in!) or the humiliating "agnostic" (meaning you are an I-don't-know). Describing alternative spiritual beliefs that don't begin with a negative doesn't exist.

After fuming about this in the boundless birth / growth / procreation / death all around me at the farm, I return to Ann Arbor for a round of discussions with Ralph Williams, the officially acknowledged best teacher at the University of Michigan and an expert on religion. "How," I ask him, "can we describe our lack of belief in God or gods without using 'atheist,' a word that automatically announces a lack of something?" Like the impossibility of describing plants without reference to animals, or a primary color unpaired with something that same color, the word stymies one in the negative. Finding a single term like "believer" to mean "faith in nature apart from any deity" should be easy, right?

After lots of false starts failed to piph, I came across a dead coon being consumed by maggots and came up with "Participant," as in someone who finds the divine in participating in the laws of nature and the universe: ashes to ashes, dust to dust, flesh to maggots, lives to the memories of others. Will "Participant" sweep the world's languages? Doubtful. But it's better than naturist, which often means nudist; universalist, which means nothing; or anything else Williams and I have come up with. Yet. Patience may be required. For us in the animal kingdom, everything about plants seems to take forever. So why try to rush the acceptance of a new term to describe a kingdom beyond kingdoms? No need to stay tuned, you poor animal; you won't live long enough.

AT OVERLOOK FARM, leaving God out of it is easy. Life, death and the afterlife go on nonstop all by themselves. If there's a book of Revelations to consult, I find it in what the kingdom of death has to say about life and afterlife. For example, it was natural to me as a human to call the storm that destroyed much of the forest around Overlook Farm in 2002 a holocaust. I grew up with the gruesome newsreels of concentration camp dead (and parts of them) being bulldozed into mass graves — just as we bulldozed the trunks and the limbs of downed trees. I've also had the experience of being invited to the little town in the Ruhr where the Eisendraths came from. When the Nazi holocaust eliminated nearly every

trace of the Jews in Germany and Eastern Europe, that was it. No seed of many families was left behind. Regeneration would depend on adults moving back. But that's the human form of reforestation. As I scrambled around after the storm with a small crew of reforesters—two of them under ten years old and all of them mostly Mayan-speakers—I thought about the fundamental characteristic of trees and how that had doomed them. An entire community killed in a few ferocious minutes because none of the individuals could crouch, or even bend very much, let alone run away. But my focus was so narrowly on restoration that I couldn't see what had really happened that August day, not to mention what's going on naturally, now, eight months later.

Everyone knows plants breathe, grow, eat and drink, procreate and compete. Some know they feel, too, and in general share about fifty percent of their genes with animals. What plants don't do is move, at least in terms of walking, flying, swimming or slithering their entire bodies from one place to another. If born in a spot with too much shade, too bad for them; they won't thrive even though a perfect place may be just a foot or two away.

Still, the movement of plants is something you can almost see, but not quite. Tendrils—that perfect word for something so tender that its entire, impossibly delicate surface is a sensing network for detecting solid structure for support—secure what the rest of the plant needs by turning themselves into fasteners strong as plastic pull-ties. You can nearly watch a sweet pea do this. Or bamboos that shoot up with a speed that my generation learned could drill through the strapped-down prostate bodies of prisoner GIs.

Some botanical strategies are unmatchable by anything that could scamper to the sun. One is their time scale. They perform the same life processes familiar in any animal or human, but on a schedule so radically unfamiliar as to obscure the much more compelling similarities. Infant maple, ash and beech will sprout so thickly under their parent trees as to be a kind of lawn. Year after year, decade on decade, they remain only four or five inches tall and can wait this way indefinitely. Unlike, say, Henry David Thoreau, the deliberative, dour-faced New Englander who gave himself precisely two years, two months and two days in a lifetime of forty-five years to understand the entire world as reflected in the water, woods and sky near Walden Pond. That's plenty of time to research and write a short book based, like this one, on what one sees, hears, feels and thinks while in self-imposed semi-isolation. And, although a human lifetime of nearly a half-century was then respectable, periods of one year or fifty are absurdly short by tree time.

Peter Wohlleben devoted a career to the scientific study of trees. While managing German forests he permitted himself poetic observation and let it enliven his book, *The Hidden Life of Trees*. He notes that beeches, maples, ashes and oaks are just hitting stride at one hundred. And while the eggs of mobile creatures eventually develop into beings with legs, wings, fins and slither scales to slip through life, trees are also dependent on eggs. Some float, others propeller themselves. The cleverest develop an indigestible shell, then just let themselves get devoured by birds and beasts. After being carried several feet—or many miles—without packing much of their own nourishment internally (like bird eggs), they hatch encased in someone else's excrement, excellent food.

Among the mobile, human males produce seed on a scale that falls far short of trees, but is still impressive at 290 million sperm a day. Only a number so small as to be as statistically irrelevant as the solar eclipses you'll see in a lifetime ever get to make contact with the other half of a gamete necessary to germinate, however. Why? Limited room at the local uterus—at least compared to trees.

The difference this makes towers all around you—shimmering, turning colors, rustling, sometimes falling on your car, yet somehow managing to hide in plain sight. Only when delayed-action-photography speeds up the sex and dining habits of living things that have leaves for lungs does the resemblance become comprehensible. Somehow, though, the perception doesn't illuminate understanding. It's usually filed away in mental categories reserved for "art" or "science" instead of "Holy shit! This changes how I see life," where it belongs.

Let's call the fruiting season of a tree its estrus. Each year it produces trillions of fertilized seeds, most of which are destroyed by disease, predator molds, too much water or too little, and still leaving billions among the surviving. Of these, only millions find a decent place to sprout. Every year. A holocaust by wind or lumbering finds the adults defenseless because it strikes at the mobility factor, the way Nazi extermination found those who were too rooted to move. Think of their children, the ones who developed from that pathetically small number of implanted seeds. Most of them died with their parents. In our woods, the ethnic cleansing among maples, beeches and ashes provided better—far better—conditions for their offspring. Suddenly they had enough sun, water and food. They were like the children sent abroad before it was too late by parents bound for Auschwitz.

AFTER THE 2002 STORM I found a new fascination with the furious regeneration that unfolded on those stricken hillsides, the valley between them and far, far beyond. As predicted, the woods responded furiously to insult. The creepers didn't just creep—full sun made racers and booby trappers of them as they clambered up the few remaining trees and smothered the crisscross of log carcasses on the ground. Walking the woods was like upstream wading the trout streams hereabouts, where the bottoms are still festooned with half-buried timbers from the lumber era and bristling with sticks left sharp by beavers—the current turns the hazards downstream, meaning against a fisherman wading the other way, a natural version of the punji-stick booby traps of the Viet Cong.

Nursing the newly-planted meant first finding them, often not until they're down underfoot. Needles in haystacks may present problems, but at least the haystack is not made of prickles. I emerge from these painful quests torn, a little bloody, winded, yes, but mysteriously satisfied. These quests: Are they missions of mercy for the young trees? Psychic recovery? Recovery of some feeling of control? To enrich eventual grandchildren? Three years on, I'm still at it and it's clear the now-present grandchildren are no more than a deterrent from looking silly to myself. I ride up the valley on an ATV, hoping to see a crown reaching for light above the tangle, like an infant peering over the edge of a playpen. My botanical wards are for my own satisfaction, and in height they're catching up to me.

On a hillside I find a red oak strapped to the ground in position to die. Here was an impressive nursery recruit, grown from a twig to a full inch at the base of the trunk and at least fifteen feet tall. A survivor of jungle combat? No, nothing tropical or exotic here, just the repeated on-slaughts that in plant time are like wave after wave of cavalry attacks on the strategic resources of light, water and nutrients. Grasses cut sunlight by filtering and absorb the surface necessities of a seedling tree. Then, burdock with leaves so broad that a local potter imprints individual ex-amples to make ceramic trays; and smothering, leathery mullein leaves capable of crushing as well as suffocating. This little oak had somehow survived them all. Then came the raspberries.

About those spines that educated your childish fingers all those years ago ... they're not, as someone assuredly told you, mere defenses to pro-tect seeds delectable to nearly every member of the animal kingdom, in-cluding you. They also give the plant offensive weaponry, equipping it to drag down and suffocate young trees; trees that if allowed to grow would suffocate them with the same killer shade technique. Alone, a raspberry or blackberry stalk catches branches, leaves and bark with simple friction. And they are almost never alone. In patches, the prickles bind with the strength of Velcro and can support themselves to a height of six feet or more. Picture a cat-o-nine-tails whip with tiny spikes embedded: Angled outward by gravity, blown by the wind, or pushed by passing animals, the killing range of blackberry plants can reach a twelve-foot diameter. Catching something to support them triggers a second move, like a py-thon that stuns with a bite, then weighs down prey with its body until breath ends and digestion begins.

In open areas, berry stalks can bind themselves into entire roof-sized sheets at heights from a few feet to head-height above the ground. To penetrate this structure you need body armor, gloves and a clipper. Also patience, commitment, lots of time and the delusion of a man who knows he has maybe twenty more years playing nursemaid to a forest that won't look as he wants it for another 150. Nevermind. Onward tilting at these particular windmills I've happily gone, several times a year, pruning red oaks and black cherries to get their top branches above deer browse level and spraying them with an odoriferous repellent until they do.

The threatened oak's descent to the dead leaves of the forest floor had been gradual enough to not snap it. Wrestled down the previous season, the new growth from limbs pinned for months beseech help. I cut the berry stalks and, happily, the young trunk accepts being uprighted to freedom position. Damn, nothing to stake it with, so I tie it to a nearby something and affix orange marking tape to signal a successful ambulance run. More permanent help can come later.

Rescues like this give me an irrational chill. Am I a Schindler to living things facing death because of an inability to flee? My motivation is both unexamined and unimportant. And on this occasion I can't say I was sobbing with Samaritan joy, but I was most definitely thinking about limbs without the strength to beg, or maybe even the will to do so. That spring in Ann Arbor, early in the kind of bright day that makes you whistle on your morning walk, I'd heard enough of a "plop" to stop and turn around. A young man lay motionless, on his back, at the base of a tall parking structure. A closer look revealed the bloody wrist badges of a suicide attempt previous to his jump. His eyes were wide open and blue as the sky. There was nothing I could do except bear witness as the light of life left those eyes, living tissue's moment of final capitulation before being reabsorbed into oblivion.

The boy's deadroom was the open cement street. The byway to one of a different order led through brambles at the farm. Deer like to make trails under the brambles; an ingenious tactic serving travel and cuisine concurrently as they can eat the young berry shoots along their surveyed track before they grow spikes. I often follow deer trails because they take me closest to the trees in greatest danger of being fatally skinned by passing bucks with itchy antler velvet. They make the going easier—if you obey the traffic signals. Traffic signals? Through a berry tangle, the paths are distinctly one-way streets as the stalks are bent in one direction. Going the other way is like wading upstream in a river of snags. On the deer trail, the "current" is the passing bodies that angle bramble spines the same way.

Today I am hacking, clipping, cursing my way through a tangle that had to be brought down to my height in order to reach an oak that had managed to get its head above the rest, but was being threatened by elderberry growing thick as one of those Rousseau dreamscapes with palms and lions. I paused for a pee. This is often when I spot an elusive mushroom, and it's invariably when ducks suddenly come within range. And so it was that I looked at the landscape in new way and spotted something different. The line of sight wasn't long, just down to my right boot, but it happened to penetrate a bramble roof as intricately interlaced as the ceiling of a Gothic cathedral.

I had blundered into an abode arranged for admirable privacy. Curled slightly, legs under rib cage, the full skeleton of a buck lay on a platform exactly his size, a sepulcher facing back over the valley. The undergrowth was smoothly mattressed down within range of tempting green shoots: canapés within convenient range of a favorite chaise. That deer—and probably others—had made an escape tunnel under the bramble tops where evasion could be fast and unseen. All the stems on that path led straight to this place, even after a winter of snow. Clearly, this was the well-used hideout of choice. It was a buck's man-cave, where it had gone to die.

It's teeth and antlers said it had been in prime shape when it died, ruling out age or disease. No sign of broken legs, so it probably hadn't been hit by a car up on Mountain Road. The agent of death was most likely a hunter getting to know that buck, as the Spanish philosopher Ortega y Gasset would have approved, including staking out its territory and noting its paths while carefully avoiding leaving a scent. Everything had to have been done just right in order to get close enough. And then? Maybe luck intervened the wrong way for the hunter. Maybe the buck moved—it doesn't take much to throw off a telescopic sight by a few inches.

It's no accident that a kill shot is a called a "true shot." In thick undergrowth like this, getting off a true shot is as chancy as finding meaning in a boy's suicide, reconciling conflicting religions or discovering "the only way" to approach fishing. One thing was sure: This creature was a "participant" in the flow of nature. Its tissues, bones (and who knows? maybe spirit) were being recycled by the fellow inhabitants of Overlook Farm, returning them to its essence. Is that enough for me, to participate? It is, and further, when possible, to leave some sort of record of having done so. There was nothing to do about the boy, but with the deer, I could help.

The antlers were the most stately I'd ever seen here, ten points and broad. Miraculously, they were un-gnawed by the porcupines that usually make short work of anything full of salts and calcium. I asked our favorite taxidermist to leave them attached to the whole skull and to hinge the jaw so it could open and close. "Do you plan to talk with it?" he asked, skeptical, but amenable. Not really. On the other hand, discussing ultimates with a buck skull seems as plausible as accepting sermons on the mount. I keep it on a living room table close to where I read, sip, dream.

A MINNOWER AND THE LADY
WHO SAVED ME

July, 1993

You see the Steve Sloops of the world on early-morning business drives. Out there in the soft lake mists they are doing something in small boats the same gray as the water and air. In fact, the water, glassy before the first breeze troubles it, shades into the sky without a line, like linoleum rolled right up a wall. You? You are off to do something inside, perhaps in a car, enclosed; the Sloops are outside, free.

A few years back a Brit named Leslie Thomas wrote a whole book about this predicament called *The Adventures of Goodnight & Loving*. George Goodnight, ordinary commuter, "missed another day of summer" when the train cleared London and he saw the man fishing beside the green river.

> *His heart, his eyes and his mouth fell simultaneously. At 6:30 the man was unfailingly there and even when George was required to stay late and it was 8:30 or even 9, there he was with his rod, as if he had spitefully waited. Even when George looked down he could not resist looking up again. Staring from the train he would have given quite a lot to see that stranger topple into the weeds and water just as they travelled by. To see his tackle splash, to view his hat floating away. Damn him.*

This is the sort of book that finds you when leave your normal job-life and wake up one morning at a place like Overlook Farm. The message about who is free in this world and who's not floats out there in Lake Charlevoix just as it does for Goodnight on the Thames, plain as a fishing bobber. Goodnight, who heretofore considered himself respectably successful and therefore free, does not test the proposition intentionally. Instead, the moment of revelation takes form after a mechanical breakdown on the motorway. He just walks off into a farmer's field. By the time his adventures—none of them about fishing; all involving travel and women—bring him full circle, he has become the damnable fisherman in all ways except a literal identity swap. He is free, but that's because his life, as he knew it, is gone.

What Sloop does down there in the weed shallows is catch bait. It's unlikely you'd ever see him because, unlike the fictional counterpart on the banks of the Thames near the railroad tracks, he doesn't like to hear the rush of passing humanity and so looks for places where he can launch his outboard beyond all that. Not even the paved roads have much traffic during his commuting times; to work about 3 AM, home three hours later. The boat doesn't need running lamps to warn other craft away; it's never out deeper than four feet of water and always in the weeds. Anyway, the brightness, even starlight, would spook the minnows. Painted the color of lake muck, it disappears.

He comes off the water in the morning gray. You might catch sight of him setting off for the indoor part of his existence as a nurse in Petoskey. I've never heard him say an ungentle word about his charges, who include the criminally insane. To Sloop, the Minnower, the real loony bin is everything between the weed shallows and the hospital wards. Someplace like where you might be going right now.

Sloop's minnow operation has no name, nor did the tackle-and-gun shop he ran out of his basement for a decade or so. The lettering on the junked steel rowboat that served as a billboard, where his gravel met the nearest pavement at Deer Lake Road, just said "Bait," with characteristic understatement.

With the flow of a good-sized spring, Sloop had fashioned a series of ponds and holding bins for a variety of swimming wares as intricately arranged as the tie racks at Brooks Brothers. Your answer to "What're you after?" tells him the size: five-inch baby suckers for pike, slightly smaller for walleye. Brown trout means big shiners, which don't grow beyond three inches; perch and bass, smaller still. Minnows are to him what game birds were a century ago to the bounty hunters who iced them under blocks cut from frozen lakes in early spring for rail shipment to the markets of New York and Chicago. In slow schools, Sloop's tiny quarry darken the lake bed the way clouds of passenger pigeons blotted the sun from the fields, as unmindful of danger from above as the pigeons were from below.

When I met him in the late 1970s, Sloop's spirit lived with those reassuring schools of tiny fish, but as a bait man he was already a remnant, like the last of the pigeons. Nobody did it that way anymore, just as nobody thought of raising a pig in a condo for bacon. He had become a wholesaler, delivering tank-loads of shimmering treasure to the marinas where the "live bait" sign was a minor message in places that also offered cheesedogs, gasoline, engine service, cold drinks and life preservers. But we dealt with him as a vertically-integrated supply chain, albeit a short one, leading from lake shallows to minnow ponds, to us. Oh, yes, but another pond, the biggest, he reserved for the fat, slow, beautiful rainbows he raised like, well, a condo dweller might fatten a hog. Sloop could do anything with fish, the extent of which covered the floors, walls, beams and counters of the respectable ranch house he'd downgraded to look like a shack-cum-natural history exhibition. The creatures he caught, trapped, shot, stuffed and mounted gazed from everywhere, as though they were still in the wilderness and you were the intruder.

A university friend—a social scientist whose life and life truths depend on "data"—heard me describe Sloop and instantly informed me that my discovery fell into a well-recognized group called "marginals," on whom the data were definitive. His interest ended with identification / categorization / quantification. For the boys and me, however, that's where interest began and the potential for more interest seemed infinite. What else could this amazing person do? Actually, the learning started with the clear impression that if the boys and I were out to explore his world, he would consider us an interesting adjunct to himself and his boys. Step one: gear, and a lesson in the economics of marginals.

A DECADE OR SO before we moved home and the boys grew old enough to be treated — sort of — like expedition buddies, Michigan's vital tourism and the related sport fisheries were beset by a new situation: too many fish and the wrong kind. Like most alien species in the Great Lakes, the silvery sardine-sized things called alewives arrived via the St. Lawrence Seaway. (Don't bother to look up the name. According to the *Oxford English Dictionary* it's been in use since 1672 without anyone knowing who the original ale wife was, or anything else.) Alewives are prone to massive die-offs that leave miles-long stretches of beach quilted with dead fish stitched together by their skeletons and saturated by putrescine and cadaverine, the perfectly-named chemicals responsible for death stink. If you're advertising vacations on pristine beaches, alewives are a big, smelly problem.

In any of the places in Europe we'd lived, an alewife problem would have been assigned to a study committee, that would then have devolved the issue to other committees, *ad nauseum.* In our new home, the head of Michigan's Department of Conservation turned it over to Fisheries Director Howard Tanner with instructions that became legendary: "Do something spectacular." He did. "I sat in the chair most of the night," he told the *Grand Rapids Press,* "and it dawned on me." More than half a million coho smolts were promptly released into tributaries of Lake Michigan. Other species of salmon followed. Relying on inspiration over lengthy research — like which fish would best use ocean-size lakes in place of the sea in their life cycles — Tanner & Co. simply released millions of each, in essence letting the fish themselves decide where to live and what to eat. Result? Other problems, most of them good. Marinas couldn't keep lures in stock. They ran out of gasoline and beer. Local governments had to build boat launches, parking places and public toilets. Tanner's brainstorm nearly doubled the tourist season. To us, this kind of problem-solving seemed wonderfully, wondrously American.

As a child of the era when another invader, the lamprey eel, had eliminated most of the large fish from the Great Lakes, the coho, Chinook, pink and Atlantic salmon meant far more than joy on the water and at the table. They re-created the excitement I'd sampled with my grandfather. These behemoths could be four-feet long and weigh twenty-five pounds! "A piece of the bottom?" we called our first one. Obviously, heavy, mysterious gear would be essential for pursuit. Sloop, of course, knew all.

There were reels capable of holding more line than I had ever seen spooled, let alone a fish big and strong enough to pull out three football fields of it. There were rods to attach the reels at one end and lures to be pulled from it at the other. Something called "down-riggers," the brainstorm of a guy Sloop knew in Traverse City, kept the lures at a certain level. Brilliant, because once you found where the fish were, you wanted to keep the bait there. Sloop had them all, plus heavy, hand-crank machines and the ten-pound lead balls that attached to the end of yet more wires.

All of this ran into serious money, or would have. Sloop apologized that the reels were made in Korea, which clearly embarrassed him. He repeated it so often, along with his inability to find affordable American brands heavy enough for the job, that I wondered whether shame underlay something even more inexplicable. To Sloop, it didn't seem right to charge more for these foreign things than what he had paid for them, or at least to a fellow American. Not even when I offered more in exchange for a lesson explaining techniques and general coaching. To Sloop, a man who had found his refuge / pulpit and considered his flock those who loved the same mysteries he loved, charging more than he had paid was heresy. These were transactions of the soul.

Nevertheless, the relationship spread over seasons, then years. Big fish gear led to small fish gear as we got into trout fishing in the streams. Here I was finally able to contribute something to the exchange. I'd fallen in love with bamboo rods, but there was a problem: small, light ones were impossible to find unless you were willing to spend big on antiques. I wasn't. I planned to use the rods, not hang them on a wall. They would be instruments of the exploration of a new world, a path to the sensation of feeling each wile and lunge from creatures strong beyond their size and as beautiful as the places where they are found. Six feet of split bamboo ended in a tip no bigger around than the average leaf stem. The whole thing—cork handle and all—could be mailed with two, first class stamps. Where to find such things?

Sloop thought the whole idea was crazy until he made me the first one. He took the heavy, nine-foot rod I'd paid $5 for at a garage sale, threw away the butt and first section and made a magic wand from the last two. The *life spirit* was there: I could feel the fish literally in the palm of my hand, not just from tugs at the tip. Sloop made them, I broke them, he made more.

What I mostly paid him was in my admitted humiliation and an invited openness to tease. He found me an easy target and I made sure the teasing was one-way. In the background, I knew, was something we shared in the most awkward way imaginable—and that something surfaced during one of the rare times I went out on a stream with him. It was the upper Jordan: shallow, fast, full of snags from the lumbering years and all that followed. We were testing his early versions of the laughable "teensy" rods. I was in my waders and vest. Sloop wore an ammo pouch for tackle, shorts and Vietnam-issue combat boots. I made long, slow casts, often as not hooking something way above the surface or under water. Sloop wielded his more businesslike rod like an M-16; short jabs under the banks where his targets lurked. Neither of us caught a decent fish that day, but I learned why silence had been the right language where our shared war was concerned.

THE FIRST WISP OF THE WAR in Vietnam reached my consciousness in the fall of 1958, when both the war and my level of world-aware-
ness were inchoate. I arrived in New Haven to begin a full scholarship
at Yale as a member of the United States Marine Corps Platoon Leaders
Class (PLC) program. At seventeen, I had been thrilled to be at my father's alma mater, joining an outfit redolent of resplendent uniforms and
my favorite uncle's World War II service in the South Pacific. As for the
actual fighting, a few American advisors were helping deal with an in-
surgency. America had never lost a war. How could this not be thrilling?

By the next fall, I had enrolled in a large political science class taught
by a young firebrand with reputed glamorous CIA connections to whom
we gave standing ovations for lectures describing how various nations
could and should be beneficially invaded by the U.S. I didn't see Prof.
Bradley Westerfield after Yale until an accidental reunion forty years later.
Having no reason to think he remembered me, let alone knew that I'd
became a foreign correspondent, I was astonished to hear, "Oh, I know
what you did at *Time*, Charlie." Warily, I added that while I'd found his
analytical framework helpful, I hadn't bought his whole act.

"Cheney did," he said with a tight little smile about my contemporary
and Yale dropout who, as vice president, became architect of the Global
War on Terror.

As an undergraduate absorbing Westerfield-ism, I was, of course, also
encountering the war doubters, the cynics and the just plain realists who
pointed out that "after the Marines give you four years where you want
to be, you give them four years wherever they put you." It wasn't the
where or even the doing *what*, it was the time involved. It was just that
simple: I dropped PLC. That didn't mean the war dropped me, however.
By 1962, when I graduated, "the conflict in Southeast Asia" was not yet
a fully-fledged American war, but the possibility was easily imagined. In
graduate schools like the University of Michigan's, a corrosive element
was added to the unremitting pressure of the draft: low grades could lose
you your deferment. Still, my War in Vietnam was all about not going to
the war in Vietnam in any guise, be it as soldier, or later, journalist.

It's no accident that the draft ended with the Vietnam War. By then
it was clear that elections could not be won if hundreds of thousands

of young men were being shipped off against their will, some of them later to appear as televised images in family living rooms in bandages or body bags. No credible reason beyond political expediency ever surfaced for losses on that scale. Vietnam proved the difficulty of maintaining home-front backing to fight large colonial-style wars with an army of conscripts. Henceforth American soldiers often engaged in actions with justifications equally dubious, but at least, at this writing, never without having volunteered.

Vietnam corroded the country's general self-image and my personal sense of what being a patriot might be. It warped the academic world I had recently left and the profession I was entering. For male graduate students who were, or soon would be, subject to the draft, a new grading system began protecting them. Out went A-to-F rating. In came a system that started at A and stopped at B for all but egregious work, in that B was the letter grade average necessary to maintaining graduate student deferments: a C could easily mean "the meatgrinder" of Vietnam. For professors, untrained for such decisions, the choice between academic standards and political implications was often agonizing. Not surprisingly, the "bell curve" shifted decidedly toward "pass."

In journalism, the situation was similar. The war's early stages were covered by a generation of reporters who had never known a conflict that so tore at the loyalties and expectations inherited from the Second World War. Even in Korea—similarly without a direct threat to American security and fought by draftees—the goal was territorial, not "hearts-and-minds" psychological; its prosecution, honorable. But in Vietnam, "American interests" could not be verified. Reporters found themselves dependent on an American command they simply could not trust. With "victory just around the corner" belied by an inability to demonstrate gains on the ground, Secretary of Defense Robert S. MacNamara adapted accounting procedures he brought from the Ford Motor Company, substituting supposed tallies of dead enemy combatants for sales figures. The "body counts," however, were soon shown to be padded with non-combatants and children. Convinced they were being lied to in order to force them into reporting false messages to their audiences, many correspondents substituted battlefield accounts of their own and casualty figures that they, themselves could verify. To help end the perceived madness tearing at the country, editors reversed the traditional policy of refusing to dwell, or even report, the personal foibles of political leaders, most recently and famously the sexual adventures of President John F. Kennedy.

I was as guilty as anyone else. Assigned to cover Spiro T. Agnew's 1968 campaign for vice president, my cover story in *Time* stooped to note the irrelevant but certainly unfriendly fact that his wife's maiden name, Judenfeint, translated as "enemy of Jews." To suggest a cast of mind I felt repellent, subsequent reporting concentrated less on his policy statements than his reference to a Japanese-American reporter for the *Baltimore Sun* as "the fat Jap," his calling intellectuals "pointy headed" and his branding of Hubert Humphrey as "squishy soft on Communism." My editors loved it.

The changes in academic grading systems eventually subsided post-Vietnam. Not so *ad hominum* political reporting. It steadily grew, reinforcing justification for publishing unauthorized government data that had been unthinkable before Vietnam. Publication of the "Pentagon Papers," a secret history compiled by MacNamara that demonstrated with hard data that the war was being lost at a gruesome cost to my generation of troops and journalists while the government, said otherwise. To reporters, Watergate proved that a new duplicity had spread home from foreign battlefields to domestic politics. It hasn't stopped and it challenges the notion of objectivity, even of truth, itself.

WARS OFTEN BEGIN OFFSTAGE, like the U.S. embargo of oil and scrap steel pointing the Japanese command toward Pearl Harbor, a first step in taking what was needed by force. The unlikely setting for my offstage events was my tiny grad school apartment on East Jefferson Street in Ann Arbor. Its total floor space was about the size of a king-size bed and contained, in addition to a cot-size bed, a desk and a two-tray fridge with a coffee pot on top. As was so often the case, I was playing the banjo to avoid the law books when a neighbor burst through my door with news that changed everything: John Fitzgerald Kennedy had been shot.

Even so, another year would go by, nearly to the day, before the journalist in me truly woke up. I opened my eyes on that cot of a bed, stared at the ceiling and thought, "Yesterday was my last day for law school." Law school seemed tediously unrelated to the real drama of life. I would switch to the field that Kennedy's assassination brought suddenly into focus. I would enter Michigan's journalism master's program and become a reporter; specifically, a foreign correspondent. Formalities completed, I left for the farm, where loose thoughts tended to settle during and after the four-hour drive in the beloved, if functionally unheated, MGB roadster I called BéBé.

READY TO OCCUPY BALTIMORE AND WASHINGTON, D.C.

Please fast forward again about the same length of time, with me again lying on that soft sliver wedged into a corner, this time with the additional comfort of a girl with the blonde good looks of a famous namesake actress (not Marilyn) and the merit of ignoring how much taller she was. The telephone next to the Voss typewriter on my painted-grey desk rang about midnight. It was Frances McTiernan, clerk of Selective Service Board #109 in St. Louis.

There were three levels of appeal for keeping the II-A student deferment that had kept me out of the jungles: You could deal with the first two by mail, but if Selective Service was not impressed, your third and last chance was a Presidential Appeal that required meeting face-to-face with twelve "friends and neighbors" in your home area. They would decide whose classification would become I-A, the ticket to war. Back in 1965, I'd outlined the reasons why the Local #109 should refer my case to the President of the United States: I had an internship with the *Baltimore Evening Sun*, an academic extension of the Master's Degree in Journalism I'd just earned at the University of Michigan. This, I explained, would be followed by service to my country as a foreign correspondent.

"Mr. Eisendrath," said the chairman with a quota to reach, "you already have plenty of education and your country needs you in Southeast Asia."

But Leland Stowe had taught me well. A former World War II correspondent famous for his coverage in Norway and Finland, he had turned professor and, at Michigan, had taken me under his wing. There, he revealed the innermost secret of successfully reporting important people and institutions: "Get to know the secretaries." So on the way out of Local #109, I dropped by the counter, behind which sat a classic blue-haired lady with an expression I couldn't read in detail apart from that it seemed to say, "Ask no favors." But, but, might she consider calling me, collect, of course, whenever my classification changed? No matter to what? Wouldn't that be just prompt notice of something I would soon get by mail?

She said nothing. A few weeks later however, the long-distance operator asked whether I would accept charges for a collect call from St. Louis. There I was, standing naked in the dark for a call that stripped away everything. Nude is nude; naked is exposed.

"This is Frances McTiernan of Selective Service Local Board number one-oh-nine." A pause, then, "Charles, run!"

Artists make a living comparing the nudes to the naked, but most of us learn it at moments like that one. I had done the ordinary thing of answering a phone in the dark with no time nor reason to put clothes on. A split second later they somehow meant protection. Frances McTiernan had switched on the Klieg lights of my generation to sweep my tiny bedroom. I felt much closer to the grandmotherly clerk of Selective Service Local Board #109 than the companion with whom I could exchange only the body's intimacies.

Possibly she saved my life; she most certainly saved the life I intended, exposing herself to charges, possibly ranging up to treason. Until you received official notice of reclassification, you could avoid being drafted by joining a unit of the reserves — if you could find one with an opening. The next morning I was on a plane for Baltimore, where I would start my internship at the end of the semester. First stop however, was not the city room of a newspaper: I went directly from the airport to the day room of headquarters detachment, 29th Infantry Division, Maryland National Guard. The Fifth Regiment Armory was a forbidding colossus in stone.

Somewhere inside, I hoped, was a unit that would allow me to join and thus make good on a last chance to stay out of Vietnam.

Why, asked the officers of a Military Police Unit, should they enlist me with so many others clamoring for the few slots available? Because, I told them, I could make them look like Napoleon Bonaparte in the pages of the *Evening Sun*. I had done my homework. As political appointees in the Maryland Department of Corrections, some of the officers of this particular unit knew that looking good in the local paper supplied a boost for moving up in the bureaucracy available to few others.

FROM ELSEWHERE in these essays you may recall how a storm in a northern Michigan forest in 2002 left a scene that reminded me of the battlefield at Verdun in 1916. Life's pivotal images are like that — personal versions of universal art and literature. An illustrated boyhood book on *The World's Ten Greatest Battles* introduced the great World War I slaughter. Verdun transfixed me long before I majored in modern European history, or covered France as a correspondent, or visited the battlefield. Stalemated in the west, the Germans devised strategy based as much on psychology as logistics. They would advance just a few miles into lightly defended northeastern France — they only wanted it to look like a move toward Paris — then dug in on high ground overlooking a valley and waited. They knew that French pride could not abide their holding a single hectare of sacred soil. They also understood that the French government, already panicked, would have trouble dealing with the stupendous losses they meant to inflict. Germany would bleed France out of the war.

The first parts worked. French *poilus* ("hairy ones," equivalent to grunts) hurled themselves through gas and artillery, against the barbed wire and bayonets, generally uphill. Paris newspapers urged them on, trumpeting the dubious new theory that élan alone would break the German lines. Massive and unreported cases of wholesale mutinies and French troops killing their own officers followed repeated failures. I'm reminded of this battle and how everything changed abruptly the next year each time I listen to "Over There" on the Overlook Farm player piano that dates from the same era. Until the doughboys arrived with their innocence, their optimism, their gay ditties and endless supplies of food and matériel, France teetered. My boyhood book included a drawing of the *Chemin des Dames*, a little street where artillery shells buried the *poilus* alive, their fixed bayonets sticking out of mud like grave markers. Maybe it was then that something in me determined that whatever life would bring me, I would not let it end that way.

Vietnam seemed to me like an American Verdun, only even more pointless because we had not been attacked and no enemy held American territory. Vietnam held nothing we needed, strategically or otherwise. My generation was being asked—ordered—to muster courage for the killing game because our government, like the French Third Republic, lacked the courage to admit that the costs were not worth the sacrifice although, ultimately, it was the Germans who retreated. I pictured Vietnam as a whirlpool that deflected the course of my life. And even though I had managed to avoid the vortex—neither fighting nor directly covering the war—I was among those who hovered in the outer rings, thrashing to keep out of the suck-hole, but unable to swim beyond an impossible pull. There was no calm water.

Nineteen months after Mrs. McTiernan's phone call, I'd met Julia and we'd married. Four months into our marriage I reported for basic training. That's when we realized that our togetherness might be an early Vietnam casualty. Except for a few reservist "pretty boys" (all of us white), everyone in Charlie Company would ship out to Danang shortly after Ft. Dix. There was a real chance that the rest of us would follow if the Guard was "nationalized" in the regular army—and that seemed increasingly likely when the 29th was mobilized to occupy parts of Baltimore and Washington D.C. during the riots following Martin Luther King's assassination. Not to worry, I told my new bride. We would go to Canada. I'd been sent to summer camp in Algonquin Park, Ontario, as a kid, then worked there; I knew people and we'd be okay.

Her response was as simple and life-path important as those few words from Frances McTiernan. Julia was a Cardozo, the proud Sephardic Jewish family with a legacy in North America pre-dating the United States by a century and a half, a clan that includes the author of the famous welcome on the Statue of Liberty and one of the most revered justices in the history of the Supreme Court. Her father headed the Association of American Law Schools; her brother was a naval officer serving on an attack boat in the Mekong Delta. I could hide my jitters from Julia, but Vietnam revealed a fissure that underlay our relationship—on one side was a Mandarin legacy loyal to institutions and precedent, on the other a born skeptic who would follow what seemed true when the institutions seemed wrong. Julia could not, would not, flee to Canada. I might have to.

Sometimes important doors swing ever so quietly. An old woman who had never spoken to me before had opened one with a whisper in the dark at the other end of a telephone line. With those two words I suddenly knew her better than most people in my life, and because of her I rushed into an existence that would have been moot without her warning. Another woman, young and known well enough to marry, closed a door equally succinctly, defining limits more closely and permanently than anything I'd ever experienced. I feared losing Julia so soon after finding her. Most of all, however, I feared something Vietnam was forcing me to learn about myself.

We all knew about the drugs, the low morale and the nonsensical rationale for the war. After more than a year in the National Guard—some of it in the quasi-combat situation of riot duty—I had come to know the Guard officers who would be giving the orders, the ones I had promised to make look like Napoleon. By now, I also knew that several came from the crony system permeating the Baltimore Department of Corrections. As a clerk typist in the orderly room of a military police detachment, I didn't have to eavesdrop; they laid out their incompetence, racism and exploitation of inmates as I quietly filled out the endless forms. Could I trust men in combat whom I wouldn't believe as a reporter? It was all too easy to imagine a sort of personal Verdun in the jungles of Vietnam. I would be in the position of prison inmates receiving orders to enhance their careers, possibly at the expense of my life. But unlike them, I would be armed and trained to kill. I thought I knew what I might do. And I knew that no matter what happened, I would never be same person. That realization so shocked and terrified me—mortified is probably the best word—that I still hadn't confided it to anyone, Julia included, twenty-two years later.

STEVE SLOOP AND I were aboard *Cherry Baron*, fishing for Chinook salmon on a day trip from the Overlook Farm mooring. Our approaches were as different as two men can have while doing the same thing on a twenty-two-foot lobster boat. He had two rods out on one downrigger, each festooned with several lures. On the other, I had a bamboo fly rod with a single spoon. We trolled at two knots as a full sun sizzled into the Lake Michigan horizon, taking the last breeze with it. As suddenly and unexpectedly as fish strike, we were on 'Nam, and I told him what I had confessed to no others: that I had imaged killing one of my own officers to stay alive. To Sloop, the details mattered no more than which lure might kill a fish, and there was no reason to doubt him about either.

GI's coined the word "fragging" to refer to the lethal fragments that exploding hand grenades spew in all directions, a plausible explanation for the 1,000 or so "accidental" casualties among commanders within the ranks. Drafted into the infantry, Sloop told of choppering into jungle clearings, boots hanging outside at treetop level, the cannon going and the fear pounding so hard he didn't need earplugs. Sloop had flown into the vortex. I had evaded it, because even if drastic action saved my life, it would be a life spiritually maimed. I would not take that chance. I knew I could never master Sloop's nonchalance. "Nobody knows who fragged lots of them officers," he said in an offhand way. "It was no big deal."

UNTIL WHAT, EXACTLY, DO WE PART?

July, 2006

I n a thirty-three-year marriage, imminent death was one of the few life experiences we had not faced together. Odd, then, wasn't it, that we weren't thinking about each other when it came. Julia said her mind went blank. That's the way she liked it on take-off, this woman who had somehow avoided airplanes until I proposed and flew her to Overlook Farm to meet my parents, explaining that my dream of foreign correspondence was a life full of adventures for both of us. It didn't seem necessary to discuss how we'd travel. She went along, but continued to hate, fear and avoid any but obligatory flights. The one that ended up nose down and afire in a Costa Rican jungle was one of the unavoidables.

As a sixtieth birthday present to me, Ben, temporarily rich with America Online stock options, proposed an exotic, everything-paid fishing trip with no input tolerated beyond a response to, "Are you in or are you out?" That had always been my challenge, so this was a big role reversal. Another was having convinced Julia to come along. Hunting of all kinds—including the hunting of fish—had become the central metaphor in my relationships with Ben and Mark, especially concerning how each of us deals with the unknown. For judging luck and resilience, nothing beats trying to understand something ultimately unknowable and doing it under the close scrutiny of others. In nearly all cases, the comforts were too few, the days too long, the talk too male, the behavior too insane and the flights too iffy to attract Julia. For this one, however, she proclaimed herself "in."

The week at a hilltop villa with a pool overlooking the jungle and the Pacific had had everything—bird/butterfly/monkey watching, hilarious family cooking adventures with our new daughter-in-law and, as advertised, amazing fishing. Packing up, I told Julia that even with all the good things that had been done for me in a life of privileged satisfaction, I could think of only one gesture to equal this gift trip from Ben—the one from my grandfather when I was nine. Like with my sons, my strongest ties to Pops had been knotted around fishing. He loved it, and loved that I loved it. My parents boarded me on "The Panama Limited" in the caverns of Chicago's Central Railroad Station, all alone for the two-day ride to Ft. Myers, Florida. I was sent on my way with a tip sufficient that the Pullman porter smiled broadly—but without the knowledge that Pops was ill, maybe terminally so. Even less so that this might have prompted the invitation.

The feeling of pride that my grandfather wanted me to join him on Gasparilla Island, and was confident that I could make the trip alone, overwhelmed all else. It remains a perfect example of fishing-trip recall: the mental screen calls up all sorts of images, all of them wonderful, and mostly *without* fish. On the way home, we traveled together as far as St. Louis, where my grandparents lived. (More images: watching Grandma crochet; irritating, homeworky mathematical drills with Pops, who never stooped to anything so parent-like with a rod in his hand.) I stayed with them overnight. Then, on the platform at Delmar Station, only my grandmother waved me home. Pops wasn't feeling well. I knew—mysteriously, but for sure—that I would never see him again. And didn't. Lesson: Never miss a fishing trip and nevermind the fish.

IN COSTA RICA, jungle-watching in our own villa and an easy, sandy walk to the Pacific was the main enticement for Julia. Although she had become a creditable fly fisherwoman, this more often than not did not involve actually catching something. By her own cheerful admission she misses most strikes, because while the fish rises to her fly, she's more involved with a flower on the stream bank, a cloud formation, a bird, butterfly, mosses or one of those exquisite arrangements of driftwood and flora that are the special marks of the small streams around Overlook.

Eliza, who Mark added to our "father-son," sleep-at-close-quarters Ungava expeditions before they were married, or even engaged, was also "in" for Costa Rica, as his wife. We all shared the villa, the van and the perfect small plane flying conditions for the first leg home: breezy, with single-scoop vanilla clouds.

If you fly often with Canadian bush pilots, you naturally eyeball the take-off route and where you'll make the turn, checking the clearance of shoreline trees, mountains, whatever. You'll have a look at the baggage: Can this thing really take off with all that crap? Does the load look balanced? Is it strapped in tightly enough to keep barrels of oil, weaponry, food and booze in place? You'll watch the pilot's checkout routine, try to evaluate it; although, if you're not a pilot, it's like judging grammar in a language you don't speak. But, if nothing really egregious strikes you, you'll then position yourself for an uncomfortable little chat—unnerving not because of what you ask, but how close your nose is to his mouth. Kissing close. Closer than hetero men ever get and much closer than hunters normally tolerate. Why? Because if you smell alcohol, you delay the flight or cancel it. In the same way, if a duck hunting trip involves an unfamiliar guide and a long, cold boat ride in a marsh that I can't navigate myself, I'll do the same.

That day—11:21 AM, Monday, December 20, 2000, in Nosara—everything checked out. The landing strip was nothing more than a section of two-lane pavement in the jungle. Except for a lean-to, there were few niceties against the elements and none whatsoever for any fire or medical needs that might arise. It looked long enough, and smooth.

We wouldn't know about the bad fuel until a few minutes after take-off. It would be weeks before Mark recalled what he'd overheard from the only non-Eisendrath passenger, an expat Californian. The woman was a routine commuter between the coast and the capital, San José, and she joked about the pilot's amusing habit of performing a signature "varOOOM" turn over his girlfriend's bed. On this particular morning, our captain had apparently left it with enough reluctance to have made his late arrival by car look airborne, too.

I am assigned the co-pilot's seat. As the plane gains speed, I note with satisfaction that the route toward San José, where we would meet the flight home, was to the right, directly away from the mountain that defines the skyline for miles around Nosara. No obstacles, and as a bonus we'll get a last view of our fishing grounds and the villa.

But we don't go straight. We bank sharp and left in a steep climb, over the bedroom, toward the mountain. It looks like the pilot can reach out his window and run his fingers through the treetops. Within a couple of minutes, however, he has other things on his mind, or rather one thing—the starboard engine. It has stopped. I don't notice it, maybe because the prop is well behind my line of sight. Maybe because there's a good deal else going on. The pilot begins frantic things with his hands and feet, pumping and pulling, turning controls. One of them is between us, just under his seat. In Canada, that's where a seaplane's trim wheel is; something I associate with a calm, leveling out of the plane. But this was a frantic spinning of a valve—which I later learn probably saved our lives. He's shutting down the flow of engine fuel from tanks located a wing-length away from us, just in front of my knees. That's where fires often begin.

"Sheet…Oh sheet!" the pilot hisses, and it is suddenly clear we're going down. As we fall from 500 feet, gaining speed, there is no movie screaming, no flashbacks nor instant regrets, no desperate hand-grasping. My job, it seems to me (Why? Does part of my brain insist there will be a story to write later?), is to figure out precisely which trees we were likely to hit as the plane is pummeled ever faster by three successive downdrafts; none with the usual lifts in between. I spot the trees just ahead, two beautifully symmetrical crowns overlying the surrounding tropical jungle. First contact makes eerily familiar sounds as palm fronds brush the aluminum tail of the Cessna, like the first splash of waves on the rear of seaplane pontoons. In Canada, that had been a signal to flash thumbs up to each other after sometimes hairy flights. "Piece of cake" floats gently to my mind, the way some minor satisfaction of the day reappears just before sleep.

I wake up with the jungle at my knees. The instruments are gone. The propeller and engine are gone. My first images are tangled roots, fronds, dirt. How did all that get there? It's a perfect representation, I think later, for the shocking jumble of familiar elements that bring us to critical junctures of life, including how it ends.

"THEY'RE ALIVE!" WE MADE PAGE ONE IN *LA NACIÓN*...
THE WRONG WAY. THE ARROW POINTS TO MY SEAT.

The second image is fire. It's close enough on the right to feel heat; somewhat farther away to the left, beyond the window and the body—I take him for dead—of the pilot. I'm focused on the window because I won't be able to crawl through mine. His looks doable.

The third image is out-of-body wonder at my hands. I watch them doing things while another part of my brain tells me—slowly, deliberately—that these can't be my hands because look what they're doing! Confronted with having to fix things mechanical in a hurry, my hands invariably fumble. I've watched them fail me countless times, unable to intervene. But present circumstances lie beyond the range of usual variables and the normal me is clearly not in charge. Calmly, slowly, deliberately and without error, these hands detect how to disengage from the jumble of seatbelt. Freed, I wriggle over the pilot and out his window. Ben is right behind. Behind him, I hear Mark, Eliza and Julia shouting as they open the rear door.

IF YOU FLY in small planes frequently, you can't help but imagine crashing and my "piece-of-cake" response may be a typical reality evasion. But, instead of a picture of us in some nice, soft dream-on landing in the forest canopy, giggling as we climbed down about how preposterous it would have been to die, the plane tore through the greenery and crashed at full speed. Newspaper photos show the plane noseless and pointed down, but with the wings roughly level. Oddly, infuriatingly, it was pilot error that saved us. Had he not veered to salute his girlfriend's bedroom, requiring that deep bank the opposite way from our destination, we would have flipped in the direction of the dead engine. We would have come in wings level—as actually happened—but upside down and most likely decapitated.

What kind of survival fight did we put up? We jumped, and then we scrambled, and then began the long inventory of wounds. To our collective amazement, none of us was burned and the plane did not explode—the last correction to the TV/movie version we all carry around but repress each time we board. Did I say we scrambled? That's what we intended, but with what turned out to be seventeen fractures—five in her back—Julia had to be carried. My entire left side had closed down in shock paraplegia, as had Mark's leg, and Eliza was deeply cut, but between the two of them they managed it. Ben was actually moving normally, but he wasn't scrambling either; there was too much help to be rendered.

If you are hunters—as we all were but Julia—our escape wriggles were all too familiar: rabbits hit in the leg, deer in the gut, ducks in the wing, all of them scramble for a little more life. We call a *coup de grâce*, a mercy shot, because it prevents additional suffering on the way to an inevitable end. Yet would it not be more "merciful" to allow a creature a few more moments of life, even if wracked? After all, if it wasn't worth the effort, the effort would not be made. Yet another comfortable assumption popped that day: we survived, and so, conceivably, might the creatures we wound.

How badly hurt was Julia? The survival clarity that guided my fingers through the mess of jammed seatbelt canvas and ruined cockpit metal also miraculously returned me to lessons I don't remember ever having learned in my inglorious military career. But there it was! Basic infantry combat first aid from thirty-five years ago, meant for Vietnam, again miraculously guiding my hands right there on the jungle floor. Julia was most concerned with the hundreds of bee-like ants that had swarmed into her hair when the plane dislodged their nest. To her eternal irritation — she still scolds me for this — I recognized irrelevant preoccupation as a good sign. The dying do not talk about mere discomfort. Suddenly, another image from a forgotten past: a Black Ft. Dix drill sergeant shouting, "Give 'em air when they hurt bad, men. Questions last thing they need with guts hangin' over! When they hamburger, they need a answer! I say a answer. Just one! Someone got it, they give it, and anyone else get the fuck away and shut the fuck up." I shooed everyone away.

The right ankle was bad, but no in-depth investigation necessary. Her toes! Could she move her toes? Each toe? Yes? Conclusion: However bad her back was — and it was obviously very, very bad — the spinal cord hadn't snapped. But keeping it intact from the crash site to the nearest clinic would mean immobilizing that gelatinous piece of Julia's communications system.

By this time, villagers had begun appearing. Like my grunt medicine, my Spanish magically returned and I yelled for them to see about the pilot, who was dragged free and lived. It also helped to prevent anyone from picking Julia up and damaging her further; We would load her into a van some other way. How about a doctor? None? How about a stretcher? *Tampoco.* A board? Sheet of plywood? Rope? We strapped her down and loaded the van. It would be two hours over jungle tracks and stream beds — no pavement, not even gravel, just mud and roots. No bridges, either. On the other hand, we learned we were lucky. The streams were low and fordable.

In one of those lucid moments between fear, pain and confusion about Julia and our other injuries (would my left side work again? Mark's leg?), I noticed that the man I'd asked to rescue the pilot had exchanged his greasy baseball hat for a classy straw fedora. I was in the act of complimenting a fellow hat person when I saw that it was mine. "Es mio," I shouted. He looked perplexed. "Da me, por favor! Pronto señor!" I got the hat back, but wasn't quick enough to realize what the neatly appropriated *sombrero* might mean for the rest of our baggage. As the villagers helped us, they also helped themselves.

I left Mark, Ben and Eliza to save what they could, then follow in a second truck while I went ahead with Julia and the pilot. After the first bumps, Julia's shrieks and the pilot's first hallucinations about what had happened focused my efforts on holding her straps tight and directing the driver to a tiny fishing base where there might be a dose or two of morphine. Deep sea fishing's dangerous, and even in these Central American boondocks, there was an emergency stock in a little box nailed to a tree.

When we try to escape—from pain, fear, danger— thoughts swim away, as if they need to flee from the bad, hurt places of our minds. Mine want go to fishing: the fishing we had just done from a shore less than a mile away. Then a whole school of thoughts, some going back decades. It's the psychological equivalent of my brain circumventing its normal hand-eye clumsiness under pressure.

TO FRESHWATER PEOPLE like me, ocean fish like the bonito seem machines made of steel. They are infinitely more powerful than anything in a stream or lake. That said, bonito are small and tuna shaped, like "Fat Man," the atomic bomb dropped over Nagasaki. The one I had hooked overwhelmed my gear … just as I'd hoped. I like to use tackle much lighter than recommended because, for me, the relationship I feel on the line is more important than the ending. I try to sense everything that's going on with the fish. That matters because I believe that true fishing—hunting—is a search for understanding. Ortega Y Gasset put it best: *Life is a terrible conflict, a grandiose and atrocious confluence. Hunting submerges man deliberately in that formidable mystery and therefore contains something of religious rite and emotion in which homage is paid to what is divine, transcendent, and in the laws of Nature.*

The bonito ran, dove, paused to send shivers up the line to my hand. I don't know how ocean fish do this, but fishing lore has it that these vibrations communicate stress to other fish, and that is certainly what you learn through your hand; nerves stretched to breaking. Sometimes this is how you feel, too. Think about your shiver before the parachute jump, the plunge into a gyrating stock market, the decision to propose.

Then the fish ran again. When unable to force line off the reel, it refused to give up the distance it had defined between itself and the source of its torment, a standoff maintained with such ragged precision that it might as well have been made of blasted earth and barbed wire. In circle after circle around the boat, the hunter waits for the slightest weakening to inch in the hunted. At such moments, I usually catch myself thinking how ironic it is; that all this superb strength and conviction should be applauded, and here I am doing everything I can to destroy it. That's why there's often such a letdown at the end, at death. It's the time between search and death when a hunter is most alive. Ortega again: *The hunter is the alert man—life as complete alertness.* More than anything, this heightened sense of being alive explains the millions of licenses to fish sold worldwide, and the billions spent using them.

On the ocean, however, there was another system on display. About ten yards in back of the bonito a black dorsal fin sliced through the waves. There was no motion in that fin except forward, as if the ocean had no whitecaps, while the bonito's every molecule strained and shivered up the line to my fingers. Hooked by its jaw, the bonito would be done-in from behind. As we watched, the line went limp.

My thoughts went limp as well when the pilot began raving, "Wh'aat eeze hoppen? I no know wh'aat eeze hoppen and where plane?" This has a good side: The racket somehow gets through Julia's shock and pain to infuriate her, distracting her from the heat (no AC) and bugs (we travel at open-window, mosquito-access speed). But between episodes of the here-and-now I keep picturing the doomed bonito, then Julia lying on the jungle floor, then the predators taking pieces of what we had to offer: in our case, at least, belongings, not biomass. Like the bonito, devoured from behind, Julia can't see the predator, either, because she can't move her head. The rest of us are too full of adrenalin to look in the right direction, and even if we had, we're too weakened or distracted to defend ourselves from our tormentors.

FOR DAYS, WEEKS, MONTHS afterwards, a mental split-screen appeared, often grabbing me back to Nosara when I thought myself firmly and fully occupied with university work in Ann Arbor: on one side was us, the predators; on the other the bonito, the prey. I tried to purge both with an op-ed piece for *The New York Times*—often the best way to understand and/or get rid of something is to write about it. They'd already used a piece about an other-worldly northern lights exhibition in Ungava, but I had trouble with this one. I couldn't get the links right between fishing, family and survival. Howell Raines, a friend and the author of *Fly Fishing through the Mid-Life Crisis*, was in charge of the op-ed page at the time. "Fishing too strong, cosmic connections too weak," he said, and he was right.

It turned out that I had trouble completing the story because the end hadn't happened yet, and wouldn't happen for a full eight months after the crash and too late to write about it for a newspaper. Epiphanies—that delicate word that seems fringed with lace—can literally, physically, knock you down.

THE STREAMS AND LAKES around Overlook Farm are my home waters and I love them even though they're broken. When people say, "the fishing isn't what it used to be," they usually have no idea how right they are. It's not just that the number and size of fish are not up to the standard made famous by Hemingway, our most famous local angler, they don't behave the same way, either, because fish reared in hatcheries are never as strong as those who have dealt with the elements from egg-stage. Actually, it's not possible to talk sensibly about whether the fishing is as good as it was "back then"—whenever that might have been—because unless you're more careful than most, you're not even discussing the same species. Most dramatically, the native grayling are extinct and the resident brook trout, fewer and comparatively tiny. Only the lake trout, steelhead and salmon fishing remain reliable, and that only because of human tinkering. Good or bad, however, anyone on a stream or a lake anywhere near Overlook Farm is not encountering a natural ecosystem and so misses important messages. They're seeing a play with missing actors.

So there I was, in waders on the bank of a stream flowing out of Pons Lake in Ungava, a stream I know in the intimate ways that most people reserve for those they love most. I needed a rock to sit on and found a big one with its base in the water. I needed a cigar and a single malt; emergency gear along with a compass to find where to go and surveyor's tape for the way back. Ben had opted out of this trip the summer following the crash, but Mark and I returned. It was our usual week when, for a brief time, the seasons for trout, arctic char and landlocked salmon coincide with ptarmigan and caribou. It's also spawning time for brook trout, and their courting colors sizzle the water — bright belly orange, racing stripes on fins, white on black for added pizazz. As a work of art, the flash draws the eye into the darker greens, blues and yellows of the twisting variegations on their backs. Much of the stream's three-mile tumble is empty; the fish are gathering in only a few spots — not always "pools" — to feed, socialize and spawn. At one shallow, unlikely juncture we'd walked by a dozen times, we discovered that a mouse fly dragged fast through fast water nearly always caught something. It was one of those "this will never work" accidents that make fishing a sport for true believers. Then we noticed that when we caught one big fish, we generally caught another, almost invariably of the other sex.

Before the last week of August 2001, that wouldn't have meant much to me, just as the thought of airplanes flying into New York office towers wouldn't have occurred to me, either. I hook a beauty; four pounds or more. We keep fish to eat and release the rest, but we're at a point in the day — after trout lunch and enough for a trout dinner — when the decision to keep could go either way.

You can usually tell gender, as well as species, from how the fish takes the fly and what it does immediately thereafter. I guessed "girlfish" — no jumping, a tendency to shake the head instead of running. On a tiny bamboo rod in a fast stream, the fish goes pretty much where it wants, including between rocks, where it will make a final stand. The choice for this one was a kind of deep, narrow sluice directly off my left boot where the water ran as smooth as light. I don't use a net. I take her behind the head, my line of sight narrowed to the wondrous black lips with white etching and the running water immediately behind. Running water where, suddenly, there *he* was. Broad of shoulder and somewhat bigger, his dorsal fin just below the surface, erect, with a forward spine sharp as a shriek. He's ready for anything, or, rather, *anything but this*. The water flows as fast as streams do, but he holds himself motionless, watching me. *Watching me*. To me, that gaze said, "We've been together a long time, give her back to me."

I did.

AT THE LATITUDE OF UNGAVA, the ice goes out in June and returns in early October. For non-migrating creatures like trout, all essentials—sex, of course, but mostly eating—must be handled in those few months. Growth is slow. A four-pound brook trout could be thirty years old, say guides like Henri Boivin, a Cree of precisely my age who is the best there is. Nobody knows if the pairs stay together during the year, or if they go their own way but select each other on the spawning gravel over repeated seasons. That leaves the answer in the realm of muse, which is another attraction of fisherman to fishing. In my musing, that trout was as old as my son Mark, and the pair had been together for the same proportion of their lives as Julia and me. In Costa Rica, had I carried myself with his dignity while I begged fate to help me rescue her from the pain and fractures of the crash, to get her back with me?

And the bonito? I could no longer not wonder if there had been another bonito, a mate to the one on my line, swimming behind and signaling back to those vibrations I'd felt off Nosara. What then? Sitting on that rock, I knew that fishing, for me, had just changed. With all the lessons Overlook Farm offered, Ungava had taken me beyond. Things would be more complicated now because of an experience dividing one side of life from the other.

Our first grandchild, a boy, was born two days after Mark and I returned from Ungava. Conceived on the Nosara trip, his middle name is Crash and he loves to fish.

Acknowledgments

Journalists have sources. What happens when the journalist is the prime source, reporting about himself? Discomfort, that's what. So in compiling my own story, I found myself uncovering the trail through others and also with them, as if tracking some elusive quarry while conversing with fellow hunters who were unaware that I had a purpose beyond the moment. Indeed, usually I didn't. Not only were these essays composed over thirty years, often long after the events described, they also were never considered part of a book until novelist Travis Holland so suggested and photographer Julie Steedman urged my adding any sort of visual that came to mind. Realization couldn't happen, however, until the right editor got hold of the project. That would be Heather Lee Shaw, whose eye, balance and counsel set the design of the book and the shape of its prose.

Another born editor, Julia, parses my thoughts before, during and after they are written down, whether long ago on international deadline or fielding some question yesterday yelled down the stairs. Ben took not only the cover photo: Thousands of his images form a sort mental mosaic that I can reference, of all miracles, through something called "The cloud." Mark's contribution is exactly the opposite. His artist's eye picks up the damnedest details, many of which inform the text as well as enliven it. From his childhood demonstration that the drawing of a figure could (did) begin with a fingertip, I learned—or maybe think I learned—where Michelangelo began outlining the figures of God giving life to Adam on the ceiling of the Sistine Chapel.

There are many others to thank, particularly for reducing error: Lore Silberman concerning her family, the Loebs, and their Charlevoix friends. Lynne Guthman Rosenthal for tone, Alvin and Patsy Ranger for local lore and how the Rangers and the Goldmans cared for *The Boss*, a floating psychological ship of state. The Charlevoix Historical Society helped. Jack Lessenberry for backstopped historical fact; Chris Porterfield checkpointed *Time* material. The cherry business was sourced through Bill Sherman, mapling with Derek Ross. Reporting my own ancestry, I turned to family archives including incomplete memoirs from my mother and her father, my "Pops." Charles M. Rice II, my first cousin and the only living relative left in St. Louis, helped keep me straight on his side of the family. Bill Bascom, teacher and writer, offered a sounding board tempered over a half-century.

For my high school yearbook mug shot, classmate editor and senior prom date Lucy Pitzman (she fully formed, me formless) selected a caption from Ralph Waldo Emerson: "In every man there is something wherein I may learn, and in that I am his pupil." I want to acknowledge that a selection from long ago still (adjusted for gender inclusion) bullseyes my approach to the essays in this book and much, much else.

Index